THE FALLACY OF SUCCESS & THE ETHICS OF ELFLAND

ESSAYS ON CULTURE, MORALITY, AND THE PARADOXES OF LIFE

G. K. CHESTERTON

FILIBOOKS.COM

Cover by: Filibooks Covers

Published by: Fili Public

Filibooks ApS

info@filibooks.com

CVR: 37100161

~

©Filibooks 2024

Original works by G. K. Chesterton are in the public domain

Paperback ISBN: 978-87-94559-18-8
Ebook ISBN: 978-87-94559-19-5

CONTENTS

THE CASE FOR THE EPHEMERAL

I cannot understand the people who take literature seriously; but I can love them, and I do. Out of my love I warn them to keep clear of this book. It is a collection of crude and shapeless papers upon current or rather flying subjects; and they must be published pretty much as they stand. They were written, as a rule, at the last moment; they were handed in the moment before it was too late, and I do not think the commonwealth would have been shaken to its foundations if they had been handed in the moment after. They must go out now, with all their imperfections on their head, or rather on mine; for their vices are too vital to be improved with a blue pencil, or with anything I can think of, except dynamite.

Their chief vice is that so many of them are very serious; because I had no time to make them flippant. It is so easy to be solemn; it is so hard to be frivolous. Let any honest reader shut his eyes for a few moments, and approaching the secret tribunal of his soul, ask himself whether he would really rather be asked in the next two hours to write the front page of *The Times*, which is full of long leading articles, or the front page of *Tit-Bits*, which is full of short jokes. If the reader is the fine conscientious fellow I take him for, he will at once reply that he would rather on the spur of the moment write ten *Times* articles than one *Tit-Bits* joke. Responsibility, a heavy and cautious responsibility of speech, is the easiest thing in the world; anybody can do it. That is why so many tired, elderly, and wealthy men go in for politics. They are responsible, because they have not the strength of mind left to be irresponsible. It is more dignified to sit still than to dance the Barn Dance. It is also easier. So in these easy pages I keep myself on the whole on the level of *The Times*: it is only occasionally that I leap upwards almost to the level of *Tit-Bits*.

I resume the defence of this indefensible book. These articles have another disadvantage arising from the scurry in which they were written; they are too long-winded and elaborate. One of the great disadvantages of hurry is that it takes such a long time. If I have to start for Highgate this day week, I may perhaps go the shortest way. If I have to start this minute, I shall almost certainly go the longest. In these essays (as I read them over) I feel frightfully annoyed with myself for not getting to the point more quickly; but I had not enough leisure to be quick. There are several maddening cases in which I took two or three pages in attempting to describe an attitude of which the essence could be expressed in an epigram; only there was no time for epigrams. I do not repent of one shade of opinion here expressed; but I feel that they might have been expressed so much more briefly and precisely. For instance, these pages contain a sort of recurring protest against the boast of certain writers that they are merely recent. They brag that their philosophy of the universe is the last philosophy or the new philosophy, or the advanced and progressive philosophy. I have said much against a mere modernism. When I use the word "modernism," I am not alluding specially to the current quarrel in the Roman Catholic Church, though I am certainly astonished at any intellectual group accepting so weak and unphilosophical a name. It is incomprehensible to me that any thinker can calmly call himself a modernist; he might as well call himself a Thursdayite. But apart altogether from that particular disturbance, I am conscious of a general irritation expressed against the people who boast of their advancement and modernity in the discussion of religion. But I never succeeded in saying the quite clear and obvious thing that is really the matter with modernism. The real objection to modernism is simply that it is a form of snobbishness. It is an attempt to crush a rational opponent not by reason, but by some mystery of superiority, by hinting that one is specially up to date or particularly "in the know." To flaunt the fact that we have had all the last books from Germany is simply vulgar; like flaunting the fact that we have had all the last bonnets from Paris. To introduce into philosophical discussions a sneer at a creed's antiquity is like introducing a sneer at a lady's age. It is caddish because it is irrelevant. The pure modernist is merely a snob; he cannot bear to be a month behind the fashion.

Similarly I find that I have tried in these pages to express the real objection to philanthropists and have not succeeded. I have not seen the quite simple objection to the causes advocated by certain wealthy idealists; causes of which the cause called teetotalism is the strongest case. I have used many abusive terms about the thing, calling it Puritanism, or superciliousness, or aristocracy; but I have not seen and stated the quite simple objection to philanthropy; which is that it is religious persecution. Religious persecution does not consist in thumbscrews or fires of Smithfield; the essence of religious persecution is this: that the man who happens to have material power in the State, either by wealth or by official position, should govern his fellow-citizens not according to their religion or philosophy, but according to his own. If, for instance, there is such a thing as a vegetarian morality, then I say in the emphatic words of the arrogant French marquis before the French Revolution, "Let them eat grass." Perhaps that French oligarch was a humanitarian; most oligarchs are. Perhaps when he told the peasants to eat grass he was recommending to them the hygienic simplicity of a vegetarian restaurant. But that is an irrelevant, though most fascinating, speculation. The point here is that if a nation is really vegetarian let its government force upon it the whole horrible weight of vegetarianism. Let its government give the national guests a State vegetarian banquet. Let its government, in the most literal and awful sense of the words, give them beans. That sort of tyranny is all very well; for it is the people tyrannising over all the persons. But "temperance reformers" are like a small group of vegetarians who should silently and systematically act on an ethical assumption entirely unfamiliar to the mass of the people. They would always be giving peerages to greengrocers. They would always be appointing Parliamentary Commissions to enquire into the private life of butchers. Whenever they found a man quite at their mercy, as a pauper or a convict or a lunatic, they would force him to add the final touch to his inhuman isolation by becoming a vegetarian. All the meals for school children will be vegetarian meals. All the State public houses will be vegetarian public houses. There is a very strong case for vegetarianism as compared with teetotalism. Drinking one glass of beer cannot by any philosophy be drunkenness; but killing one animal can, by this philosophy, be murder. The objection to both processes is not that the two creeds, teetotal and vegetarian, are not admissible; it is simply that they are not admitted. The thing is religious persecution because it is not based on the existing religion of the democracy. These people ask the poor to accept in practice what they know perfectly well that the poor would not accept in theory. That is the very definition of religious persecution. I was against the Tory attempt to force upon ordinary Englishmen a Catholic theology in which they do not believe. I am even more against the attempt to force upon them a Mohamedan morality which they actively deny.

Again, in the case of anonymous journalism I seem to have said a great deal without getting out the point very clearly. Anonymous journalism is dangerous, and is poisonous in our existing life simply because it is so rapidly becoming an anonymous life. That is the horrible thing about our contemporary atmosphere. Society is becoming a secret society. The modern tyrant is evil because of his elusiveness. He is more nameless than his slave. He is not more of a bully than the tyrant of the past; but he is more of a coward. The rich publisher may treat the poor poet better or worse than the old master workman treated the old apprentice. But the apprentice ran away and the master ran after him. Nowadays it is the poet who pursues and tries in vain to fix the fact of responsibility. It is the publisher who runs away. The clerk of Mr. Solomon gets the sack; the beautiful

Greek slave of the Sultan Suliman also gets the sack; or the sack gets her. But though she is concealed under the black waves of the Bosphorus, at least her destroyer is not concealed. He goes behind golden trumpets riding on a white elephant. But in the case of the clerk it is almost as difficult to know where the dismissal comes from as to know where the clerk goes to. It may be Mr. Solomon or Mr. Solomon's manager, or Mr. Solomon's rich aunt in Cheltenham, or Mr. Solomon's rich creditor in Berlin. The elaborate machinery which was once used to make men responsible is now used solely in order to shift the responsibility. People talk about the pride of tyrants; but we in this age are not suffering from the pride of tyrants. We are suffering from the shyness of tyrants; from the shrinking modesty of tyrants. Therefore we must not encourage leader-writers to be shy; we must not inflame their already exaggerated modesty. Rather we must attempt to lure them to be vain and ostentatious; so that through ostentation they may at last find their way to honesty.

The last indictment against this book is the worst of all. It is simply this: that if all goes well this book will be unintelligible gibberish. For it is mostly concerned with attacking attitudes which are in their nature accidental and incapable of enduring. Brief as is the career of such a book as this, it may last just twenty minutes longer than most of the philosophies that it attacks. In the end it will not matter to us whether we wrote well or ill; whether we fought with flails or reeds. It will matter to us greatly on which side we fought.

COCKNEYS AND THEIR JOKES

A writer in the Yorkshire Evening Post is very angry indeed with my performances in this column. His precise terms of reproach are, "Mr. G. K. Chesterton is not a humourist: not even a Cockney humourist." I do not mind his saying that I am not a humourist--in which (to tell the truth) I think he is quite right. But I do resent his saying that I am not a Cockney. That envenomed arrow, I admit, went home. If a French writer said of me, "he is no metaphysician: not even an English metaphysician," I could swallow the insult to my metaphysics, but I should feel angry about the insult to my country. So I do not urge that I am a humourist; but I do insist that I am a Cockney. If I were a humourist, I should certainly be a Cockney humourist; if I were a saint, I should certainly be a Cockney saint. I need not recite the splendid catalogue of Cockney saints who have written their names on our noble old City churches. I need not trouble you with the long list of the Cockney humourists who have discharged their bills (or failed to discharge them) in our noble old City taverns. We can weep together over the pathos of the poor Yorkshireman, whose county has never produced some humour not intelligble to the rest of the world. And we can smile together when he says that somebody or other is "not even" a Cockney humourist like

Samuel Johnson or Charles Lamb. It is surely sufficiently obvious that all the best humour that exists in our language is Cockney humour. Chaucer was a Cockney; he had his house close to the Abbey. Dickens was a Cockney; he said he could not think without the London streets. The London taverns heard always the quaintest conversation, whether it was Ben Jonson's at the Mermaid or Sam Johnson's at the Cock. Even in our own time it may be noted that the most vital and genuine humour is still written about London. Of this type is the mild and humane irony which marks Mr. Pett Ridge's studies of the small grey streets. Of this type is the simple but smashing laughter of the best tales of Mr. W. W. Jacobs, telling of the smoke and sparkle of the Thames. No; I concede that I am not a Cockney humourist. No; I am not worthy to be. Some time, after sad and strenuous after-lives; some time, after fierce and apocalyptic incarnations; in some strange world beyond the stars, I may become at last a Cockney humourist. In that potential paradise I may walk among the Cockney humourists, if not an equal, at least a companion. I may feel for a moment on my shoulder the hearty hand of Dryden and thread the labyrinths of the sweet insanity of Lamb. But that could only be if I were not only much cleverer, but much better than I am. Before I reach that sphere I shall have left behind, perhaps, the sphere that is inhabited by angels, and even passed that which is appropriated exclusively to the use of Yorkshiremen.

No; London is in this matter attacked upon its strongest ground. London is the largest of the bloated modern cities; London is the smokiest; London is the dirtiest; London is, if you will, the most sombre; London is, if you will, the most miserable. But London is certainly the most amusing and the most amused. You may prove that we have the most tragedy; the fact remains that we have the most comedy, that we have the most farce. We have at the very worst a splendid hypocrisy of humour. We conceal our sorrow behind a screaming derision. You speak of people who laugh through their tears; it is our boast that we only weep through our laughter. There remains always this great boast, perhaps the greatest boast that is possible to human nature. I mean the great boast that the most unhappy part of our population is also the most hilarious part. The poor can forget that social problem which we (the moderately rich) ought never to forget. Blessed are the poor; for they alone have not the poor always with them. The honest poor can sometimes forget poverty. The honest rich can never forget it.

I believe firmly in the value of all vulgar notions, especially of vulgar jokes. When once you have got hold of a vulgar joke, you may be certain that you have got hold of a subtle and spiritual idea. The men who made the joke saw something deep which they could not express except by something silly and emphatic. They saw something delicate which they could only express by something indelicate. I remember that Mr. Max Beerbohm (who has every merit except democracy) attempted to analyse the jokes at which the mob laughs. He divided them into three sections: jokes about bodily humiliation, jokes about things alien, such as foreigners, and jokes about bad cheese. Mr. Max Beerbohn thought he understood the first two forms; but I am not sure that he did. In order to understand vulgar humour it is not enough to be humorous. One must also be vulgar, as I am. And in the first case it is surely obvious that it is not merely at the fact of something being hurt that we laugh (as I trust we do) when a Prime Minister sits on his hat. If that were so we should laugh whenever we saw a funeral. We do not laugh at the mere fact of something falling down; there is nothing humorous about leaves falling or the sun going down. When our house falls down we do not laugh. All the birds of the air might drop around us in a perpetual shower like a hailstorm without arousing a smile. If you really ask yourself why we laugh at a man sitting down suddenly in the street you will discover that the reason is not only recondite, but ultimately religious. All the jokes about men sitting down on their hats are really theological jokes; they are concerned with the Dual Nature of Man. They refer to the primary paradox that man is superior to all the things around him and yet is at their mercy.

Quite equally subtle and spiritual is the idea at the back of laughing at foreigners. It concerns the almost torturing mirth of a thing being like oneself and yet not like oneself. Nobody laughs at what is entirely foreign; nobody laughs at a palm tree. But it is funny to see the familiar image of God disguised behind the black beard of a Frenchman of the black face of a Negro. There is nothing funny in the sounds that are wholly inhuman, the howling of wild beasts or of the wind. But if a man begins to talk like oneself, but all the syllables come out different, then if one is a man one feels inclined to laugh, though if one is a gentleman one resists the inclination.

Mr. Max Beerbohm, I remember, professed to understand the first two forms of popular wit, but said that the third quite stumped him. He could not see why there should be anything funny about bad cheese. I can tell him at once. He has missed the idea because it is subtle and philosophical, and he was looking for something ignorant and foolish. Bad cheese is funny because it is (like the foreigner or the man fallen on the pavement) the type of the transition or transgression across a great mystical boundary. Bad cheese symbolises the change from the inorganic to the organic. Bad cheese symbolises the startling prodigy of matter taking on vitality. It symbolises the origin of life itself. And it is only about such solemn matters as the origin of life that the democracy condescends to joke. Thus, for instance, the democracy jokes about marriage, because marriage is a part of mankind. But the democracy would never deign to joke about Free Love, because Free Love is a piece of priggishness.

As a matter of fact, it will be generally found that the popular joke is not true to the letter, but it is true to the spirit. The vulgar joke is generally in the oddest way the truth and yet not the fact. For instance, it is not in the least true that mothers-in-law are as a class oppressive and intolerable; most of them are both devoted and useful. All the mothers-in-law I have ever had were admirable. Yet the legend of the comic papers is profoundly true. It draws attention to the fact that it is much harder to be a nice mother-in-law than to be nice in any other conceivable relation of life. The caricatures have drawn the worst mother-in-law a monster, by way of expressing the fact that the best mother-in-law is a problem. The same is true of the perpetual jokes in comic papers about shrewish wives and henpecked husbands. It is all a frantic exaggeration, but it is an exaggeration of a truth; whereas all the modern mouthings about oppressed women are the exaggerations of a falsehood. If you read even the best of the intellectuals of to-day you will find them saying that in the mass of the democracy the woman is the chattel of her lord, like his bath or his bed. But if you read the comic literature of the democracy you will find that the lord hides under the bed to escape the wrath of his chattel. This is not the fact, but it is much nearer the truth. Every man who is married knows quite well, not only that he does not regard his wife as a chattel, but that no man can conceivably ever have done so. The joke stands for an ultimate truth, and that is a subtle truth. It is not very easy to state correctly. It can, perhaps, be most correctly stated by saying that, even if the man is the head of the house, he knows he is the figure-head.

But the vulgar comic papers are so subtle and true that they are even prophetic. If you really want to know what is going to happen to the future of our democracy, do not read the modern sociological prophecies, do not read even Mr. Wells's Utopias for this purpose, though you should certainly read them if you are fond of good honesty and good English. If you want to know what will happen, study the pages of Snaps or Patchy Bits as if they were the dark tablets graven with the oracles of the gods. For, mean and gross as they are, in all seriousness, they contain what is entirely absent from all Utopias and all the sociological conjectures of our time: they contain some hint of the actual habits and manifest desires of the English people. If we are really to find out what the democracy will ultimately do with itself, we shall surely find it, not in the literature which studies the people, but in the literature which the people studies.

I can give two chance cases in which the common or Cockney joke was a much better prophecy than the careful observations of the most cultured observer. When England was agitated, previous to the last General Election, about the existence of Chinese labour, there was a distinct difference between the tone of the politicians and the tone of the populace. The politicians who disapproved of Chinese labour were most careful to explain that they did not in any sense disapprove of Chinese. According to them, it was a pure question of legal propriety, of whether certain clauses in the contract of indenture were not inconsistent with our constitutional traditions: according to them, the case would have been the same if the people had been Kaffirs or Englishmen. It all sounded wonderfully enlightened and lucid; and in comparison the popular joke looked, of course, very poor. For the popular joke against the Chinese labourers was simply that they were Chinese; it was an objection to an alien type; the popular papers were full of gibes about pigtails and yellow faces. It seemed that the Liberal politicians were raising an intellectual objection to a doubtful document of State; while it seemed that the Radical populace were merely roaring with idiotic laughter at the sight of a Chinaman's clothes. But the popular instinct was justified, for the vices revealed were Chinese vices.

But there is another case more pleasant and more up to date. The popular papers always persisted in representing the New Woman or the Suffragette as an ugly woman, fat, in spectacles, with bulging clothes, and generally falling off a bicycle. As a matter of plain external fact, there was not a word of truth in this. The leaders of the movement of female emancipation are not at all ugly; most of them are extraordinarily good looking. Nor are they indifferent to art or decorative costume; many of them are alarmingly attached to these things. Yet the popular instinct was right. For the popular instinct was that in this movement, rightly or wrongly, there was an element of indifference to female dignity, of a quite new willingness of women to be grotesque. These women did truly despise the pontifical quality of woman. And in our streets and around our Parliament we have seen the stately woman of art and culture turn into the comic woman of Comic Bits. And whether we think the exhibition justifiable or not, the prophecy of the comic papers is justified; the healthy and vulgar masses were conscious of a hidden enemy to their traditions who has now come out into the daylight, that the scriptures might be fulfilled. For the two things that a healthy person hates most between heaven and hell are a woman who is not dignified and a man who is.

ON AMERICAN MORALS

America is sometimes offered to us, even by Americans (who ought to know better), as a moral example. There are indeed very real American virtues; but this virtuous attitude is hardly one of them. And if anyone wants to know what a welter of weakness and inconsequence the moral mind of America can sometimes be, he may be advised to look, not so much to the Crime Wave or the Charleston, as to the serious idealistic essays by highbrows and cultural critics, such as one by Miss Avis D. Carlson on `Wanted: A Substitute for Righteousness.' By righteousness she means, of course, the narrow New England taboos; but she does not know it. For the inference she draws is that we should recognize frankly that `the standard abstract right and wrong is moribund.' This statement will seem less insane if we consider, somewhat curiously, what the standard abstract right and wrong seems to mean -- at least in her section of the States. It is a glimpse of an incredible world.

She takes the case of a young man brought up `in a home where there was an attempt to make dogmatic cleavage of right and wrong.' And what was the dogmatic cleavage? Ah, what indeed! His elders told him that some things were right and some wrong; and for some time he accepted this strange assertion. But when he leaves home he finds that, `apparently perfectly nice people do the things he has been taught to think evil.' Then follows a revelation. `The flowerlike girl he envelops in a mist of romantic idealization smokes like an imp from the lower regions and pets like a movie vamp. The chum his heart yearns towards cultivates a hip-flask, etc.' And this is what the writer calls a dogmatic cleavage between right and wrong!

The standard of abstract right and wrong apparently is this. That a girl by smoking a cigarette makes herself one of the company of the fiends of hell. That such an action is much the same as that of a sexual vampire. That a young man who continues to drink fermented liquor must necessarily be `evil' and must deny the very existence of any difference between right and wrong. That is the `standard of abstract right and wrong' that is apparently taught in the American home. And it is perfectly obvious, on the face of it, that it is not a standard of abstract right or wrong at all. That is exactly what it is not. That is the very last thing any clear-headed person would call it. It is not a standard; it is not abstract; it has not the vaguest notion of what is meant by right and wrong. It is a chaos of social and sentimental accidents and associations, some of them snobbish, all of them provincial, but, above all, nearly all of them concrete and connected with a materialistic prejudice against particular materials. To have a horror of tobacco is not to have an abstract standard of right; but exactly the opposite. It is to have no standard of right whatever; and to make certain local likes and dislikes as a substitute. We need not be very surprised if the young man repudiates these meaningless vetoes as soon as he can; but if he thinks he is repudiating morality, he must be almost as muddle-headed as his father. And yet the writer in question calmly proposes that we should abolish all ideas of right and wrong, and abandon the whole human conception of a standard of abstract justice, because a boy in Boston cannot be induced to think that a nice girl is a devil when she smokes a cigarette.

If the rising generation were faced with no worse doubts and difficulties than this, it would not be very difficult to reconcile them to the traditions of truth and justice. But I think the episode is worth mentioning, merely because it throws a ray of light on the moral condition of American Culture, in the decay of Puritanism. And when next we are told that the idealism of America is to set a `standard' by which England must transform herself, it will be well to remember what is apparently meant by a standard and an ideal; and that the fire of idealism seems both to begin and end in smoke.

Incidentally, I must say I can bear witness to this queer taboo about tobacco. Of course numberless Americans smoke numberless cigars; a great many others eat cigars, which seems to me a more occult pleasure. But there does exist an extraordinary idea that ethics are involved in some way; and many who smoke really disapprove of smoking. I remember once receiving two American interviewers on the same afternoon; there was a box of cigars in front of me and I offered one to each in turn. Their reaction (as they would probably call it) was very curious to watch. The first journalist stiffened suddenly and silently and declined in a very cold voice. He could not have conveyed more plainly that I had attempted to corrupt an honorable man with a foul and infamous indulgence; as if I were the Old Man of the Mountain offering him hashish that would turn him into an assassin. The second reaction was even more remarkable. The second journalist first looked doubtful; then looked sly; then seemed to glance about him nervously, as if wondering whether we were alone, and then said with a sort of crestfallen and covert smile: `Well, Mr. Chesterton, I'm afraid I have the habit.'

As I also have the habit, and have never been able to imagine how it could be connected with morality or immorality, I confess that I plunged with him deeply into an immoral life. In the course of our conversation, I found he was otherwise perfectly sane. He was quite intelligent about economics or architecture; but his moral sense seemed to have entirely disappeared. He really thought it rather wicked to smoke. He had no `standard of abstract right or wrong'; in him it was not merely moribund; it was apparently dead. But anyhow, that is the point and that is the test. Nobody who has an abstract standard of right and wrong can possibly think it wrong to smoke a cigar. But he had a concrete standard of particular cut and dried customs of a particular tribe. Those who say Americans are largely descended from the American Indians might certainly make a case out of the suggestion that this mystical horror of material things is largely a barbaric sentiment. The Red Indian is said to have tried and condemned a tomahawk for committing a murder. In this case he was certainly the prototype of the white man who curses a bottle because too much of it goes into a man. Prohibition is sometimes praised for its simplicity; on these lines it may be equally condemned for its savagery. But I myself do not say anything so absurd as that Americans are savages; nor do I think it would matter much if they were descended from savages. It is culture that counts and not ethnology; and the culture that is concerned here derives indirectly rather from New England than from Old America. Whatever it derives from, however, this is the thing to be noted about it: that it really does not seem to understand what is meant by a standard of right and wrong. It is a vague sentimental notion that certain habits were not suitable to the old log cabin or the old hometown. It has a vague utilitarian notion that certain habits are not directly useful in the new amalgamated stores or the new financial gambling-hell. If his aged mother or his economic master dislikes to see a young man hanging about with a pipe in his mouth, the action becomes a sin; or the nearest that such a moral philosophy can come to the idea of a sin. A man does not chop wood for the log hut by smoking; and a man does not make dividends for the Big Boss by smoking; and therefore smoking has a smell as of something sinful. Of what the great theologians and moral philosophers have meant by a sin, these people have no more idea than a child drinking milk has of a great toxicologist analyzing poisons. It may be a credit of their virtue to be thus vague about vice. The man who is silly enough to say, when offered a cigarette, `I have no vices,' may not always deserve the rapier-thrust of the reply given by the Italian Cardinal, `It is not a vice, or doubtless you would have it.' But at least the Cardinal knows it is not a vice; which assists the clarity of his mind. But the lack of clear standards among those who vaguely think of it as a vice may yet be the beginning of much peril and oppression. My two American journalists, between them, may yet succeed in adding the sinfulness of cigars to the other curious things now part of the American Constitution.

I would therefore venture to say to Miss Avis Carlson that the quarrel in question does not arise from the Yankee Puritans having too much morality, but from their having too little. It does not arise from their drawing too hard and fast a line of distinction between right and wrong, but from their being much to loose and indistinct. They go by associations and not by abstractions. Therefore they classify smoking with vamping or a flask in the pocket with sin in the soul. I hope at least that some of the Fundamentalists will succeed in being a little more fundamental than this. The men of Tennessee are supposed to be very anxious to draw the line between men and monkeys. They are also supposed by some to be rather too anxious to draw the line between black men and white men. May I be allowed to hope that they will succeed in drawing a rather more logical line between bad men and good men? Something of the the difference and the difficulty may be seen by comparing the old Ku Klux Klan with the new Klu Klux Klan. The old secret society may have been justified or not; but it had a definite object: it was directed against somebody. The new secret society seems to have been directed against anybody; often against anybody who drank; in time, for all I know, against anybody who smoked. It is this sort of formless fanaticism that is the great danger of the American Temperament; and it is well to insist that if men must persecute, they will be more clear-headed if they persecute for a creed.

THE GOD IN THE CAVE

*"The place that the shepherds found was not an
academy or an abstract republic; it was not a
place of myths... explained or explained away.
It was a place of dreams come true."*

Traditions in art and literature and popular fable have quite sufficiently attested, as has been said, this particular paradox of the divine being in the cradle. Perhaps they have not so clearly emphasised the significance of the divine being in the cave. Curiously enough, indeed, tradition has not very clearly emphasised the cave. It is a familiar fact that the Bethlehem scene has been represented in every possible setting of time and country of landscape and architecture; and it is a wholly happy and admirable fact that men have conceived it as quite different according to their different individual traditions and tastes. But while all have realised that it was a stable, not so many have realised that it was a cave. Some critics have even been so silly as to suppose that there was some contradiction between the stable and the cave; in which case they cannot know much about caves or stables in Palestine. As they see differences that are not there it is needless to add that they do not see differences that are there. When a well-known critic says, for instance, that Christ being born in a rocky cavern is like Mithras having sprung alive out of a rock, it sounds like a parody upon comparative religion. There is such a thing as the point of a story, even if it is a story in the sense of a lie. And the notion of a hero appearing, like Pallas from the brain of Zeus, mature and without a mother, is obviously the very opposite of the idea of a god being born like an ordinary baby and entirely dependent on a mother. Whichever ideal we might prefer, we should surely see that they are contrary ideals. It is as stupid to connect them because they both contain a substance called stone as to identify the punishment of the Deluge with the baptism in the Jordan because they both contain a substance called water. Whether as a myth or a mystery, Christ was obviously conceived as born in a hole in the rocks primarily because it marked the position of one outcast and homeless....

It would be vain to attempt to say anything adequate, or anything new, about the change which this conception of a deity born like an outcast or even an outlaw had upon the whole conception of law and its duties to the poor and outcast. It is profoundly true to say that after that moment there could be no slaves. There could be and were people bearing that legal title, until the Church was strong enough to weed them out, but there could be no more of the pagan repose in the mere advantage to the state of keeping it a servile state. Individuals became important, in a sense in which no instruments can be important. A man could not be a means to an end, at any rate to any other man's end. All this popular and fraternal element in the story has been rightly attached by tradition to the episode of the Shepherds; the hinds who found themselves talking face to face with the princes of heaven. But there is another aspect of the popular element as represented by the shepherds which has not perhaps been so fully developed; and which is more directly relevant here.

Men of the people, like the shepherds, men of the popular tradition, had everywhere been the makers of the mythologies. It was they who had felt most directly, with least check or chill from philosophy or the corrupt cults of civilisation, the need we have already considered; the images that were adventures of the imagination; the mythology that was a sort of search; the tempting and tantalising hints of something half-human in nature; the dumb significance of seasons and special places. They had best understood that the soul of a landscape is a story, and the soul of a story is a personality. But rationalism had already begun to rot away these really irrational though imaginative treasures of the peasant; even as a systematic slavery had eaten the peasant out of house and home. Upon all such peasantries everywhere there was descending a dusk and twilight of disappointment, in the hour when these few men discovered what they sought. Everywhere else Arcadia was fading from the forest. Pan was dead and the shepherds were scattered like sheep. And though no man knew it, the hour was near which was to end and to fulfil all things; and, though no man heard it, there was one far-off cry in an unknown tongue upon the heaving wilderness of the mountains. The shepherds had found their Shepherd.

And the thing they found was of a kind with the things they sought. The populace had been wrong in many things; but they had not been wrong in believing that holy things could have a habitation and that divinity need not disdain the limits of time and space. And the barbarian who conceived the crudest fancy about the sun being stolen and hidden in a box, or the wildest myth about the god being rescued and his enemy deceived with a stone, was nearer to the secret of the cave and knew more about the crisis of the world, than all those in the circle of cities round the Mediterranean who had become content with cold abstractions or cosmopolitan generalisations; than all those who were spinning thinner and thinner threads of thought out of the transcendentalism of Plato or the orientalism of Pythagoras. The place that the shepherds found was not an academy or an abstract republic; it was not a place of myths allegorised or dissected or explained or explained away. It was a place of dreams come true. Since that hour no mythologies have been made in the world. Mythology is a search....

The philosophers had also heard. It is still a strange story, though an old one, how they came out of orient lands, crowned with the majesty of kings and clothed with something of the mystery of magicians. That truth that is tradition has wisely remembered them almost as unknown quantities, as mysterious as their mysterious and melodious names; Melchior, Caspar, Balthazar. But there came with them all that world of wisdom that had watched the stars in Chaldea and the sun in Persia; and we shall not be wrong if we see in them the same curiosity that moves all the sages. They would stand for the same human ideal if their names had really been Confucius or Pythagoras or Plato. They were those who sought not tales but the truth of things; and since their thirst for truth was itself a thirst for God, they also have had their reward. But even in order to understand that reward, we must understand that for philosophy as much as mythology, that reward was the completion of the incomplete....

The Magi, who stand for mysticism and philosophy, are truly conceived as seeking something new and even as finding something unexpected. That sense of crisis which still tingles in the Christmas story and even in every Christmas celebration, accentuates the idea of a search and a discovery. For the other mystical figures in the miracle play, for the angel and the mother, the shepherds and the soldiers of Herod, there may be aspects both simpler and more supernatural, more elemental or more emotional. But the Wise Men must be seeking wisdom; and for them there must be a light also in the intellect. And this is the light; that the Catholic creed is catholic and that nothing else is catholic. The philosophy of the Church is universal. The philosophy of the philosophers was not universal. Had Plato and Pythagoras and Aristotle stood for an instant in the light that came out of that little cave, they would have known that their own light was not universal. It is far from certain, indeed, that they did not know it already. Philosophy also, like mythology, had very much the air of a search. It is the realisation of this truth that gives its traditional majesty and mystery to the figures of the Three Kings; the discovery that religion is broader than philosophy and that this is the broadest of religions, contained within this narrow space....

We might well be content to say that mythology had come with the shepherds and philosophy with the philosophers; and that it only remained for them to combine in the recognisation of religion. But there was a third element that must not be ignored and one which that religion for ever refuses to ignore, in any revel or reconciliation. There was present in the primary scenes of the drama that Enemy that had rotted the legends with lust and frozen the theories into atheism, but which answered the direct challenge with something of that more direct method which we have seen in the conscious cult of the demons. In the description of that demon-worship, of the devouring detestation of innocence shown in the works of its witchcraft and the most inhuman of its human sacrifice, I have said less of its indirect and secret penetration of the saner paganism; the soaking of mythological imagination with sex; the rise of imperial pride into insanity. But both the indirect and the direct influence make themselves felt in the drama of Bethlehem. A ruler under the Roman suzerainty, probably equipped and surrounded with the Roman ornament and order though himself of eastern blood, seems in that hour to have felt stirring within him the spirit of strange things. We all know the story of how Herod, alarmed at some rumour of a mysterious rival, remembered the wild gesture of the capricious despots of Asia and ordered a massacre of suspects of the new generation of the populace. Everyone knows the story; but not everyone has perhaps noted its place in the story of the strange religions of men. Not everybody has seen the significance even of its very contrast with the Corinthian columns and Roman pavement of that conquered and superficially civilised world. Only, as the purpose in this dark spirit began to show and shine in the eyes of the Idumean, a seer might perhaps have seen something like a great grey ghost that looked over his shoulder; have seen behind him filling the dome of night and hovering for the last time over history, that vast and fearful fact that was Moloch of the Carthaginians; awaiting his last tribute from a ruler of the races of Shem. The demons in that first festival of Christmas, feasted also in their own fashion.

THE EXTRAORDINARY CABMAN

From time to time I have introduced into this newspaper column the narration of incidents that have really occurred. I do not mean to insinuate that in this respect it stands alone among newspaper columns. I mean only that I have found that my meaning was better expressed by some practical parable out of daily life than by any other method; therefore I propose to narrate the incident of the extraordinary cabman, which occurred to me only three days ago, and which, slight as it apparently is, aroused in me a moment of genuine emotion bordering upon despair.

On the day that I met the strange cabman I had been lunching in a little restaurant in Soho in company with three or four of my best friends. My best friends are all either bottomless sceptics or quite uncontrollable believers, so our discussion at luncheon turned upon the most ultimate and terrible ideas. And the whole argument worked out ultimately to this: that the question is whether a man can be certain of anything at all. I think he can be certain, for if (as I said to my friend, furiously brandishing an empty bottle) it is impossible intellectually to entertain certainty, what is this certainty which it is impossible to entertain? If I have never experienced such a thing as certainty I cannot even say that a thing is not certain. Similarly, if I have never experienced such a thing as green I cannot even say that my nose is not green. It may be as green as possible for all I know if I have really no experience of greenness. So we shouted at each other and shook the room; because metaphysics is the only thoroughly emotional thing. And the difference between us was very deep, because it was a difference as to the object of the whole thing called broad-mindedness or the opening of the intellect. For my friend said that he opened his intellect as the sun opens the fans of a palm tree, opening for opening's sake, opening infinitely for ever. But I said that I opened my intellect as I opened my mouth, in order to shut it again on something solid. I was doing it at the moment. And as I truly pointed out, it would look uncommonly silly if I went on opening my mouth infinitely, for ever and ever*.

Now when this argument was over, or at least when it was cut short (for it will never be over), I went away with one of my companions, who in the confusion and comparative insanity of a General Election had somehow become a member of Parliament, and I drove with him in a cab from the corner of Leicester Square to the members' entrance of the House of Commons, where the police received me with a quite unusual tolerance. Whether they thought that he was my keeper or that I was his keeper is a discussion between us which still continues.

It is necessary in this narrative to preserve the utmost exactitude of detail. After leaving my friend at the House I took the cab on a few hundred yards to an office in Victoria Street which I had to visit. I then got out and offered him more than his fare. He looked at it, but not with the surly doubt and general disposition to try it on which is not unknown among normal cabmen. But this was no normal, perhaps, no human, cabman. He looked at it with a dull and infantile astonishment, clearly quite genuine. "Do you know, sir," he said, "you've only given me 1s. 8d?" I remarked, with some surprise, that I

---

* *From other writings of Chesterton, we know that the "open-minded" friend referred to here is H.G. Wells. Also, we learn from the paragraph to follow that Hilaire Belloc was another of those present at this Soho meeting. And it is quite possible, even probable, that George Bernard Shaw was also in the party.*

did know it. "Now you know, sir," said he in a kindly, appealing, reasonable way, "you know that ain't the fare form Euston." "Euston," I repeated vaguely, for the phrase at that moment sounded to me like China or Arabia. "What on earth has Euston got to do with It?" "You hailed me just outside Euston Station," began the man with astonishing precision, "and then you said ..." "What in the name of Tartarus are you talking about?" I said with Christian forbearance; "I took you at the south-west corner of Leicester Square." "Leicester Square," he exclaimed, loosening a kind of cataract of scorn, "why we ain't been near Leicester Square to-day. You hailed me outside Euston Station, and you said ..." "Are you mad, or am I?" I asked with scientific calm.

I looked at the man. No ordinary dishonest cabman would think of creating so solid and colossal and creative a lie. And this man was not a dishonest cabman. If ever a human face was heavy and simple and humble, and with great big blue eyes protruding like a frog's, if ever (in short) a human face was all that a human face should be, it was the face of that resentful and respectful cabman. I looked up and down the street; an unusually dark twilight seemed to be coming on. And for one second the old nightmare of the sceptic put its finger on my nerve. What was certainty? Was anybody certain of anything? Heavens! to think of the dull rut of the sceptics who go on asking whether we possess a future life. The exciting question for real scepticism is whether we possess past life. What is a minute ago, rationalistically considered, except a tradition and a picture? The darkness grew deeper from the road. The cabman calmly gave me the most elaborate details of the gesture, the words, the complex but consistent course of action which I had adopted since that remarkable occasion when I had hailed him outside Euston Station. How did I know (my sceptical friends would say) that I had not hailed him outside Euston. I was firm about my assertion; he was quite equally firm about his. He was obviously quite as honest a man as I, and a member of a much more respectable profession. In that moment the universe and the stars swung just a hair's breadth from their balance, and the foundations of the earth were moved. But for the same reason that I believe in Democracy, for the same reason that I believe in free will, for the same reason that I believe in fixed character of virtue, the reason that could only be expressed by saying that I do not choose to be a lunatic, I continued to believe that this honest cabman was wrong, and I repeated to him that I had really taken him at the corner of Leicester Square. He began with the same evident and ponderous sincerity, "You hailed me outside Euston Station, and you said ..."

And at this moment there came over his features a kind of frightful transfiguration of living astonishment, as if he had been lit up like a lamp from the inside. "Why, I beg your pardon, sir," he said. "I beg your pardon. I beg your pardon. You took me from Leicester Square. I remember now. I beg your pardon." And with that this astonishing man let out his whip with a sharp crack at his horse and went trundling away. The whole of which interview, before the banner of St. George I swear, is strictly true.

I looked at the strange cabman as he lessened in the distance and the mists. I do not know whether I was right in fancying that although his face had seemed so honest there was something unearthly and demoniac about him when seen from behind. Perhaps he had been sent to tempt me from my adherence to those sanities and certainties which I had defended earlier in the day. In any case it gave me pleasure to remember that my sense of reality, though it had rocked for an instant, had remained erect.

ON TURNPIKES AND MEDIEVALISM

Opening my newspaper the other day, I saw a short but emphatic leaderette entitled `A Relic of Medievalism'. It expressed a profound indignation upon the fact that somewhere or other, in some fairly remote corner of this country, there is a turnpike-gate, with a toll. It insisted that this antiquated tyranny is insupportable, because it is supremely important that our road traffic should go very fast; presumably a little faster than it does. So it described the momentary delay in this place as a relic of medievalism. I fear the future will look at that sentence, somewhat sadly and a little contemptuously, as a very typical relic of modernism. I mean it will be a melancholy relic of the only period in all human history when people were proud of being modern. For though to-day is always to-day and the moment is always modern, we are the only men in all history who fell back upon bragging about the mere fact that to-day is not yesterday. I fear that some in the future will explain it by saying that we had precious little else to brag about. For, whatever the medieval faults, they went with one merit. Medieval people never worried about being medieval; and modern people do worry horribly about being modern.

To begin with, note the queer, automatic assumption that it must always mean throwing mud at a thing to call it a relic of medievalism. The modern world contains a good many relics of medievalism, and most of us would be surprised if the argument were logically enforced even against the things that are commonly called medieval. We should express some regret if somebody blew up Westminster Abby, because it is a relic of medievalism. Doubts would trouble us if the Government burned all existing copies of Dante's *Divine Comedy* and Chaucer's *Canterbury Tales*, because they are quite certainly relics of medievalism. We could not throw ourselves into unreserved and enthusiastic rejoicing even if the Tower of Giotto were destroyed as a relic of medievalism. And only just lately, in Oxford and Paris (themselves, alas! relics of medievalism), there has been a perverse and pedantic revival of the Thomist Philosophy and the logical method of the medieval Schoolmen. Similarly, curious and restless minds, among the very youngest artists and art critics, have unaccountably gone back even farther into the barbaric period than the limit of the Tower of Giotto, and are even now telling us to look back to the austerity of Cimabue and Byzantine diagrams of the Dark Ages. These relics must be more medieval even than medievalism.

But, in fact, this queer phrase would not cover only what is commonly called medievalism. If a relic of medievalism only means something that has come down to us from medieval times, such writers would probably be surprised at the size and solidity of the relics. If I told these honest pressmen that the Press is a relic of medievalism, they would probably prove their love of a cliché by accusing me of a paradox. But it is at least certain that the Printing Press is a relic of medievalism. It was discovered and established by entirely medieval men, steeped in medieval ideas, stuffed with the religion and social spirit of the Middle Ages. There are no more typically medieval words than those noble words of the eulogy that was pronounced by the great English printer on the great English poet; the words of Caxton upon Chaucer. If I were to say that Parliament is a relic of medievalism, I should be on even stronger ground; for, while the Press did at least come at the end of the Middle Ages, the Parliaments came much more nearly at the beginning of the Middle

Ages. They began, I think, in Spain and the provinces of the Pyrenees; but our own traditional date, connecting them with the revolt of Simon de Montfort, if not strictly accurate, does roughly represent the time. I need not say that half the great educational foundations, not only Oxford and Cambridge, but Glasgow and Paris, are relics of medievalism. It would seem rather hard on the poor journalistic reformer if he is not allowed to pull down a little turnpike-gate till he has proved his right to pull down all these relics of medievalism.

Next we have, of course, the very considerable historic doubt about whether the turnpike-gate is a relic of medievalism. I do not know what was the date of this particular turnpike; but turnpikes and tolls of that description were perhaps most widely present, most practically enforced, or, at least, most generally noted, in the eighteenth century. When Pitt and Dundas, both of them roaring drunk, jumped over a turnpike-gate and were fired at with a blunderbuss, I hope nobody will suggest that those two great politicians were relics of medievalism. Nobody surely could be more modern than Pitt and Dundas, for one of them was a great financial statesman, depending entirely on the bankers, and the other was a swindler. It is possible, of course, that some such local toll was really medieval, but I rather doubt whether the journalist even inquired whether it was medieval. He probably regards everything that happened before the time of Jazz and the Yellow Press as medieval. For him medieval only means old, and old means bad; so that we come to the last question, which ought to have been the first question, of whether a turnpike really is necessarily bad. If we were really relics of medievalism--that is, if we had really been taught to think--we should have put that question first, and discussed whether a thing is bad or good before discussing whether it is modern or medieval. There is no space to discuss it here at length, but a very simple test in the matter may be made. The aim and effect of tolls is simply this: that those who use the roads shall pay for the roads. As it is, the poor people of a district, including those who never stir from their villages, and hardly from their firesides, pay to maintain roads which are ploughed up and torn to pieces by the cars and lorries of rich men and big businesses, coming from London and the distant cities. It is not self-evident that this is a more just arrangement than that by which wayfarers pay to keep up the way, even if that arrangement were a relic of medievalism. Lastly, we might well ask, is it indeed so certain that our roads suffer from the slowness of petrol traffic; and that, if we can only make every sort of motor go faster and faster, we shall all be saved at last? That motors are more important than men is doubtless an admitted principle of a truly modern philosophy; nevertheless, it might be well to keep some sort of reasonable ratio between them, and decide exactly how many human beings should be killed by each car in the course of each year. And I fear that a mere policy of the acceleration of traffic may take us beyond the normal modern recognition of murder into something resembling a recognition of massacre. And about this, I for one still have a scruple; which is probably a relic of medievalism.

GOVERNMENT AND THE RIGHTS
OF MAN

I could never see why a man who is not free to open his mouth to drink should be free to open it to talk. Talking does far more direct harm to other people. The village suffers less directly from the village drunkard than it might from the village tale bearer, or the village tub-thumper, or the village villain who seduces the village maiden. These and twenty other types of evil are done simply by talking; it is certain that a vast amount of evil would be prevented if we all wore gags. And the answer is not to deny that slander is a social poison, or seduction a spiritual murder. The answer is that, unless a man is allowed to talk, he might as well be a chimpanzee who is only able to chatter. In other words, if a man loses the responsibility for these rudimentary functions and forms of freedom, he loses not only his citizenship, but his manhood.

But there are other personal liberties still permitted us, more elaborate and civilized than that simple human speech which is still closely akin to the chatter of the chimpanzees. By some official oversight, which I am quite unable to explain, we are still allowed to write private letters if we put them in public pillar-boxes. The Postmaster-General does not write all our letters for us; even the local postman has as yet no such local powers. I cannot conceive how it is that reformers have failed to note the need for uniting, reorganizing, coordinating, codifying, and linking up all this complex, chaotic, and wasteful system, or lack of system. There must be vast amounts of overlapping, with some six young gentlemen writing letters to one young lady. There must be a terribly low educational standard, with all sorts of poor people allowed to put into a private letter any spelling or grammar they like. There must be a number of bad psychological habits being formed, by foolish people writing their sons in the Colonies or their mothers in the workhouse. And all this anarchy and deterioration could be stopped by the simple process of standardisation of all correspondence. I know if I use the word "standardisation," Mr. H.G. Wells will welcome it and begin to think of it seriously [indeed there opens before me a vista of vast social reform].

On the face of it, the first and most obvious method would be for the Government to send round official forms for our friendly correspondence, to be filled up like the forms about insurance or Income Tax. Here and there, even in the most model communication, there would be words left blank, which the individual might be allowed to fill out himself. I have a half-formed ideal of an official love letter, printed in the manner of "I ________you," so that the citizen might insert "love," or "like," or "adore," with a view to the new civil marriage; or "renounce," or "repudiate," or "execrate," with a view to the newer and more civil divorce. But even these blanks for verbal variation must be admitted with caution; for the aim of the whole reform is to raise the general level of all correspondence to a height unattainable by the majority of the people as yet.

It may be hinted that I plead for this reform with the passion of self interest, for it would enable me to neglect my correspondence in theory as I already neglect it in practice. I very seldom write to anybody; and I never write to the people I like best. About them I do not trouble, for they understand. But there are unanswered letters from total strangers about which I feel a remorse. Some day I shall make a list of the people I should have liked to answer, or advertise for them by such details as I can remember them. If I had any money I should like to leave them millions of it when I die. It may be said that I should get off cheaply, if the government would sent round to all these people an official card in my name [instead].

But I am not really converted to my own project, even by my own failure. I am not really convinced of the necessity of standardised correspondence, either by the existence of criminal letters or my own criminal neglect of letters. If or when, in some strange mood at some distant date, I should actually answer a letter, I should still prefer to answer it myself. even if I had nothing to write except an apology for not writing, I should prefer my self-abasement to have the character of self-determination.

It is a most extraordinary fact that all modern talk about self-determination is applied to everything except the self. It is applied to the State but it is not applied to the very thing to which its verbal formula professes to apply. I, for one, do believe in that mystical doctrine of democracy, which pre-supposes that England has a soul, or that France has a self. But surely it is much more obvious and ordinary fact that Jones has a self and Robinson has a self. And the question I have here discussed under the parable of the Post Office is not the question of whether there are abuses in drink or diet, as there are calumny and blackmail in any pillar-box or postman's bag. It is the question of whether in these days the claims of government are to leave anything whatever of the rights of man.

CONCERNING A STRANGE CITY

Everyone has his own private and almost secret selection among the examples of the mysterious power of words, the power which a certain verbal combination has over the emotions and even the soul. It is commonplace that literature has a charm, not merely in the sense of the charm of a woman, but of the charms of a witch. Historical scholars question how the ignorant imagination of the Dark Ages distorted the poet Virgil into a magician. One answer to the question, possibly, is that he was one. Theologians and philosophers debate about the inspiration of scripture, but perhaps the most philosophical argument, for saying that certain scriptural sayings are inspired, is simply that they sound like it. The great lines of the poets are like landscapes or visions, but the same strange light can be found not only in the high places of poetry but also in quite obscure corners of prose.

I can only express what I mean by saying that it is the finite part of the image that really suggests infinity. Most worthy and serious people, instead of saying the spiritual place, would say the spiritual world. Some dismal and disgusting people, instead of saying the spiritual place, would say the spiritual plane. The immediate chill and disenchantment of this change is due to a vague but vivid sense that the spiritual thing has become less real. A world sounds like an astronomical diagram, and a plane sounds like a geometrical diagram. Both of these are abstractions, but a place is not an abstraction, but a reality. The spiritual thrill is all in the idea that the place is a place, however spiritual, that it is some strange city where the sky touches the earth, or where eternity contrives to live on: the borderland of time and space.

In the mind of man, if not in the nature of things, there seems to be some connection between concentration and reality. When we want to ask, in natural language, whether a thing really exists or not, we ask if it is really "there" or not. We say "there", even if we do not clearly understand where. A man cannot enter a house by five doors at once; he might do it if he were in an atmosphere. But he does not want to be in an atmosphere. He has a stubborn sub-conscious belief that an animal is greater than an atmosphere. As a thing rises in the scale of things, it tends to localize and even narrow its natural functions. A man cannot absorb his sustenance through all his pores like a sponge or some low sea-organisms; he cannot take in an atmosphere of beef, or an abstract essence of buns. Any buns thrown at him, as at the bear at the zoo, must be projected with such skill as to hit a particular hole in his head. In nature, in a sense, there is choice even before there is will . The plant or bulb narrows itself and pierces at one place rather than at another and all growth is a pattern of such green wedges. But however it be with these lower things, there has always been this spearlike selection and concentration in man's conception of higher things. Compared with that, there is something not only vague but vulgar in most of the talk about infinity. The pantheist is right up to a certain point, but so is the sponge.

Both vitally and verbally, this infinity is the enemy of all that is fine. Such philological points are sometimes more than pedantries or mere puns. And it is more than a pedantic pun to say that most things that are fine are finite. We testify to it when we talk of a beautiful thing having refinement or having finish. It is brought to an end like the blade of a beautiful sword, not only to its end in the sense of its cessation but to its end in the sense of its aim. All fine things are in this sense finished, even when they are eternal.

Poetry is committed to this concentration fully as much as religion: fairyland has always been as local, one might say as parochial, as Heaven. And if religion were removed tomorrow the poets would only begin to act as the pagans acted. They would begin to say "Lo, here", and "Lo, there", from the incurable itch of the idea that something must be somewhere, and not merely anywhere. Even if it were in some sense found to be in everything, it would still be in everything and not merely in all.

NEGATIVE AND POSITIVE MORALITY

A vast amount of nonsense is talked against negative and destructive things. The silliest sort of progressive complains of negative morality, and compares it unfavorably with positive morality. The silliest sort of conservative complains of destructive reform and compares it unfavorably with constructive reform. Both the progressive and the conservative entirely neglect to consider the very meaning of the words "yes" and "no". To give the answer "yes" to one question is to imply the answer "no" to another question. To desire the construction of something is to desire the destruction of whatever prevents its construction. This is particularly plain in the fuss about the "negative" morality of the Ten Commandments. The truth is that the curtness of the Commandments is an evidence, not of the gloom and narrowness of a religion but of its liberality and humanity. It is shorter to state the things forbidden than the things permitted precisely because most things are permitted and only a few things are forbidden. An optimist who insisted on a purely positive morality would have to begin by telling a man that he might pick dandelions on a common and go on for months before he came to the fact that he might throw pebbles into the sea. In comparison with this positive morality the

Ten Commandments rather shine in that brevity which is the soul of wit.

But of course the fallacy is even more fundamental than this. Negative morality is positive morality, stated in the plainest and therefore the most positive way. If I am told not to murder Mr. Robinson, if I am stopped in the very act of murdering Mr. Robinson, it is obvious that Mr. Robinson is not only spared, but in a sense renewed, and even created. And those who like Mr. Robinson, among them my reactionary romanticism might suggest the inclusion of Mrs. Robinson, will be well aware that they have recovered a living and complex unity. And similarly, those who like European civilisation, and the common code of what used to be called Christendom, will realize that salvation is not negative, but highly positive, and even highly complex. They will rejoice at its escape, long before they have leisure for its examination. But, without examination, they will know that there is a great deal to be examined, and a great deal that is worth examination. Nothing is negative except nothing. It is not our rescue that was negative, but only the nothingness and annihilation from which we were rescued.

On the other side there is the same fallacy about merely destructive reform. It could be applied just as easily to the merely destructive war. In both cases destruction may be essential to the avoidance of destruction, and also to the very possibility of construction. Men are not merely destroying a ship in order to have a shipwreck; they may be merely destroying a tree in order to have a ship. To complain that we spent four years in the Great War in mere destruction is to complain that we spent them in escaping from being destroyed. And it is, once again, to forget the fact that the failure of the murderer means the life of a positive and not a negative Mr. Robinson. If we take the imaginary Mr. Robinson as a type of the average modern man in Western Europe, and study him from head to foot, we shall find defects as well as merits. And in the whole civilisation we have saved, we shall find defects that amounts to diseases. Its feet, if not of clay, are certainly in clay, stuck in the mud of a materialistic industrial destitution and despair. To say it is a positive good and glory to have saved Mr. Robinson from strangling is to miss the whole meaning of human life. It is to forget every good as soon as we have saved it, that is, to lose it as soon as we have got it. Progress of that kind is a hope that is the enemy of faith, and a faith that is the enemy of charity.

When our hopes for the coming time seem disturbed or doubtful, and peace chaotic, let us remember that it is really our disappointment that is an illusion. It is our rescue that is a reality. Our grounds for gratitude are really far greater than our powers of being grateful. It is in the mood of a noble sort of humility, and even a noble sort of fear, that new things are really made. We adorn things most when we love them most. And we love them most when we have nearly lost them.

DEMOCRACY AND INDUSTRIALISM

It grows plainer, every day, that those of us who cling to crumbling creeds and dogmas, and defend the dying traditions of the Dark Ages, will soon be left alone defending the most obviously decaying of all those ancient dogmas: the idea called Democracy. It has taken not quite a lifetime, roughly my own lifetime, to bring it from the top of its success, or alleged success, to the bottom of its failure, or reputed failure. By the end of the nineteenth century, millions of men were accepting democracy without knowing why. By the end of the twentieth century, it looks as if millions of people will be rejecting democracy, also without knowing why. In such a straight, strictly logical and unwavering line does the Mind of Man advance along the great Path of Progress.

Anyhow, at the moment, democracy is not only being abused, but being very unfairly abused. Men are blaming universal suffrage, merely because they are not enlightened enough to blame original sin. There is one simple test for deciding whether popular political evils are due to original sin. And that is to do what none or very few of these modern malcontents are doing; to state any sort of moral claim for any other sort of political system. The essence of democracy is very simple and, as Jefferson said, self-evident. If ten men are wrecked together on a desert island, the community consists of those ten men, their welfare is the social object, and normally their will is the social law. If they have not a natural claim to rule themselves, which of them has a natural claim to rule the rest? To say that the cleverest or boldest will rule is to beg the moral question. If his talents are used for the community, in planning voyages or distilling water, then he is the servant of the community; which is, in that sense, his sovereign. If his talents are used against the community by stealing rum or poisoning water, why should the community submit to him? And is it in the least likely that it will? In such a simple case as that, everybody can see the popular basis of the thing, and the advantage of government by consent. The trouble with democracy is that it has never, in modern times, had to do with such a simple case as that. In other words, the trouble with democracy is not democracy. It is certain artificial anti-democratic things that have, in fact, thrust themselves into the modern world to thwart and destroy democracy.

Modernity is not democracy; machinery is not democracy; the surrender of everything to trade and commerce is not democracy. Capitalism is not democracy; and is admittedly, by trend and savour, rather against democracy. Plutocracy by definition is not democracy. But all these modern things forced themselves into the world at about the time, or shortly after the time, when great idealists like Rousseau and Jefferson happened to have been thinking about the democratic ideal of democracy. It is tenable that the ideal was too idealist to succeed. It is not tenable that the ideal that failed was the same as the realities that did succeed. It is one thing to say that a fool went into a jungle and was devoured by wild beasts; it is quite another to say that he himself survives as the one and only wild beast. Democracy has had everything against it in practice, and that very fact may be something against it in theory. It may be argued that it has human life against it. But, at any rate, it is quite certain that it has modern life against it. The industrial and scientific world of the last hundred years has been much more unsuitable a setting for the experiment of the self-government than would have been found in old conditions of agrarian or even nomadic life. Feudal manorial life was a not a democracy; but it could have been much more easily turned into a democracy. Later peasant life, as in France or Switzerland, actually has been quite easily turned into a democracy. But it is horribly hard to turn what is called modern industrial democracy into a democracy.

That is why many men are now beginning to say that the democratic ideal is no longer in touch with the modern spirit. I strongly agree; and I naturally prefer the democratic ideal, which is at least an ideal, and therefore, an idea, to the modern spirit, which is simply modern, therefore, already becoming ancient. I notice that the cranks, whom it would be more polite to call the idealists, are already hastening to shed this ideal. A well-known Pacifist, with whom I argued in Radical papers in my Radical days, and who then passed as a pattern Republican of the new Republic, went out of his way the other day to say, 'The voice of the people is commonly the voice of Satan.' The truth is that these Liberals never did really believe in popular government, any more than in anything else that was popular, such as pubs or the Dublin Sweepstake. They did not believe in the democracy they invoked against kings and priests. But I did believe in it; and I do believe in it, though I much preferred to invoke it against prigs and faddists. I still believe it would be the most human sort of government, if it could be once more attempted in a more human time.

Unfortunately, humanitarianism has been the mark of an inhuman time. And by inhumanity I do not mean merely cruelty; I mean the condition in which even cruelty ceases to be human. I mean the condition in which the rich man, instead of hanging six or seven of his enemies because he hates them, merely beggars and starves to death six or seven thousand people whom he does not hate, and has never seen, because they live at the other side of the world. I mean the condition in which the courtier or pander of the rich man, instead of excitedly mixing a rare, original poison for the Borgias, or carving exquisite ornamental poignard for the political purposes of the Medici, works monotonously in a factory turning out a small type of screw, which will fit into a plate he will never see; to form part of a gun he will never see; to be used in a battle he will never see, and about the merits of which he knows far less than the Renaissance rascal knew about the purposes of the poison and the dagger. In short, what is the matter with industrialism is indirection; the fact that nothing is straightforward; that all its ways are crooked even when they are meant to be straight. Into this most indirect of all systems we tried to fit the most direct of all ideas. Democracy, an ideal which is simple to excess, was vainly applied to a society which was complex to the point of craziness. It is not so very surprising that such a vision has faded in such an environment. Personally, I like the vision; but it takes all sorts to make a world, and there actually are human beings, walking about quite calmly in the daylight, who appear to like the environment.

THE IDEAL OF A LEISURE STATE

Among the strange and rather stiff antics of the rather antiquated art of party journalism is the duty laid upon the good party man of trying to disagree with his opponents when they have the impudence to agree with him. He not only has to insist that they are wrong; he has to deny their right to be right. Even when you have to admit that your antagonist is talking sense, even when you pride yourself on talking exactly the same sense, you have to deny that it is sensible of him to talk sense. Or you deny that it is sense in the same sense; or sense in the true sense of the word. More often you simply imply that it is inconsistent and irrational in him to talk sense, because it is his whole duty and high function in State to talk nonsense. It is his business to be wrong; it is his business to be beaten; he is the invisible playmate, who sides with the Frenchman and never can win. That he should suddenly side with his own country, or win the approval of his own critics, is regarded as a form of cheating. Twice lately I have noticed a party leader saying things that any sensible person would say, but not allowed by the Opposition Press to say them, because he was not supposed to be a sensible person. One of them was when Mr. Baldwin pointed out the appalling peril of directly declaring war on all Trade Unionists at the very moment when we are supposed to be persuading them not to be Bolshevists. The other was when Mr. George Lansbury said to the effect that the dole was a deplorable necessity, because every man in the world ought to grow up expecting to work. But the conventional journalists, instead of agreeing with Mr. Landsbury, sneered at him for agreeing with them.

Well, that way of working against Bolshevism will have its Nemesis; the Nemesis of all nonsense, which is neglect. A new generation will go straight to the problems and forget all about the party quarrels. If we want to know what the future will be like, as far as anybody can know it, we must begin at the springs of thought and theory, the sources of the river, and not merely potter about in the swamps where it straggles away into its last labyrinthine delta of lobbying and intrigue. We must consider what ideas there are in the world at present, and in what way they are likely to mould the future. Now Mr. George Lansbury, whether consciously or not, really touched on one of the most important of these intellectual conflicts, which so often precede political and even military conflicts. And the position which he took up upon that matter was that of a conservative or a traditionalist; or as some on the otherside would say, of a Tory.

The controversy I mean has nothing to do with Socialism or Capitalism. It is a question about the nature of human life, even of ideal human life, which cuts across all these things and would probably divide Socialism into two camps. It is something which some speculators have already begun to discuss under the name of "The Leisure State." It is something which was suggested, perhaps, in the title and work of Mr. H.G. Wells called "The World Set Free." It does not mean the world set free from the sceptre or the sabre; it means the world set free from the spade and the ploughshare. It means that it might be possible so to organize machinery that the whole life of man on the earth should be one of leisure and not of labour. I will not pretend to discuss whether it would be mechanically possible. But it is time we began to discuss whether it is morally desirable. I am entirely at one with the Socialists in wishing to give most men less work and some men more work. But the abstract question

propounded here is not that question; it is whether, if we could, we would give nobody any work. It assumes for the sake of argument the dark and dubious principle that labour-saving devices will save labour. It asks whether, even then, we always want to save labour. We talk of paying too much for labour; should we or should we not pay too much for idleness?

Many of the idealists can only conceive of an idle humanity as an ideal humanity. They talk as if no man could ever rest until he reached Utopia; or as if a really long holiday were something like heaven, utterly distant and divine. Their social philosophy is that of the hearty and humorous epitaph of the charwoman, who had gone on to do nothing for ever and ever. But even now it is by no means certain that those who are not charwomen really become any more hearty and humorous by doing nothing for ever and ever. A vast amount of stuffy and sentimental humbug has been uttered in favour of the Gospel of Work. As it was said that Carlyle talked a great deal in praise of silence, it may also be respectfully affirmed that he idled away a great deal of his time meditating on the virtues of labour. Work is not necessarily good for people; overwork is very bad for people; and both often begin with a bad motive and come to a bad end. Many a modern industrialist has prided himself on being as industrious as he was industrial. And it meant little more than that he was ready to sweat himself, as well as his neighbors, when he wanted to swindle his neighbors. Many a modern man has lived by the Gospel of Work, when it meant the spirit that will always work against the Gospel. A great deal of harm has been done by setting up these oily machines as models for mankind. I would not point to these ideal industrious men; I would turn away men's eyes from the painful picture of the Industrious Apprentice; I would veil their faces lest they should be disturbed by the repulsive appearance of the man who Attended These Classes and Is Making Big Money Now. I would hastily remove this deplorable person; but would gently remind the Utopians that he is not the only kind of person who is deplorable.

Now, the Leisure State exists already. It can be represented at any sort of function such as is called a State Banquet or State Ball. The

World Set Free exists already. It exists in the world that specially claims to call itself the world. It exists in the world which Socialists and Utopians specially claim to call worldly. We are in a position even now to judge pretty well, in a general fashion, what is the effect on human beings having nothing particular to do. The "world" is already set free, if that is freedom; but is it exactly what the Utopians want to demand as freedom? It is undoubtedly an idle society, but is it an ideal society? Is Utopia to be found in Belgravia any more than in Bohemia? Are the rich all good or better than anybody else? Are they all clever or cleverer than anybody else? Are they even all free and happy, or all freer and happier than anybody else? And though there are good and clever and free and happy people among the idle rich, as there are among the idle poor, not to mention the industrious poor, I think it is broadly true that most of us have found that the most sincere and sensible people were people who earned their own living. I agree therefore with Mr. Landbury in differing from those who would perpetuate eternal unemployment combined with universal doles, and who call that ignominious combination The World Set Free.

But there is another strong objection which I, one of the laziest of all the children of Adam, have against the Leisure State. Those who think it could be done argue that a vast machinery using electricity, water-power, petrol, and so on, might reduce the work imposed on each of us to a minimum. It might, but it would also reduce our control to a minimum. We should ourselves become parts of a machine, even if the machine only used those parts once a week. The machine would be our master; for the machine would produce our food, and most of us could have no notion of how it was really being produced. A free man would rather be a peasant rising at dawn to put more work on his own field. In other words, in the social formula to which we are all accustomed, the peasant has control over the means of production. The occasional adjunct to the intermittent machine would have no control whatever over his own leisure, but less over his own life. Machinery organized in that fashion would have to be organized from an official centre; and no more controlled by its adjuncts

than the tiniest of the little wheels can wind a watch. The leisured persons might be many things in their long hours of leisure. It is not impossible, by the parallel of plutocracy, that they might be profligates, perverts, drugtakers, dram-drinkers, pessimists, and suicides. But they might all be poets and artists and philosophers. They would not be citizens.

THE FALLACY OF SUCCESS

There has appeared in our time a particular class of books and articles which I sincerely and solemnly think may be called the silliest ever known among men. They are much more wild than the wildest romances of chivalry and much more dull than the dullest religious tract. Moreover, the romances of chivalry were at least about chivalry; the religious tracts are about religion. But these things are about nothing; they are about what is called Success. On every bookstall, in every magazine, you may find works telling people how to succeed. They are books showing men how to succeed in everything; they are written by men who cannot even succeed in writing books. To begin with, of course, there is no such thing as Success. Or, if you like to put it so, there is nothing that is not successful. That a thing is successful merely means that it is; a millionaire is successful in being a millionaire and a donkey in being a donkey. Any live man has succeeded in living; any dead man may have succeeded in committing suicide. But, passing over the bad logic and bad philosophy in the phrase, we may take it, as these writers do, in the ordinary sense of success in obtaining money or worldly position. These writers profess to tell the ordinary man how he may succeed in his trade or speculation--how, if he is a builder, he may

succeed as a builder; how, if he is a stockbroker, he may succeed as a stockbroker. They profess to show him how, if he is a grocer, he may become a sporting yachtsman; how, if he is a tenth-rate journalist, he may become a peer; and how, if he is a German Jew, he may become an Anglo-Saxon. This is a definite and business-like proposal, and I really think that the people who buy these books (if any people do buy them) have a moral, if not a legal, right to ask for their money back. Nobody would dare to publish a book about electricity which literally told one nothing about electricity; no one would dare publish an article on botany which showed that the writer did not know which end of a plant grew in the earth. Yet our modern world is full of books about Success and successful people which literally contain no kind of idea, and scarcely and kind of verbal sense.

It is perfectly obvious that in any decent occupation (such as bricklaying or writing books) there are only two ways (in any special sense) of succeeding. One is by doing very good work, the other is by cheating. Both are much too simple to require any literary explanation. If you are in for the high jump, either jump higher than any one else, or manage somehow to pretend that you have done so. If you want to succeed at whist, either be a good whist-player, or play with marked cards. You may want a book about jumping; you may want a book about whist; you may want a book about cheating at whist. But you cannot want a book about Success. Especially you cannot want a book about Success such as those which you can now find scattered by the hundred about the book-market. You may want to jump or to play cards; but you do not want to read wandering statements to the effect that jumping is jumping, or that games are won by winners. If these writers, for instance, said anything about success in jumping it would be something like this: "The jumper must have a clear aim before him. He must desire definitely to jump higher than the other men who are in for the same competition. He must let no feeble feelings of mercy (sneaked from the sickening Little Englanders and Pro-Boers) prevent him from trying to *do his best*. He must remember that a competition in jumping is distinctly competitive, and that, as Darwin has gloriously demonstrated, THE WEAKEST GO TO THE

WALL." That is the kind of thing the book would say, and very useful it would be, no doubt, if read out in a low and tense voice to a young man just about to take the high jump. Or suppose that in the course of his intellectual rambles the philosopher of Success dropped upon our other case, that of playing cards, his bracing advice would run-- "In playing cards it is very necessary to avoid the mistake (commonly made by maudlin humanitarians and Free Traders) of permitting your opponent to win the game. You must have grit and snap and *go in to win*. The days of idealism and superstition are over. We live in a time of science and hard common sense, and it has now been definitely proved that in any game where two are playing IF ONE DOES NOT WIN THE OTHER WILL." It is all very stirring, of course; but I confess that if I were playing cards I would rather have some decent little book which told me the rules of the game. Beyond the rules of the game it is all a question either of talent or dishonesty; and I will undertake to provide either one or the other--which, it is not for me to say.

Turning over a popular magazine, I find a queer and amusing example. There is an article called "The Instinct that Makes People Rich." It is decorated in front with a formidable portrait of Lord Rothschild. There are many definite methods, honest and dishonest, which make people rich; the only "instinct" I know of which does it is that instinct which theological Christianity crudely describes as "the sin of avarice." That, however, is beside the present point. I wish to quote the following exquisite paragraphs as a piece of typical advice as to how to succeed. It is so practical; it leaves so little doubt about what should be our next step--

> The name of Vanderbilt is synonymous with wealth gained by modern enterprise. 'Cornelius,' the founder of the family, was the first of the great American magnates of commerce. He started as the son of a poor farmer; he ended as a millionaire twenty times over.
>
> He had the money-making instinct. He seized his opportunities, the opportunities that were given by the application of the steam-engine to ocean traffic, and by the birth of railway locomotion in the

wealthy but underdeveloped United States of America, and consequently he amassed an immense fortune.

Now it is, of course, obvious that we cannot all follow exactly in the footsteps of this great railway monarch. The precise opportunities that fell to him do not occur to us. Circumstances have changed. But, although this is so, still, in our own sphere and in our own circumstances, we *can* follow his general methods; we can seize those opportunities that are given us, and give ourselves a very fair chance of attaining riches.

In such strange utterances we see quite clearly what is really at the bottom of all these articles and books. It is not mere business; it is not even mere cynicism. It is mysticism; the horrible mysticism of money. The writer of that passage did not really have the remotest notion of how Vanderbilt made his money, or of how anybody else is to make his. He does, indeed, conclude his remarks by advocating some scheme; but it has nothing in the world to do with Vanderbilt. He merely wished to prostrate himself before the mystery of a millionaire. For when we really worship anything, we love not only its clearness but its obscurity. We exult in its very invisibility. Thus, for instance, when a man is in love with a woman he takes special pleasure in the fact that a woman is unreasonable. Thus, again, the very pious poet, celebrating his Creator, takes pleasure in saying that God moves in a mysterious way. Now, the writer of the paragraph which I have quoted does not seem to have had anything to do with a god and I should not think (judging by his extreme unpracticality) that he had ever been really in love with a woman. But the thing he does worship--Vanderbilt --he treats in exactly this mystical manner. He really revels in the fact his deity Vanderbilt is keeping a secret from him. And it fills his soul with a sort of transport of cunning, an ecstasy of priestcraft, that he should pretend to be telling to the multitude that terrible secret which he does not know.

Speaking about the instinct that makes people rich, the same writer remarks--

In the olden days its existence was fully understood. The Greeks
enshrined it in the story of Midas, of the 'Golden Touch.' Here was a
man who turned everything he laid his hands upon into gold. His
life was a progress amidst riches. Out of everything that came in his
way he created the precious metal. 'A foolish legend,' said the
wiseacres if the Victorian age. 'A truth,' say we of to-day. We all know
of such men. We are ever meeting or reading about such persons
who turn everything they touch into gold. Success dogs their very
footsteps. Their life's pathway leads unerringly upwards. They
cannot fail.

Unfortunately, however, Midas could fail; he did. His path did not
lead unerringly upward. He starved because whenever he touched a
biscuit or a ham sandwich it turned to gold. That was the whole point
of the story, though the writer has to suppress it delicately, writing so
near to a portrait of Lord Rothschild. The old fables of mankind are,
indeed, unfathomably wise; but we must not have them expurgated
in the interests of Mr. Vanderbilt. We must not have King Midas
represented as an example of success; he was a failure of an unusually painful kind. Also, he had the ears of an ass. Also (like most other
prominent and wealthy persons) he endeavoured to conceal the fact.
It was his barber (if I remember right) who had to be treated on a
confidential footing with regard to this peculiarity; and his barber,
instead of behaving like a go-ahead person of the Succeed-at-all-costs
school and trying to blackmail King Midas, went away and whispered
this splendid piece of society scandal to the reeds, who enjoyed it
enormously. It is said that they also whispered it as the winds swayed
them to and fro. I look reverently at the portrait of Lord Rothschild; I
read reverently about the exploits of Mr. Vanderbilt. I know that I
cannot turn everything I touch to gold; but then I also know that I
have never tried, having a preference for other substances, such as
grass, and good wine. I know that these people have certainly
succeeded in something; that they have certainly overcome somebody; I know that they are kings in a sense that no men were ever
kings before; that they create markets and bestride continents. Yet it

always seems to me that there is some small domestic fact that they are hiding, and I have sometimes thought I heard upon the wind the laughter and whisper of the reeds.

At least, let us hope that we shall all live to see these absurd books about Success covered with a proper derision and neglect. They do not teach people to be successful, but they do teach people to be snobbish; they do spread a sort of evil poetry of worldliness. The Puritans are always denouncing books that inflame lust; what shall we say of books that inflame the viler passions of avarice and pride? A hundred years ago we had the ideal of the Industrious Apprentice; boys were told that by thrift and work they would all become Lord Mayors. This was fallacious, but it was manly, and had a minimum of moral truth. In our society, temperance will not help a poor man to enrich himself, but it may help him to respect himself. Good work will not make him a rich man, but good work may make him a good workman. The Industrious Apprentice rose by virtues few and narrow indeed, but still virtues. But what shall we say of the gospel preached to the new Industrious Apprentice; the Apprentice who rises not by his virtues, but avowedly by his vices?

CHEESE

My forthcoming work in five volumes, `The Neglect of Cheese in European Literature,' is a work of such unprecedented and laborious detail that it is doubtful whether I shall live to finish it. Some overflowings from such a fountain of information may therefore be permitted to springle these pages. I cannot yet wholly explain the neglect to which I refer. Poets have been mysteriously silent on the subject of cheese. Virgil, if I remember right, refers to it several times, but with too much Roman restraint. He does not let himself go on cheese. The only other poet that I can think of just now who seems to have had some sensibility on the point was the nameless author of the nursery rhyme which says: `If all the trees were bread and cheese' - which is indeed a rich and gigantic vision of the higher gluttony. If all the trees were bread and cheese there would be considerable deforestation in any part of England where I was living. Wild and wide woodlands would reel and fade before me as rapidly as they ran after Orpheus. Except Virgil and this anonymous rhymer, I can recall no verse about cheese. Yet it has every quality which we require in an exalted poetry. It is a short, strong word; it rhymes to `breeze' and `seas' (an essential point); that it is emphatic in sound is admitted even by the civilization of the modern cities. For their citizens, with no apparent intention except emphasis, will often say `Cheese it!' or even `Quite the cheese.' The substance itself is imaginative. It is ancient - sometimes in the individual case, always in the type and custom. It is simple, being directly derived from milk, which is one of the ancestral drinks, not lightly to be corrupted with soda-water. You know, I hope (though I myself have only just thought of it), that the four rivers of Eden were milk, water, wine, and ale. Aerated waters only appeared after the Fall.

But cheese has another quality, which is also the very soul of song. Once in endeavouring to lecture in several places at once, I made an eccentric journey across England, a journey of so irregular and even illogical shape that it necessitated my having lunch on four successive days in four roadside inns in four different counties. In each inn they had nothing but bread and cheese; nor can I imagine why a man should want more than bread and cheese, if he can get enough of it. In each inn the cheese was good; and in each inn it was different. There was a noble Wensleydale cheese in Yorkshire, a Cheshire cheese in Cheshire, and so on. Now, it is just here that true poetic civilization differs from that paltry and mechanical civilization that holds us all in bondage. Bad customs are universal and rigid, like modern militarism. Good customs are universal and varied, like native chivalry and self-defence. Both the good and the bad civilization cover us as with a canopy, and protect us from all that is outside. But a good civilization spreads over us freely like a tree, varying and yielding because it is alive. A bad civilization stands up and sticks out above us like an umbrella - artificial, mathematical in shape; not merely universal, but uniform. So it is with the contrast between the substances that vary and the substances that are the same wherever they penetrate. By a wise doom of heaven men were commanded to eat cheese, but not the same cheese. Being really universal it varies from valley to valley. But if, let us say, we compare cheese to soap (that vastly inferior substance), we shall see that soap tends more and more to be merely Smith's Soap or Brown's Soap, sent automatically all over the world. If the Red Indians have soap it is Smith's Soap. If the Grand Lama has soap it is Brown's Soap. There is nothing subtly and strangely Buddhist, nothing tenderly Tibetan, about his soap. I fancy the Grand Lama does not eat cheese (he is not worthy), but if he does it is probably a local cheese, having some real relation to his life and outlook. Safety matches, tinned foods, patent medicines are sent all over the world; but they are not produced all over the world. Therefore there is in them a mere dead identity, never that soft play of variation which exists in things produced everywhere out of the soil, in the milk of the kine, or the fruits of the orchard. You can get a whisky and soda at every outpost of the Empire: that is why so many Empire builders go mad. But you are not tasting or touching any environment, as in the cider of Devonshire or the grapes of the Rhine. You are not approaching Nature in one of her myriad tints of mood, as in the holy act of eating cheese.

When I had done my pilgrimage in the four wayside public-houses I reached one of the great northern cities, and there I proceeded, with great rapidity and complete inconsistency, to a large and elaborate restaurant, where I knew I could get a great many things besides bread and cheese. I could get that also, however; or at least I expected to get it; but I was sharply reminded that I had entered Babylon, and left England behind. The waiter brought me cheese, indeed, but cheese cut up into contemptibly small pieces; and it is the awful fact that instead of Christian bread, he brought me biscuits. Biscuits - to one who had eaten the cheese of four great countrysides! Biscuits - to one who had proved anew for himself the sanctity of the ancient wedding between cheese and bread! I addressed the waiter in warm and moving terms. I asked him who he was that he should put asunder those whom Humanity had joined. I asked him if he did not feel, as an artist, that a solid but yielding substance like cheese went naturally with a solid, yielding substance like bread; to eat it off biscuits is like eating it off slates. I asked him if, when he said his prayers, he was so supercilious as to pray for his daily biscuits. He gave me generally to understand that he was only obeying a custom of Modern Society. I have therefore resolved to raise my voice, not against the waiter, but against Modern Society, for this huge and unparalleled modern wrong.

THE GREAT SHIPWRECK AS ANALOGY

The tragedy of the great shipwreck is too terrific for any analogies of mere fancy. But the analogy which springs to the mind between the great modern ship and our great modern society that sent it forth--this analogy is not a fancy. It is a fact; a fact perhaps too large and plain for the eyes easily to take in. Our whole civilization is indeed very like the TITANIC; alike in its power and its impotence, it security and its insecurity. Technically considered, the sufficiency of the precautions are a matter for technical inquiry. But psychologically considered, there can be no doubt that such vast elaboration and system induce a frame of mind which is inefficient rather than efficient. Quite apart from the question of whether anyone was to blame, the big outstanding fact remains: that there was no sort of sane proportion between the provision for luxury and levity, and the extent of the provision for need and desperation. The scheme did far too much for prosperity and far too little for distress--just like the modern State. Mr. Veneering, it will be remembered, in his electoral address, "instituted a new and striking comparison between the State and a ship"; the comparison, if not new, is becoming a little too striking. By the time you have made your ship as big as a commonwealth it does become very like a ship--rather like a sinking ship.

For there is a real connection between such catastrophes and a certain frame of mind which refuses to expect them. A rough man going about the sea in a small boat may make every other kind of mistake: he may obey superstitions; he may take too much rum; he may get drunk; he may get drowned. But, cautious or reckless, drunk or sober, he cannot forget that he is in a boat and that a boat is as dangerous a beast as a wild horse. The very lines of the boat have the swift poetry of peril; the very carriage and gestures of the boat are those of a thing assailed. But if you make your boat so large that it does not even look like a boat, but like a sort of watering-place, it must, by the deepest habit of human nature, induce a less vigilant attitude of the mind. An aristocrat on board ship who travels with a garage for his motor almost feels as if he were travelling with the trees of his park. People living in open-air cafes sprinkled with liqueurs and ices get as far from the thought of any revolt of the elements as they are from that of an earthquake under the Hotel Cecil. The mental process is quite illogical, but it is quite inevitable. Of course, both sailors and passengers are intellectually aware that motors at sea are often less useful than life-boats, and that ices are no antidote to icebergs. But man is not only governed by what he thinks but by what he chooses to think about; and the sights that sink into us day by day colour our minds with every tint between insolence and terror. This is one of the worst evils in that extreme separation of social classes which marks the modern ship--and State.

But whether or no our unhappy fellow-creatures on the TITANIC suffered more than they need from this unreality of original outlook, they cannot have had less instinct of actuality than we have who are left alive on land: and now that they are dead they are much more real than we. They have known what papers and politicians never know-- of what man is really made, and what manner of thing is our nature at its best and worst. It is this curious, cold, flimsy incapacity to conceive what a THING is like that appears in so many places, even in the

comments on this astounding sorrow. It appears in the displeasing
incident of Miss Sylvia Pankhurst, who, immediately after the disaster,
seems to have hastened to assure the public that men must get no
credit for giving the boats up to women, because it was the "rule" at
sea. Whether this was a graceful thing for a gay spinster to say to eight
hundred widows in the very hour of doom is not worth inquiry here,
Like cannibalism, it is a matter of taste. But what chiefly astonishes
me in the remark is the utter absence which it reveals of the rudi-
ments of political thought. What does Miss Pankhurst imagine a "rule"
is--a sort of basilisk? Some hundreds of men are, in the exact and
literal sense of the proverb, between the devil and the deep sea. It is
their business, if they can make up their minds to it, to accept the
deep sea and resist the devil. What does Miss Pankhurst suppose a
"rule" could do to them in such extremities? Does she think the
captain would fine every man sixpence who expressed a preference
for his life? Has it occurred to her that a hundredth part of the ship's
population could have thrown the captain and all the authorities into
the sea? But Miss Pankhurst's remark although imbecile, is informing.
Now I see the abject and idolatrous way in which she uses the word
"rule," I begin to understand the abject and idolatrous way in which
she uses the word "vote." She cannot see that wills and not words
control events. If ever she is in a fire or shipwreck with men below a
certain standard of European morals, she will soon find out that the
existence of a rule depends on whether people can be induced to obey
it. And if she ever has a vote in the very low state of European politics,
she will very soon find out that its importance depends on whether
you can induce the man you vote for to obey his mandate or any of his
promises. It is vain to rule if your subjects can and do disobey you. It is
vain to vote if your delegates can and do disobey you.

But, indeed, a real rule can do without such exceptions as the
Suffragettes; de minimis non curat lex. And if the word "rule" be used
in the wider sense of an attempt to maintain a certain standard of
private conduct out of respect for public opinion, we can only say
that not only is this a real moral triumph, but it is, in our present
condition, rather a surprising and reassuring one. It is exactly this

corporate conscience that the modern State has dangerously neglected. There was probably more instinctive fraternity and sense of identical interests, I will say, not on an old skipper's vessel, but on an old pirate's, than there was between the emigrants, the aristocrats, the journalists, or the millionaires who set out to die together on the great ship. That they found in so cruel a way their brotherhood and the need of man for the respect of his neighbour, this is a dreadful fact, but certainly the reverse of a degrading one. The case of Mr. Stead, which I feel with rather special emotions, both of sympathy and difference, is very typical of the whole tragedy. Mr. Stead was far too great and brave a man to require any concealment of his exaggerations or his more unbalanced moods; his strength was in a flaming certainty, which one only weakens by calling sincerity, and a hunger and thirst for human sympathy. His excess, we may say, with real respect, was in the direction of megalomania; a childlike belief in big empires, big newspapers, big alliances--big ships. He toiled like a Titan for that Anglo-American combination of which the ship that has gone down may well be called the emblem. And at the last all these big things broke about him, and somewhat bigger things remained: a courage that was entirely individual; a kindness that was entirely universal. His death may well become a legend.

ON GARGOYLES

ALONE at some distance from the wasting walls of a disused abbey I found half sunken in the grass the grey and goggle-eyed visage of one of those graven monsters that made the ornamental water-spouts in the cathedrals of the Middle Ages. It lay there, scoured by ancient rains or striped by recent fungus, but still looking like the head of some huge dragon slain by a primeval hero. And as I looked at it, I thought of the meaning of the grotesque, and passed into some symbolic reverie of the three great stages of art.

I

Once upon a time there lived upon an island a merry and innocent people, mostly shepherds and tillers of the earth. They were republicans, like all primitive and simple souls; they talked over their affairs under a tree, and the nearest approach they had to a personal ruler was a sort of priest or white witch who said their prayers for them. They worshipped the sun, not idolatrously, but as the golden crown of the god whom all such infants see almost as plainly as the sun.

Now this priest was told by his people to build a great tower, pointing to the sky in salutation of the Sun-god; and he pondered long and heavily before he picked his materials. For he was resolved to use nothing that was not almost as clear and exquisite as sunshine itself; he would use nothing that was not washed as white as the rain can wash the heavens, nothing that did not sparkle as spotlessly as that crown of God. He would have nothing grotesque or obscure; he would not even have anything emphatic or even anything mysterious. He would have all the arches as light as laughter and as candid as logic. He built the temple in three concentric courts, which were cooler and more exquisite in substance each than the other. For the outer wall was a hedge of white lillies, ranked so thick that a green stalk was hardly to be seen; and the wall within that was of crystal, which smashed the sun into a million stars. And the wall within that, which was the tower itself, was a tower of pure water, forced up in an everlasting fountain; and upon the very tip and crest of that foaming spire was one big and blazing diamond, which the water tossed up eternally and caught again as a child catches a ball.

"Now," said the priest, "I have made a tower which is a little worthy of the sun."

II

But about this time the island was caught in a swarm of pirates; and the shepherds had to turn themselves into rude warriors and seamen; and at first they were utterly broken down in blood and shame; and the pirates might have taken the jewel flung up for ever from their sacred fount. And then, after years of horror and humiliation, they gained a little and began to conquer because they did not mind defeat. And the pride of the pirates went sick within them after a few unexpected foils; and at last the invasion rolled back into the empty seas and the island was delivered. And for some reason after this men began to talk quite differently about the temple and the sun. Some, indeed, said, "You must not touch the temple; it is classical; it is perfect, since it admits no imperfections." But the others answered,

"In that it differs from the sun, that shines on the evil and the good and on mud and monsters everywhere. The temple is of the noon; it is made of white marble clouds and sapphire sky. But the sun is not always of the noon. The sun dies daily; every night he is crucified in blood and fire."

Now the priest had taught and fought through all the war, and his hair had grown white, but his eyes had grown young. And he said, "I was wrong and they are right. The sun, the symbol of our father, gives life to all those earthly things that are full of ugliness and energy. All the exaggerations are right, if they exaggerate the right thing. Let us point to heaven with tusks and horns and fins and trunks and tails so long as they all point to heaven. The ugly animals praise God as much as the beautiful. The frog's eyes stand out of his head because he is staring at heaven. The giraffe's neck is long because he is stretching towards heaven. The donkey has ears to hear-let him hear."

And under the new inspiration they planned a gorgeous cathedral in the Gothic manner, with all the animals of the earth crawling all over it, and all the possible ugly things making up one common beauty, because they all appealed to the god. The columns of the temple were carved like necks of giraffes; the dome was like an ugly tortoise; and the highest pinnacle was a monkey standing on his head with his tail pointing at the sun. And yet the whole was beautiful, because it was lifted up in one living and religious gesture as a man lifts his hands in prayer.

III

But this great plan was never properly completed. The people had brought up on great wagons the heavy tortoise roof and the huge necks of stone, and all the thousand and one oddities that made up that unity, the owls and the efts and the crocodiles and the kangaroos, which hideous by themselves might have been magnificent if reared in one definite proportion and dedicated to the sun. For this was Gothic, this was romantic, this was Christian art; this was the whole advance of Shakespeare upon Sophocles. And that symbol which was to crown it all, the ape upside down, was really Christian; for man is the ape upside down.

But the rich, who had grown riotous in the long peace, obstructed the thing, and in some squabble a stone struck the priest on the head and he lost his memory. He saw piled in front of him frogs and elephants, monkeys and giraffes, toadstools and sharks, all the ugly things of the universe which he had collected to do honour to God. But he forgot why he had collected them. He could not remember the design or the object. He piled them all wildly into one heap fifty feet high; and when he had done it all the rich and influential went into a passion of applause and cried, "This is real art! This is Realism! This is things as they really are!"

THAT, I fancy is the only true origin of Realism. Realism is simply Romanticism that has lost its reason. This is so not merely in the sense of insanity but of suicide. It has lost its reason; that is its reason for existing. The Old Greeks summoned godlike things to worship their god. The medieval Christians summoned all things to worship theirs, dwarfs and pelicans, monkeys and madmen. The modern realists summon all these million creatures to worship their god; and then have no god for them to worship. Paganism was in art a pure beauty; that was the dawn. Christianity was a beauty created by controlling a million monsters of ugliness; and that in my belief was the zenith and the noon. Modern art and science practically mean having the million monsters and being unable to control them; and I will venture to call that the disruption and the decay. The finest lengths of the Elgin marbles consist of splendid horses going to the temple of a virgin. Christianity, with its gargoyles and grotesques, really amounted to saying this: that a donkey could go before all the horses of the world when it was really going to the temple. Romance means a holy donkey going to the temple. Realism means a lost donkey going nowhere.

The fragments of futile journalism or fleeting impression which are here collected are very like the wrecks and riven blocks that were piled in a heap round my imaginary priest of the sun. They are very like that grey and gaping head of stone. Yet I will venture to make even of these trivial fragments the high boast that I am a medievalist and not a modern. That is, I really have a notion of why I have collected all the nonsensical things there are. I have not the patience nor perhaps the constructive intelligence to state the connecting links between all these chaotic papers. But it could be stated. This row of shapeless and ungainly monsters which I now set before the reader does not consist of separate idols cut out capriciously in lonely valleys or various islands. These monsters are meant for the gargoyles of a definite cathedral. I have to carve the gargoyles, because I can carve nothing else; I leave to others the angels and the arches and the spires. But I am very sure of the style of the architecture and of the consecration of the church.

SKEPTICISM AND SPIRITUALISM

Glancing over several papers of late, I see such headings as "Another Medium Exposed," and "Another Spiritualistic Fraud." The easy and conventional comments made upon the matter by the journalists seem to me to be singularly lacking in a logical sense, and there seems to be an underlying assumption in all such comments that the more often you discover a dishonest medium or a fraudulent seance, the more you have diminished the credit or probability of spiritualism. I have never been at a seance in my life, and I never had, and probably never shall have, anything to do with the specific set of people who call themselves spiritualists. But as a mere matter of intellectual justice or mental lucidity, it is desirable to protest against this confused argument which connects the proved falsity of knaves with the probable falsity of psychic phenomena. The two things have no logical connection whatever. No conceivable number of false mediums affects the probability of the existence of real mediums one way or the other. This is surely obvious enough. No conceivable number of forged bank-notes can disprove the existence of the Bank of England. If anything, the argument might as well be turned the other way,; we might say with rather more reason that as all hypocrisies are the evil fruits of public virtue, so in the same way the more real spiritualism there is in the world the more false spiritualism there is likely to be.

In fact, the mere abstract rationality of this problem is very wrongly discussed. For instance, it is always considered ludicrous and a signal for a burst of laughter if the spiritualists say that a seance has been spoiled by the presence of a skeptic, or that an attitude of faith is necessary to encourage the psychic communications. But there is nothing at all unreasonable or unlikely about the idea that doubt might discourage and faith encourage spiritual communications, if there are any. The suggestion does not make spiritualism in abstract logic any more improbable. All that it does make it is more difficult. There is nothing foolish or fantastic about the supposition that a dispassionate person acts as a deterrent to passionate truths. Only it happens to make it much harder for any dispassionate person to find out what is true. There are a thousand practical parallels. An impartial psychologist studying the problem of human nature could, no doubt, learn a great deal from a man and woman making love to each other in his presence. None the less, it is unfortunately the fact that no man and woman would make love to each other in the presence of an impartial psychologist. Students of physiology and surgery might learn something from a man suddenly stabbing another man on a platform in a lecture-theater. But no man would stab another man on a platform in a lecture-theater. A schoolmaster would learn much if the boys would be boys in his presence; but they never are boys in his presence. An educationalist studying infancy might make important discoveries if he could hear the things said by a baby when absolutely alone and at his ease with his mother. But it is quite obvious that the mere entrance of a great ugly educationalist (they are an ugly lot) would set the child screaming with terror.

The problem, then, of skepticism and spiritual ecstacies is a perfectly human and intelligible problem to state, though it may be a difficult problem to solve. It is exactly as if a man pointed at some lady (you can choose the lady out of your own acquaintance at your own discretion) and said with marked emphasis, "Under no circumstance could I address a sonnet to that lady." We might reply, "Oh, yes;

if you fell in love with her you might feel inclined to do so." He would be fully justified in replying (with tears in his eyes), "But I cannot fall in love with her by any imaginable process." But he would not be logically justified in replying "Oh, that is all nonsense. You want me to give up my judgment, and become a silly partisan." The whole question under discussion is what would happen if he did become a partisan. In the same way, the skeptic who is expelled with bashed hat and tattered coat-tails from a spiritualistic seance has a perfect right to say (with or without tears in his eyes) "But why blame me for unbelief? I cannot manage to believe in such things by any imaginable process." But he has no logical right to say that it could not have been his skepticism that spoilt the seance, or that there was anything at all unphilosophical in supposing that it was. An impartial person is a good judge of many things, but not of all. He is not (for instance) a good judge of what it feels like to be partial.

For my own part, what little I resent in what little I have seen of spiritualism is altogether the opposite element. I do not mind spiritualism, in so far as it is fierce and credulous. In that it seems to me to be akin to sex, to song, to the great epics and the great religions, to all that has made humanity heroic. I do not object to spiritualism in so far as it is spiritualistic. I do object to it in so far as it is scientific. Conviction and curiosity are both very good things. But they ought to have two different houses. There have been many frantic and blasphemous beliefs in this old barbaric earth of ours; men have served their deities with obscene dances, with cannibalism, and the blood of infants. But no religion was quite so blasphemous as to pretend that it was scientifically investigating its god to see what he was made of. Bacchanals did not say, "Let us discover whether there is a god of wine." They enjoyed wine so much that they cried out naturally to the god of it. Christians did not say, "A few experiments will show us whether there is a god of goodness." They loved good so much that they knew that it was a god. Moreover, all the great religions always loved passionately and poetically the symbols and machinery by which they worked --the temple, the colored robes, the altar, the symbolic flowers, or the sacrificial fire. It made these things beautiful:

it laid itself open to the charge of idolatry. And into these great ritual religions there has descended, whatever the meaning of it, the thing of which Sophocles spoke, "The power of the gods, which is mighty and groweth not old." When I hear that the spiritualists have begun to carve great golden wings upon their flying tables, I shall recognize the atmosphere of a faith. When I hear them accused of worshipping a planchet made of ivory and sardonyx (whatever that is) I shall know that they have become a great religion. Meanwhile, I fear I shall remain one of those who believe in spirits much too easily ever to become a spiritualist. Modern people think the supernatural so improbable that they want to see it. I think it so probable that I leave it alone. Spirits are not worth all this fuss; I know that, for I am one myself. . .

UPON THIS ROCK

To a Roman Catholic the Roman Catholic Church is simply the Christian religion; the gift of Christ to St. Peter and his successors of a right to answer at all times all questions about what it really is; a thing surrounded at the edge of its own wide domain by various severed fragments of its own substance; consisting of people who for different reasons deny that right to affirm what it really is, and who therefore differ among themselves, indefinitely and increasingly, about what it really is. It may be added that they differ not only about the nature of the ideal Christianity that ought to be substituted, but even about the nature of the Roman Catholicism that is to be defied. To some it is Antichrist; to some it is one branch of the Church of Christ, having authority in certain provinces but not in England or Russia; to some it is a corrupt perversion of Truth from which religion was rescued; to others a necessary historic phase through which religion had to pass; and so on. But it may be noted by the curious that though there is so much difference in the reasons given, there is something common to most of the emotions felt. The reactions to Rome are all reactions to something odd. It is a thousand things, but all things with a sort of thrill in them; a mystery, a bete noire, a strange survival, a public scandal, a private embarrassment, an open secret, a tactless topic, a sly joke, a last refuge or a leap in the dark: everything except anything that is like anything else.

To a Roman Catholic there is no particular difference between those parts of the religion which Protestants and others accept and those parts which they reject. The dogmas have, of course, their intrinsic theological proportions; but in his feeling they are all one thing. The Mass is as Christian as the Gospel. The Gospel is as Catholic as the Mass. This, I fancy, is the fact which the Protestant world has found it most difficult to understand and about which some of the most unfortunate forms of ill-feeling have appeared. Yet it arises quite naturally from the actual history of the Church, which has had to contend incessantly with quite other and quite opposite heresies. She has not only had to defeat these sects to defend these doctrines, but to defeat other sects to defend other doctrines including the doctrines which these sects rightly hold so dear. It was only the Roman Catholic Church that saved the Protestant truths. It may be right to rest on the Bible, but there would be no Bible if the Gnostics had proved that the Old Testament was written by the Devil, or had littered the world with Apocryphal Gospels. It may be right to say that Jesus alone saves from sin, but nobody would be saying it if a Pelagian movement had altered the whole notion of sin. Even the very selection of dogmas which the reformers decided to preserve had only been preserved for them by the authority which they denied.

It is natural, therefore, for Catholics not to be always thinking of the antithesis of Catholic and Protestant any more than of Catholic and Pelagian. Catholicism is used to proposals to cut down the creed to a few clauses; but different people have wanted quite different clauses left and quite different clauses cut out. Thus a Catholic does not feel the special reverence paid to the Mother of God as any more of a controversial question than the divine honours paid to the Son of God; for he knows the latter was as much controverted by the Arians as the former by the Puritans. He does not feel the throne of St. Peter to be any more specially in dispute than the theology of St. Paul, for he knows that both have been disputed. There have been anti-popes;

there have been Apocryphal Gospels; there have been sects dethroning our Lady and sects dethroning our Lord. After nearly two thousand years of this sort of thing, Catholics have come to regard Catholicism as one thing, all the parts of which are in one sense equally assailed and in another sense equally unassailable.

Now it is unfortunately impossible for a Roman Catholic to state the principle without its sounding provocative and, what is much worse, superior; but unless he does state it, he does not state Roman Catholicism. Having stated it, however, in its dogmatic and defiant form, as it is his duty to do, he may afterwards suggest something of why the system seems, to those inside it, to be not so much a system as a home, and even a holiday. Thus it certainly does not mean being superior in the sense of supercilious; for in this system alone, only the saint is superior because he feels he is inferior. It does not say that all heretics are lost, for it does say that there is a common conscience by which they may be saved. But it does definitely say that he who knows the whole truth sins in accepting half the truth. Thus the Church is not a movement, like all those which have filled the world since the sixteenth century; that is, since the breakdown of the collective attempt of all Christendom to state the whole truth. It is not the movement of something trying to find its balance; it is the balance. But the point here is that even those heretics, who snatched at half-truths, seldom snatched at the same half. The original Protestants insisted on Hell without Purgatory. Their modern successors generally insist on Purgatory without Hell. Their future successors may quite possibly insist on Purgatory without Heaven. It may seem a natural sequence to the worship of Progress for its own sake, and the theory that "to travel hopefully is better than to arrive." For the Catholic each of these things may be disputed in its turn, and all will remain.

Nevertheless, in making so short a summary in a world still Protestant by tradition, it will be convenient to assume that the reader is acquainted with the Christian scheme in those features which, until lately, were common to many or most Christian bodies: the Image of God, the Fall, the necessity of Redemption, the Last Judgment, and the rest; and to describe the Catholic faith (from which all these things really come) as that world sees it, by the chief features that appear distinctive because they are disputed. I will therefore say a word or two of what would still be commonly called the marks of Roman Catholicism. I shall say very little about the greatest of all, because it is admittedly a mystery and an object of faith. Catholics believe that in the Blessed Sacrament Christ is present, not merely as a thought is present in a mind, but as a person is present in a room, veiled only from the actual senses by the appearances of bread and wine. Of its historical aspect it will be enough to say that Roman Catholics are convinced that it is spoken of in this spirit at least as early as St. Ignatius, who was roughly of the next generation to that of the Gospel. The common sense of it, it seems to me, would be to say that if the words of Christ at the Last Supper were misunderstood, they were misunderstood by the twelve Apostles. But the doctrine is so tremendous and transcendental that we cannot complain if some misunderstand it as blasphemous and extravagant. Only they cannot have it both ways. They must not turn round and complain that we claim to possess Christ as a living God by a vital process, absent from the other communions that called the process impossible. They must not grumble at our talking of Christ coming back to a heretic land with the first procession bearing the Host. There must be a difference between Christ's presence in their sense and in our sense, if they are actually shocked and staggered at our sense. A Return which they are driven to call impossible we may surely be allowed to call unique.

For practical purposes in Protestant civilization it is another fact that soars most clearly into sight, towering even over Transubstantiation. It is the Papacy that makes the Papist. For him, at least, it dates from the highly dramatic words about the Rock and the Gates of Hell; it certainly appears, to say the very least, as an admitted seat of superior authority in the debates of the first Fathers and Councils; but it was not logically and literally defined until the middle of the nineteenth century. In this sense it is true that the idea grew; but we can never make anything but nonsense out of the sort of evolution that imagines something growing out of nothing. But in so far as an eternal truth can grow, in the comprehension of men, it has grown continuously with the increase of the experience of men. The general case for a tribunal to define the truth has been touched upon already. I pointed out that long before Protestants rushed in to preserve their simple Christianity, even that simple Christianity would not have been there to preserve if there had not already been a Church tribunal to preserve it. The question then becomes one of the nature of the tribunal. Even if democracy were applicable to a revelation, there could not really be a democratic tribunal which should be deciding all the time and democratic all the time. It would not be the millions of poor and humble Catholics who would rule; it would be the officials if it were not the official. It would be a Holy Synod. Now every popular instinct Catholics possess seems to them to say that rather than have merely an official order, that is, an oligarchy, it is far more human to have a monarchy, that is, a man. It is indeed remarkable that those who broke with this purely moral monarchy generally set up a material and a rather immoral monarchy. The first great schism in the East was made by men who turned from the Popes to bow down to the Caesars and the Tsars. The last great schism in the West was made by men who attributed divine right to Henry VIII, not to mention Charles I. Those who thought the papacy too despotic did not even escape despotism.

It is needless to explain, I trust, that the only despotism of the Pope consists in the fact that all Catholics believe that God will guard him from teaching falsehood to the Church on those special and rather rare occasions when he is appealed to to end a controversy with a final statement of faith. His ordinary pronouncements, though naturally received with profound respect, are not infallible. His private character depends on his own free will, like anybody else's. He can commit sins like anybody else; he must confess sins like anybody else; and his having been Pope is nothing to his salvation. But the question is, given our need for such final decisions to save Christianity at great crises, what organ of the Church decides? The longer historical experience accumulates, the more profoundly thankful most Catholics are that the organ is a human being; a mind and not a type, a will and not a tradition or tone of a class. The best bishops ruling as a class would become a club, as a parliament does. They would have all of its scattered responsibility, all its mutual flattery, all its diffused and dangerous pride. But the responsibility of a Pope is so solitary and so solemn that a man would need to be a maniac not to be humbled by it.

Probably the Protestant world would count as the next outstanding feature, after the power of the priests to perform Mass and of the Popes to define doctrine, that other power of the priesthood which is expressed in the sacrament of Penance. The sacramental system is everywhere based on the idea that certain material acts are mystical acts; are events in the spiritual world. This mystical materialism does divide us from all those forms of idealism that hold all good to be inward and invisible and matter to be unworthy to express it. It is needless to note how this applies to the water of baptism, the oil of unction, and so on. But I am deliberately taking the sacrament which our world has most misunderstood; and, strangely enough, it is that one which is least material and most spiritual, consisting of spoken words expressing the most secret thoughts. Of all the sacraments it is, in the modern jargon, the most psychological. And the proof of it is that even the people who abolished it a few centuries ago found that they had to invent a new imitation of it a few years ago. They told the people to go to a new priest, often without credentials, and make confession generally without absolution, and they called it psychoanalysis. Catholicism would say that the lack of the confessional had produced a modern congestion and stagnation of secrets so morbid as to be reaching the verge of madness.

Broadly, it may be said that Roman Catholicism has had the idea, hitherto at least highly unique, of working mankind from the inside. There have been and are any number of external ethical and political systems directing men how to do right in the mass; there is no other that thus gets to grips with why such a system goes wrong with the individual. Most moderns are content to get hold of the plan of Utopia. This is rather like getting hold of the diary of the Utopian and learning the real reason why he does not always behave in a Utopian manner. But, of course, it is quite useless unless he produces his own diary of his own free will. Unless he really wishes it, there can be no sacrament; and unless he really repents, there is no absolution. For the history of this institution, it follows in its rough outline the same course as the other cases of the Mass and the Papacy. That is, it is undoubtedly present as an idea in the very earliest times; there are disputes about the proportion of that presence, and there need be no dispute at all that it grew more elaborate, more systematic, and more subtle with the process of experience. What is called Development is the unfolding of all the consequences and applications of an idea; but of something that is there, not of something that is not there. In this sense the Catholic Church is the one Christian body that has always believed in Evolution.

There is barely space to touch on two more of these things which are counted Popish specialties chiefly because they are counted Popish scandals. The first is the idea of asceticism and especially of celibacy. The second is the cult of the Blessed Virgin. Of the former it will be enough to say here that to most ordinary Roman Catholics, who are not called upon to practise special austerities, those examples are valuable not only as examples of heroism, but as very vivid evidences of the reality of religious hopes. Granted that for us the divine light is valued as a daily light, brightening our daily and normal affairs, yet it would not brighten them at all if we did not believe that the light was really divine. If we only believed that religion was useful, it would be of no use. Now nothing could better prove the light divine than that some should live on it as on a food; nothing could more clearly show religion to be real than that for some people it can be a substitute for other realities. We have no difficulty in believing that such people deal more directly with divine things than we, as in the case of those who enjoy directly a divine love instead of indirectly through a human love in marriage. And when we are criticized for this, we remember with some amusement that it was we who said that marriage was a divine sacrament when our critics said it was not.

Of the most popular, the most poetical and the most practically inspiring of all the distinctively Catholic traditions of Christianity, I will say very little here; indeed, I will say only one thing. The honour given to Mary as the Mother of God is, among a thousand other things, a very perfect example of the truth to which I have recurred more than once: that even what we may call the Protestant truths were only saved by the Catholic authority. Among these is the very necessary truth of the subordination of Mary to Christ, as being after all the subordination of the creature to the Creator. Nothing amuses Catholics more than the suggestion, in so much of the old Protestant propaganda, that they are to be freed from the superstition called Mariolatry, like people freed from the burden of daylight. All the spontaneous spirituality, as distinct from the necessary doctrinal orthodoxy, is on the side of the extension and even excess of this cult. If Catholics had been left to their private judgment, to their personal religious experience, to their sense of the essential spirit of Christ and Christianity, to any of the liberal or latitudinarian tests of truth, they would long ago have exalted our Lady to a height of super-human supremacy and splendour that might really have imperilled the pure monotheism in the core of the creed. Over whole tracts of popular opinion she might have been a goddess more universal than Isis. It is the authority of Rome that has prevented such Catholics from indulging in such Mariolatry; the strict definition that distinguished between a perfect woman and a divine Man. But if it were a place for expression of feeling, little doubt would be left about which way all our most direct and democratic feelings drive. I have throughout this statement ignored the meaningless affectation of impartiality. It is impossible for any man to state what he believes as if he did not believe it. But I have endeavoured to describe the most familiar features of this one religion in terms of logic not of rhetoric. And on this last matter of the doctrine touching the Virgin I will conclude without further speech. It is only reasonable that a creed presented by one who holds it should be stated with conviction; but anything I wrote on this last topic might be defaced with enthusiasm.

THE TWELVE MEN

The other day, while I was meditating on morality and Mr. H. Pitt, I was, so to speak, snatched up and put into a jury box to try people. The snatching took some weeks, but to me it seemed something sudden and arbitrary. I was put into this box because I lived in Battersea, and my name began with a C. Looking round me, I saw that there were also summoned and in attendance in the court whole crowds and processions of men, all of whom lived in Battersea, and all of whose names began with a C.

It seems that they always summon jurymen in this sweeping alphabetical way. At one official blow, so to speak, Battersea is denuded of all its C's, and left to get on as best it can with the rest of the alphabet. A Cumberpatch is missing from one street--a Chizzolpop from another--three Chucksterfields from Chucksterfield House; the children are crying out for an absent Cadgerboy; the woman at the street corner is weeping for her Coffintop, and will not be comforted. We settle down with a rollicking ease into our seats (for we are a bold, devil-may-care race, the C's of Battersea), and an oath is administered to us in a totally inaudible manner by an individual resembling an Army surgeon in his second childhood. We understand, however, that we are to well and truly try the case between our sovereign lord the King and the prisoner at the bar, neither of whom has put in an appearance as yet.

JUST WHEN I was wondering whether the King and the prisoner were, perhaps, coming to an amicable understanding in some adjoining public house, the prisoner's head appears above the barrier of the dock; he is accused of stealing bicycles, and he is the living image of a great friend of mine. We go into the matter of the stealing of the bicycles. We do well and truly try the case between the King and the prisoner in the affair of the bicycles. And we come to the conclusion, after a brief but reasonable discussion, that the King is not in any way implicated. Then we pass on to a woman who neglected her children, and who looks as if somebody or something had neglected her. And I am one of those who fancy that something had.

All the time that the eye took in these light appearances and the brain passed these light criticisms, there was in the heart a barbaric pity and fear which men have never been able to utter from the beginning, but which is the power behind half the poems of the world. The mood cannot even adequately be suggested, except faintly by this statement that tragedy is the highest expression of the infinite value of human life. Never had I stood so close to pain; and never so far away from pessimism. Ordinarily, I should not have spoken of these dark emotions at all, for speech about them is too difficult; but I mention then now for a specific and particular reason to the statement of which I will proceed at once. I speak these feelings because out of the furnace of them there came a curious realization of a political or social truth. I saw with a queer and indescribable kind of clearness what a jury really is, and why we must never let it go.

The trend of our epoch up to this time has been consistently towards specialism and professionalism. We tend to have trained soldiers because they fight better, trained singers because they sing better, trained dancers because they dance better, specially instructed laughers because they laugh better, and so on and so on. The principle has been applied to law and politics by innumerable modern writers. Many Fabians have insisted that a greater part of our political work should be performed by experts. Many legalists have declared that the untrained jury should be altogether supplanted by the trained judge.

Now, if this world of ours were really what is called reasonable, I do not know that there would be any fault to find with this. But the true result of all experience and the true foundation of all religion is this. That the four or five things that it is most practically essential that a man should know, are all of them what people call paradoxes. That is to say, that though we all find them in life to be mere plain truths, yet we cannot easily state them in words without being guilty of seeming verbal contradictions. One of them, for instance, is the unimpeachable platitude that the man who finds most pleasure for himself is often the man who least hunts for it. Another is the paradox of courage; the fact that the way to avoid death is not to have too much aversion to it. Whoever is careless enough of his bones to climb some hopeful cliff above the tide may save his bones by that carelessness. Whoever will lose his life, the same shall save it; an entirely practical and prosaic statement.

Now, one of these four or five paradoxes which should be taught to every infant prattling at his mother's knee is the following: That the more a man looks at a thing, the less he can see it, and the more a man learns a thing the less he knows it. The Fabian argument of the expert, that the man who is trained should be the man who is trusted would be absolutely unanswerable if it were really true that a man who studied a thing and practised it every day went on seeing more and more of its significance. But he does not. He goes on seeing less and less of its significance. In the same way, alas! we all go on every day, unless we are continually goading ourselves into gratitude and humility, seeing less and less of the significance of the sky or the stones.

~

Now it is a terrible business to mark a man out for the vengeance of men. But it is a thing to which a man can grow accustomed, as he can to other terrible things; he can even grow accustomed to the sun. And the horrible thing about all legal officials, even the best, about all judges, magistrates, barristers, detectives, and policemen, is not that they are wicked (some of them are good), not that they are stupid (several of them are quite intelligent), it is simply that they have got used to it.

Strictly they do not see the prisoner in the dock; all they see is the usual man in the usual place. They do not see the awful court of judgment; they only see their own workshop. Therefore, the instinct of Christian civilization has most wisely declared that into their judgments there shall upon every occasion be infused fresh blood and fresh thoughts from the streets. Men shall come in who can see the court and the crowd, and coarse faces of the policeman and the professional criminals, the wasted faces of the wastrels, the unreal faces of the gesticulating counsel, and see it all as one sees a new picture or a play hitherto unvisited.

Our civilization has decided, and very justly decided, that determining the guilt or innocence of men is a thing too important to be trusted to trained men. It wishes for light upon that awful matter, it asks men who know no more law than I know, but who can feel the things that I felt in the jury box. When it wants a library catalogued, or the solar system discovered, or any trifle of that kind, it uses up specialists. But when it wishes anything done which is really serious, it collects twelve of the ordinary men standing round. The same thing was done, if I remember right, by the Founder of Christianity.

ON LYING IN BED

Lying in bed would be an altogether perfect and supreme experience if only one had a colored pencil long enough to draw on the ceiling. This, however, is not generally a part of the domestic apparatus on the premises. I think myself that the thing might be managed with several pails of Aspinall and a broom. Only if one worked in a really sweeping and masterly way, and laid on the color in great washes, it might drip down again on one's face in floods of rich and mingled color like some strange fairy rain; and that would have its disadvantages. I am afraid it would be necessary to stick to black and white in this form of artistic composition. To that purpose, indeed, the white ceiling would be of the greatest possible use; in fact, it is the only use I think of a white ceiling being put to.

But for the beautiful experiment of lying in bed I might never have discovered it. For years I have been looking for some blank spaces in a modern house to draw on. Paper is much too small for any really allegorical design; as Cyrano de Bergerac says, "Il me faut des geants." But when I tried to find these fine clear spaces in the modern rooms such as we all live in I was continually disappointed. I found an endless pattern and complication of small objects hung like a curtain of fine links between me and my desire. I examined the walls;

I found them to my surprise to be already covered with wallpaper, and I found the wallpaper to be already covered with uninteresting images, all bearing a ridiculous resemblance to each other. I could not understand why one arbitrary symbol (a symbol apparently entirely devoid of any religious or philosophical significance) should thus be sprinkled all over my nice walls like a sort of smallpox. The Bible must be referring to wallpapers, I think, when it says, "Use not vain repetitions, as the Gentiles do." I found the Turkey carpet a mass of unmeaning colors, rather like the Turkish Empire, or like the sweetmeat called Turkish Delight. I do not exactly know what Turkish Delight really is; but I suppose it is Macedonian Massacres. Everywhere that I went forlornly, with my pencil or my paint brush, I found that others had unaccountably been before me, spoiling the walls, the curtains, and the furniture with their childish and barbaric designs.

NOWHERE DID I find a really clear space for sketching until this occasion when I prolonged beyond the proper limit the process of lying on my back in bed. Then the light of that white heaven broke upon my vision, that breadth of mere white which is indeed almost the definition of Paradise, since it means purity and also means freedom. But alas! Like all heavens, now that it is seen it is found to be unattainable; it looks more austere and more distant than the blue sky outside the window. For my proposal to paint on it with the bristly end of a broom has been discouraged - never mind by whom; by a person debarred from all political rights - and even my minor proposal to put the other end of the broom into the kitchen fire and turn it to charcoal has not been conceded. Yet I am certain that it was from persons in my position that all the original inspiration came for covering the ceilings of palaces and cathedrals with a riot of fallen angels or victorious gods. I am sure that it was only because Michelangelo was engaged in the ancient and honorable occupation of lying in bed that he ever realized how the roof of the Sistine

Chapel might be made into an awful imitation of a divine drama that could only be acted in the heavens.

The tone now commonly taken toward the practice of lying in bed is hypocritical and unhealthy. Of all the marks of modernity that seem to mean a kind of decadence, there is none more menacing and dangerous that the exaltation of very small and secondary matters of conduct at the expense of very great and primary ones, at the expense of eternal ties and tragic human morality. If there is one thing worse that the modern weakening of major morals, it is the modern strengthening of minor morals. Thus it is considered more withering to accuse a man of bad taste than of bad ethics. Cleanliness is not next to godliness nowadays, for cleanliness is made essential and godliness is regarded as an offence. A playwright can attack the institution of marriage so long as he does not misrepresent the manners of society, and I have met Ibsenite pessimist who thought it wrong to take beer but right to take prussic acid. Especially this is so in matters of hygiene; notably such matters as lying in bed. Instead of being regarded, as it ought to be, as a matter of personal convenience and adjustment, it has come to be regarded by many as if it were a part of essential morals to get up early in the morning. It is upon the whole part of practical wisdom; but there is nothing good about it or bad about its opposite.

Misers get up early in the morning; and burglars, I am informed, get up the night before. It is the great peril of our society that all its mechanisms may grow more fixed while its spirit grows more fickle. A man's minor actions and arrangements ought to be free, flexible, creative; the things that should be unchangeable are his principles, his ideals. But with us the reverse is true; our views change constantly; but our lunch does not change. Now, I should like men to have strong and rooted conceptions, but as for their lunch, let them have it sometimes in the garden, sometimes in bed, sometimes on the roof, sometimes in the top of a tree. Let them argue from the same first principles, but let them do it in a bed, or a boat, or a balloon. This alarming growth of good habits really means a too great emphasis on those virtues which mere custom can ensure, it means too little emphasis on those virtues which custom can never quite ensure, sudden and splendid virtues of inspired pity or of inspired candor. If ever that abrupt appeal is made to us we may fail. A man can get use to getting up at five o'clock in the morning. A man cannot very well get used to being burnt for his opinions; the first experiment is commonly fatal. Let us pay a little more attention to these possibilities of the heroic and unexpected. I dare say that when I get out of this bed I shall do some deed of an almost terrible virtue.

For those who study the great art of lying in bed there is one emphatic caution to be added. Even for those who can do their work in bed (like journalists), still more for those whose work cannot be done in bed (as, for example, the professional harpooners of whales), it is obvious that the indulgence must be very occasional. But that is not the caution I mean. The caution is this: if you do lie in bed, be sure you do it without any reason or justification at all. I do not speak, of course, of the seriously sick. But if a healthy man lies in bed, let him do it without a rag of excuse; then he will get up a healthy man. If he does it for some secondary hygienic reason, if he has some scientific explanation, he may get up a hypochondriac.

WHAT IS RIGHT WITH THE WORLD

The above excellent title is not of my own invention. It was suggested to me by the Editor of this paper (T.P.'s Weekly), and I consented to fill up the bill, partly because of the pleasure I have always had from the paper itself, and partly because it gives me an opportunity of telling an egotistical story, a story which may enlighten the public about the general origin of such titles.

I have always heard of the brutality of publishers and how they crush and obscure the author; but my complaint has always been that they push him forward far too much. I will not say that, so far from making too little of the author, they make too much of him; that this phrase is capable of a dark financial interpretation which I do not intend. But I do say that the prominent personalities of the literary world are very largely the creations of their publishers, in so far as they are not solely the creations of their wives. Here is a small incident out of my own existence. I designed to write a sort of essay, divided into sections, on one particular point of political error. This fallacy, though small and scholastic at first sight, seemed to me to be the real mistake in most modern sociological works. It was, briefly, the idea that things that have been tried have been found wanting. It was my purpose to point out that in the entanglements of practice this is untrue; that an old expedient may be the best thing for a new situation; that its principle may be useful though its practice was abandoned; and so on. Therefore, I claimed, we should look for the best method, the ideal, whether it is in the future or the past. I imagined this book as a drab-coloured, decorous little philosophical treatise, with no chapters, but the page occasionally broken by section-headings at the side. I proposed to call my analysis of a radical error 'What is wrong', meaning where the mistake is in our logical calculation. But I had highly capable and sympathetic publishers, whose only weakness was that they thought my unhappy monologue much more important than I did. By some confusion of ecstasy (which entirely through my own fault I failed to check) the title was changed into the apocalyptic trumpet-blast 'What's Wrong With the World'. It was divided up into three short, fierce chapters, like proclamations in a French riot. Outside there was an enormous portrait of myself looking like a depressed hairdresser, and the whole publication had somehow got the violence and instancy of a bombshell. Let it be understood that I do not blame the publishers in the least for this. I could have stopped it if I had minded my own affairs, and came out of their beautiful and ardent souls. I merely mention it as an instance of the error about publishers. They are always represented as cold and scornful merchants, seeking to keep your writers in the background. Alas (as Wordsworth so finely says), alas! the enthusiasm of publishers has oftener left me mourning.

Upon the whole, I am rather inclined to approve of this method of the publisher or editor making up the title, while the author makes up the remarks about it. Any man with a large mind ought to be able to write about anything. Any really free man ought to be able to write to order. Some of the greatest books in the world -- Pickwick, for instance -- were written to fulfil a scheme partly sketched out by a publisher. But I only brought together these two cases of title that came to me from outside because they do illustrate the necessity of some restatement in such a case. For these two titles are, when it comes to the fulfilment, at once too complex and too simple. I would never have dreamed of announcing, like some discovery of my own, what is wrong with the world. What is wrong with the world is the devil, and what is right with it is God; the human race will travel for a few more million years in all sorts of muddle and reform, and when it perishes of the last cold or heat it will still be within the limits of that very simple definition. But in an age that has confused itself with such phrases as 'optimist' and 'pessimist', it is necessary to distinguish along more delicate lines. One of the strangest things about the use of the word 'optimist' is that it is now so constantly used about the future. The house of man is criticised not as a house, but as a kind of caravan; not by what it is, but by where it is going. None are more vitally and recklessly otherworldly than those modern progressives who do not believe in another world.

Now, for the matter of that, I do not think the world is getting much better in very many vital respects. In some of them, I think, the fact could hardly be disputed. The one perfectly satisfactory element at the present crisis is that all the prophecies have failed. At least the people who have been clearly proved to be wrong are the people who were quite sure they were right. That is always a gratifying circumstance. Now why is it that all these prophecies of the wise have been confounded and why has the destiny of men taken so decisive and different a course? It is because of the very simple fact that the human race consists of many millions of two-legged and tolerably cheerful, reasonably unhappy beings who never read any books at all and certainly never hear of any scientific predictions. If they act in opposition to the scheme which science has foreseen for them, they must be excused. They sin in ignorance. They have no notion that they are avoiding what was really unavoidable. But, indeed, the phrases loosely used of that obscure mass of mankind are a little misleading. To say of the bulk of human beings that they are uneducated is like saying of a Red Indian hunter that he has not yet taken his degree. He has taken many other things. And so, sincerely speaking, there are no uneducated men. They may escape the trivial examinations, but not the tremendous examinations of existence. The dependence of infancy, the enjoyment of animals, the love of woman and the fear of death -- these are more frightful and more fixed than all conceivable forms of the cultivation of the mind. It is idle to complain of schools and colleges being trivial. In no case will a college ever teach the important things. He has learnt them right or wrong, and he has learnt them all alone.

We therefore come back to the primary truth, that what is right with the world has nothing to do with future changes, but is rooted in original realities. If groups or peoples show an unexpected independence or creative power; if they do things no one had dreamed of their doing; if they prove more ferocious or more self-sacrificing than the wisdom of the world had ever given them credit for, then such inexplicable outbursts can always be referred back to some elementary and absolute doctrine about the nature of men. No traditions in this world are so ancient as the traditions that lead to modern upheaval and innovation. Nothing nowadays is so conservative as a revolution. The men who call themselves Republicans are men walking the streets of deserted and tiny city-states, and digging up the great bones of pagans. And when we ask on what republicanism really rests, we come back to that great indemonstrable dogma of the native dignity of man. And when we come back to the lord of creation, we come back of necessity to creation; and we ask ourselves that ultimate question which St Thomas Aquinas (an extreme optimist) answered in the affirmative: Are these things ultimately of value at all?

What is right with the world is the world. In fact, nearly everything else is wrong with it. This is that great truth in the tremendous tale of Creation, a truth that our people must remember or perish. It is at the beginning that things are good, and not (as the more pallid progressives say) only at the end. The primordial things -- existence, energy, fruition -- are good so far as they go. You cannot have evil life, though you can have notorious evil livers. Manhood and womanhood are good things, though men and women are often perfectly pestilent. You can use poppies to drug people, or birch trees to beat them, stone to make an idol, or corn to make a corner; but it remains true that, in the abstract, before you have done anything, each of these four things is in strict truth a glory, a beneficent speciality and variety.

We do praise the Lord that there are birch trees growing amongst the rocks and poppies amongst the corn; we do praise the Lord, even if we do not believe in Him. We do admire and applaud the project of a world, just as if we had been called to council in the primal darkness and seen the first starry plan of the skies. We are, as a matter of fact, far more certain that this life of ours is a magnificent and amazing enterprise than we are that it will succeed. These evolutionary optimists who called themselves Meliorists (a patient and poor-spirited lot they are) always talk as if we were certain of the end, though not of the beginning. In other words, they don't know what life is aiming at, but they are quite sure it will get there. Why anybody who has avowedly forgotten where he came from should be quite so certain of where he is going to I have never been able to make out; but Meliorists are like that. They are ready to talk of existence itself as the product of purely evil forces. They never mention animals except as perpetually tearing each other to pieces; but a month in the country would cure that. They have a real giddy horror of stars and seas, as a man has on the edge of a hopelessly high precipice. They sometimes instinctively shrink from clay, fungoids, and the fresh young of animals with a quivering gesture that reveals the fundamental pessimist. Life itself, crude, uncultivated life, is horrible to them. They belong very largely to the same social class and creed as the lady who objected that the milk came to her from a dirty cow, and not from a nice clean shop. But they are sure how everything will end.

I am in precisely the opposite position. I am much more sure that everything is good at the beginning than I am that everything will be good at the end. That all this frame of things, this flesh, these stones, are good things, of that I am more brutally certain than I can say. But as for what will happen to them, that is to take a step into dogma and prophecy. I speak here, of course, solely of my personal feelings, not even of my reasoned creed. But on my instincts alone I should have no notion what would ultimately happen to this material world I think so magnificent. For all I know it may be literally and not figuratively true that the tares are tied into bundles for burning, and that as the tree falleth so shall it lie. I am an agnostic, like most people with a positive theology. But I do affirm, with the full weight of sincerity, that trees and flowers are good at the beginning, whatever happens to them at the end; that human lives were good at the beginning, whatever happens to them in the end. The ordinary modern progressive position is that this is a bad universe, but will certainly get better. I say it is certainly a good universe, even if it gets worse. I say that these trees and flowers, stars and sexes, are primarily, not merely ultimately, good. In the Beginning the power beyond words created heaven and earth. In the Beginning He looked on them and saw that they were good.

All this unavoidable theory (for theory is always unavoidable) may be popularly pulled together thus. We are to regard existence as a raid or great adventure; it is to be judged, therefore, not by what calamities it encounters, but by what flag it follows and what high town it assaults. The most dangerous thing in the world is to be alive; one is always in danger of one's life. But anyone who shrinks from this is a traitor to the great scheme and experiment of being. The pessimist of the ordinary type, the pessimist who thinks he would be better dead, is blasted with the crime of Iscariot. Spiritually speaking, we should be justified in punishing him with death. Only, out of polite deference to his own philosophy, we punish him with life.

But this faith (that existence was fundamentally and purposely good) is not attacked only by the black, consistent pessimist. The man who says that he would sooner die is best answered by a sudden blow with the poker, for the reply is rightly logical, as well as physically very effective. But there has crept through the culture of modern Europe another notion that is equally in its own way an attack on the essential rightness of the world. It is not avowedly pessimistic, though the source from which it comes (which is Buddhism) is pessimistic for those who really understand it. It can offer itself -- as it does among some of the high-minded and distinguished Theosophists -- with an air of something highly optimistic. But this disguised pessimism is what is really wrong with the world -- at least, especially with the modern world. It is essential to arrest and to examine it.

There has crept into our thoughts, through a thousand small openings, a curious and unnatural idea. I mean the idea that unity is itself a good thing; that there is something high and spiritual about things being blended and absorbed into each other. That all rivers should run into one river, that all vegetables should go into one pot -- that is spoken of as the last and best fulfilment of being. Boys are to be 'at one' with girls; all sects are to be 'at one' in the New Theology; beasts fade into men and men fade into God; union in itself is a noble thing. Now union in itself is not a noble thing. Love is a noble thing; but love is not union. Nay, it is rather a vivid sense of separation and identity. Maudlin, inferior love poetry does, indeed, talk of lovers being 'one soul', just as maudlin, inferior religious poetry talks of being lost in God; but the best poetry does not. When Dante meets Beatrice, he feels his distance from her, not his proximity; and all the greatest saints have felt their lowness, not their highness, in the moment of ecstasy. And what is true of these grave and heroic matters (I do not say, of course, that saints and lovers have never used the language of union too, true enough in its own place and proper limitation of meaning) -- what is true of these is equally true of all the lighter and less essential forms of appreciation of surprise. Division and variety are essential to praise; division and variety are what is right with the world. There is nothing specially right about mere contact and coalescence.

In short, this vast, vague idea of unity is the one 'reactionary' thing in the world. It is perhaps the only connection in which that foolish word 'reactionary' can be used with significance and truth. For this blending of men and women, nations and nations, is truly a return to the chaos and unconsciousness that were before the world was made. There is of course, another kind of unity of which I do not speak here; unity in the possession of truth and the perception of the need for these varieties. But the varieties themselves; the reflection of man and woman in each other, as in two distinct mirrors; the wonder of man at nature as a strange thing at once above and below him; the quaint and solitary kingdom of childhood; the local affections and the colour of certain landscapes -- these actually are the things that are the grace and honour of the earth; these are the things that make life worth living and the whole framework of things well worthy to be sustained. And the best thing remains; that this view, whether conscious or not, always has been and still is the view of the living and labouring millions. While a few prigs on platforms are talking about 'oneness' and absorption in 'The All', the folk that dwell in all the valleys of this ancient earth are renewing the varieties for ever. With them a woman is loved for being unmanly, and a man loved for being un-womanly. With them the church and the home are both beautiful, because they are both different; with them fields are personal and flags are sacred; they are the virtue of existence, for they are not mankind but men.

The rooted hope of the modern world is that all these dim democracies do still believe in that romance of life, that variation of man, woman and child upon which all poetry has hitherto been built. The danger of the modern world is that these dim democracies are so very dim, and that they are especially dim where they are right. The danger is that the world may fall under a new oligarchy -- the oligarchy of prigs. And if anyone should promptly ask (in the manner of the debating clubs) for the definition of a prig, I can only reply that a prig is an oligarch who does not even know he is an oligarch. A circle of small pedants sit on an upper platform, and pass unanimously (in a meeting of none) that there is no difference between the social duties of men and of women, the social instruction of men or of children. Below them boils that multitudinous sea of millions that think differently, that have always thought differently, that will always think differently. In spite of the overwhelming majority that maintains the old theory of life, I am in some real doubt about which will win. Owing to the decay of theology and all the other clear systems of thought, men have been thrown back very much upon their instincts, as with animals. As with animals, their instincts are right; but, as with animals, they can be cowed. Between the agile scholars and the stagnant mob, I am really doubtful about which will be triumphant. I have no doubt at all about which ought to be.

Europe at present exhibits a concentration upon politics which is partly the unfortunate result of our loss of religion, partly the just and needful result of our loss of our social inequality and iniquity. These causes, however, will not remain in operation for ever. Religion is returning from her exile; it is more likely that the future will be crazily and corruptly superstitious than that it will be merely rationalist.

On the other hand, our attempts to right the extreme ill-balance of wealth must soon have some issue; something will be done to lessen the perpetual torture of incompetent compassion; some scheme will be substituted for our malevolent anarchy, if it be only one of benevolent servitude. And as these two special unrests about the universe and the State settle down into more silent and enduring system, there will emerge more and more those primary and archaic truths which the dust of these two conflicts has veiled. The secondary questions relatively solved, we shall find ourselves all the more in the presence of the primary questions of Man.

For at present we all tend to one mistake; we tend to make politics too important. We tend to forget how huge a part of a man's life is the same under a Sultan and a Senate, under Nero or St Louis. Daybreak is a never-ending glory, getting out of bed is a never-ending nuisance; food and friends will be welcomed; work and strangers must be accepted and endured; birds will go bedwards and children won't, to the end of the last evening. And the worst peril is that in our just modern revolt against intolerable accidents we may have unsettled those things that alone make daily life tolerable. It will be an ironic tragedy if, when we have toiled to find rest, we find we are incurably restless. It will be sad if, when we have worked for our holiday, we find we have unlearnt everything but work. The typical modern man is the insane millionaire who has drudged to get money, and then finds he cannot enjoy even money. There is danger that the social reformer may silently and occultly develop some of the madness of the millionaire whom he denounces. He may find that he has learnt how to build playgrounds but forgotten how to play. He may agitate for peace and quiet, but only propagate his own mental agitation. In his long fight to get a slave a half-holiday he may angrily deny those ancient and natural things, the zest of being, the divinity of man, the sacredness of simple things, the health and humour of the earth, which alone make a half-holiday even half a holiday or a slave even half a man.

There is danger in that modern phrase 'divine discontent'. There is truth in it also, of course; but it is only truth of a special and secondary kind. Much of the quarrel between Christianity and the world has been due to this fact; that there are generally two truths, as it were, at any given moment of revolt or reaction, and the ancient underlying truism which is nevertheless true all the time. It is sometimes worth while to point out that black is not so black as it is painted; but black is still black, and not white. So with the merits of content and discontent. It is true that in certain acute and painful crises of oppression or disgrace, discontent is a duty and shame could call us like a trumpet. But it is not true that man should look at life with an eye of discontent, however high-minded. It is not true that in his primary, naked relation to the world, in his relation to sex, to pain, to comradeship, to the grave or to the weather, man ought to make discontent his ideal; it is black lunacy. Half his poor little hopes of happiness hang on his thinking a small house pretty, a plain wife charming, a lame foot not unbearable, and bad cards not so bad. The voice of the special rebels and prophets, recommending discontent, should, as I have said, sound now and then suddenly, like a trumpet. But the voices of the saints and sages, recommending, contentment, should sound unceasingly, like the sea.

THE ADVANTAGES OF HAVING
ONE LEG

A friend of mine who was visiting a poor woman in bereavement and casting about for some phrase of consolation that should not be either insolent or weak, said at last, "I think one can live through these great sorrows and even be the better. What wears one is the little worries." "That's quite right, mum," answered the old woman with emphasis, "and I ought to know, seeing I've had ten of 'em." It is, perhaps, in this sense that it is most true that little worries are most wearing. In its vaguer significance the phrase, though it contains a truth, contains also some possibilities of self-deception and error. People who have both small troubles and big ones have the right to say that they find the small ones the most bitter; and it is undoubtedly true that the back which is bowed under loads incredible can feel a faint addition to those loads; a giant holding up the earth and all its animal creation might still find the grasshopper a burden. But I am afraid that the maxim that the smallest worries are the worst is sometimes used or abused by people, becasue they have nothing but the very smallest worries. The lady may excuse herself for reviling the crumpled rose-leaf by reflecting with what extraordinary dignity she would wear the crown of thorns--if she had to. The gentleman may permit himself to curse the dinner and tell himself that he would behave much better if it were a mere matter of starvation. We need not deny that the grasshopper on man's shoulder is a burden; but we need not pay much respect to a gentleman who is always calling out that he would rather have an elephant when he knows there are no elephants in the country. We may concede that a straw may break the camel's back, but we like to know that it really is the last straw and not the first.

I grant that those who have serious wrongs have a real right to grumble, so long as they grumble about something else. It is a singular fact that if they are sane they almost always do grumble about something else. To talk quite reasonably about your own quite real wrongs is the quickest way to go off your head. But people with great troubles talk about little ones, and the man who complains of the crumpled rose leaf very often has his flesh full of the thorns. But if a man has commonly a very clear and happy daily life than I think we are justified in asking that he shall not make mountains out of molehills. I do not deny that molehills can sometimes be important. Small annoyances have this evil about them, that they can be more abrupt because they are more invisible; they cast no shadow before, they have no atmosphere. No one ever had a mystical premonition that he was going to tumble over a hassock. William III. died by falling over a molehill; I do not suppose that with all his varied abilities he could have managed to fall over a mountain. But when all this is allowed for, I repeat that we may ask a happy man (not William III.) to put up with pure inconveniences, and even make them part of his happiness. Of positive pain or positive poverty I do not here speak. I speak of those innumerable accidental limitations that are always falling across our path--bad weather, confinement to this or that house or room, failure of appointments or arrangements, waiting at railway stations, missing posts, finding unpunctuality when we want punctuality, or, what is worse, finding punctuality when we don't. It is of the poetic pleasures to be drawn from all these that I sing--I sing with confidence because I have recently been experimenting in the poetic pleasures which arise from having to sit in one chair with a sprained foot, with the only alternative course of stinding on one leg like a stork. A stork is a poetic simile; therefore I eagerly adopted it.

To appreciate anything we must always isolate it, even if the thing itself symbolises something other than isolation. If we wish to see what a house is it must be a house in some uninhabited landscape. If we wish to depict what a man really is we must depict a man alone in a desert or on a dark sea sand. So long as he is a single figure he means all that humanity means; so long as he is solitary he means sociability and comradeship. Add another figure and the picture is less human--not more so. One is company, two is none. If you wish to symbolize human building draw one dark tower on the horizon; if you wish to symbolize light let there be no star in the sky. Indeed, all through that strangely lit season which we call our day there is but one star in the sky-- a large, fierce star which we call the sun. One sun is splendid; six suns would be only vulgar. One Tower of Giotto is sublime; a row of Towers of Giotto would be only like a row of white posts. The poetry of art is in beholding the single tower; the poetry of nature in seeing the single tree; the poetry of love in following the single woman; the poetry of religion in worshipping the single star. And so, in the same pensive lucidity, I find the poetry of all human anatomy in standing on a single leg. To express complete and perfect leggishness the leg must stand in sublime isolation, like the tower in the wilderness. As Ibsen so finely says, the strongest leg is that which stands most alone.

This lonely leg on which I rest has all the simplicity of some Doric column. The students of architecture tell us that the only legitimate use of a column is to support weight. This column of mine fulfils its legitimate function. It supports weight. Being of an animal and organic consistency, it may even improve by the process, and during these few days that I am thus unequally balanced the helplessness or dislocation of the one leg may find compensation in the astonishing strength and classic beauty of the other leg. Mrs. Mountstuart Jenkinson in Mr. George Meredith's novel might pass by at any moment, and seeing me in the stork-like attitude would exclaim, with equal admiration and a more literal exactitude, "He has a leg." Notice how this famous literary phrase supports my contention touching this isolation of any admirable thing. Mrs. Mountstuart Jenkinson, wishing to make a clear and perfect picture of human grace, said that Sir Willoughby Patterne had a leg. She delicately glossed over and concealed the clumsy and offensive fact that he had really two legs. Two legs were superfluous and irrelevant, a reflection, and a confusion. Two legs would have confused Mrs. Mountstuart Jenkinson like two Monuments in London. That having had one good leg he should have another--this would be to use vain repetitions as the Gentiles do. She would have been as much bewildered by him as if he had been a centipede.

All pessimism has a secret optimism for its object. All surrender of life, all denial of pleasure, all darkness, all austerity, all desolation has for its real aim this separation of something so that it may be poignantly and perfectly enjoyed. I feel grateful for the slight sprain which has introduced this mysterious and fascinating division between one of my feet and the other. The way to love anything is to realize how very much otherwise it might have been. The moral of the thing is wholly exhilarating. This world and all our powers in it are far more awful and beautiful than we ever know until some accident reminds us. If you wish to perceive that limitless felicity, limit yourself if only for a moment. If you wish to realize how fearfully and wonderfully God's image is made, stand on one leg. If you want to realize the splendid vision of all visible things-- wink the other eye.

ON HOUSEHOLD GODS AND GOBLINS

Sometime ago I went with some children to see Maeterlinck's fine and delicate fairy play about the Blue Bird that brought everybody happiness. For some reason or other it did not being me happiness, and even the children were not quite happy. I will not go so far as to say that the Blue Bird was a Blue Devil, but it left us in something seriously like the blues. The children were party dissatisfied with it because it did not end with a Day of Judgment; because it was never revealed to the hero and heroine that the dog had been faithful and the cat faithless. For children are innocent and love justice; while most of us are wicked and naturally prefer mercy.

But there was something wrong about the Blue Bird, even from my more mature and corrupt point of view. There were several incidental things I did not like. I did not like the sentimental passage about the love-affair of two babes unborn; it seemed to me a piece of what may be called bad Barrie; and logically it spoilt the only meaning of the scene, which was that the babes were looking to all earthly experiences as things inconceivable. I was not convinced when the boy exclaimed, "There are no dead," for I am by no means sure that he (or the dramatist) knew what he meant by it. "I heard a voice from Heaven cry: Blessed are the dead. ..." I do not know all that is meant in that; but I think the person who said it knew. But there was something more continuous and clinging in the whole business which left me vaguely restless. And I think the nearest to a definition was that I felt as if the poet was condescending to everything; condescending to pots and pans and birds and beasts and babies.

The one part of the business which I really felt to be original and suggestive was the animation of all the materials of the household, as if with familiar spirits; the spirit of fire, the spirit of water and the rest. And even here I felt a faint difference which moved me to an imaginary comparison. I wonder that none of our medievalists has made a Morality or allegorical play founded on the Canticle of Saint Francis, which speaks somewhat similarly of Brother Fire and Sister Water. It would be a real exercise in Gothic craftsmanship and decoration to make these symbolic figures at once stiff and fantastic. If nobody else does this I shall be driven to spoil the idea myself, as I have spoiled so many other rather good ideas in my time. But the point of the parallel at the moment is merely this: that the medieval poet does strike me as having felt about fire like a child while the modern poet felt about it like a man talking to children.

Few and simple as are the words of the older poem, it does somehow convey to me that when the poet spoke of fire as untameable and strong, he felt it as something that might conceivably be feared as well as loved. I do not think the modern poet feared the nursery fire as a child who loved it might fear it. And this elemental quality in the real primitives brough back to my mind something I have always felt about this conception, which is the really fine conception in the Blue Bird: I mean something like that which the heathens embodied in the images of the household gods. The household gods, I believe, were carved out of wood; which makes them even more like the chairs and tables.

The nomad and the anarchist accuse the domestic ideal of being merely timid and prim. But this is not because they themselves are bolder or more vigorous, but simply because they do not know it well enough to know how bold and vigorous it is. The most nomadic life to-day is not the life of the desert but of the industrial cities. It is by a very accurate accident that we talk about a Street-Arab; and the Semitic description applies to not a few gutter-snipes whose gilded chariots have raised them above the gutter. They live in clubs and hotels and are often simply ignorant, I might say innocent, of the ancient life of the family, and certainly off the ancient life on the farm.

When a townsman first sees these things directly and intimately, he does not despise them as dull but rather dreads then as wild, as he sometimes takes a tame cow for a wild bull. The most obvious example is the hearth which is the heart of the home. A man living in the lukewarm air of centrally-heated hotels may be said to have never seen fire. Compared to him the housewife at the fireside is an Amazon wrestling with a flaming dragon. The same moral might be drawn from the fact that the watchdog fights while the wild dog often runs away. Of the husband, as of the house-dog, it may often said that he has been tamed into ferocity.

This is especially true of the sort of house represented by the country cottage. It is only in theory that the things are petty and prosaic; a man realistically experiencing them will feel them to be things big and baffling and involving a heavy battle with nature. When we read about cabbages or cauliflowers in the papers, and especially the comic papers, we learn to think of them as commonplace. But if a man of any imagination will merely consent to walk round the kitchen-garden for himself, and really looks at cabbages and cauliflowers, he will feel at once that they are vast and elemental things like the mountains in the clouds. He will feel somehing almost monstrous about the size and solidity of the things swelling out of that small and tidy patch of ground. There are modds in which that everyday English kitchen plot will affect him as men are affected by the reeking wealth and toppling rapidity of tropic vegetation; the green bubbles and crawling branches of a nightmare.

But whatever his mood, he will see that things so large and work so laborious cannot possibly be merely trivial. His reason no less than his imagination will tell him that the fight here waged between the family and the field is of all things the most primitive and fundamental. If that is not poetical, nothing is poetical, and certainly not the dingy Bohemianism of the artists in the towns. But the point for the moment is that even by the purely artistic test the same truth is apparent. An artist looking at these things with a free and fresh vision will at once appreciate what I mean by calling them wild rather than tame. It is true of fire, of water, of vegetation, of half a hundred other things. If a man reads about a pig, he will think of something comic and commonplace, chiefly because the word "pig" sounds comic and commonplace. If he looks at a real pig in a pigsty, he will have the sense of something too large to be alive, like a hippopotamus at the Zoo.

This is not a coincidence or a sophistry; it rests on the real and living logic of things. The family is itself a wilder thing than the State; if we mean by wildness that it is born of will and choice as elemental and emancipated as the wind. It has its own laws, as the wind has; but properly understood it is infinitely less subservient than things are under the elaborate and mechanical regulations of legalism. Its obligations are love and loyalty, but these are things quite capable of being in revolt against merely human laws; for merely human law has a great tendency to become merely inhuman law. It is concerned with events that are in the moral world what cyclones and earthquakes are in the material world.

People are not born in an infant-school any more than they die in an undertaker's shop. These prodigies are private things; and take place in the tiny theatre of the home. The public systems, the large organisation, are a mere machinery for the transport and distribution of things; they do not touch the intrinsic nature of the things themselves. If a birthday present is sent from one family to another all the legal system, and even all that we call the social system, is only concerned with the present so long as it is a parcel. Nearly all our modern sociology might be called the philosophy of parcels. For that matter, nearly all our modern descriptions of Utopia or the Great State might be called the paradise of postmen. It is in the inner chamber that the parcel becomes a present; that it explodes, so to speak, into its own radiance and real popuarity; and it is equally true, so far as that argument is concerned, whether it is a bon-bon or a bomb. The essential message is always a personal message; the important business is always private business. And this is, of course, especially with the first of all birthday presents which presents itself at birth; and it is no exaggeration to talk of a bomb as the symbol of a baby. Of course, the same is true of the tragic as the beatific acts of the domestic drama; of the spadework of the struggle for life or the Damoclean sword of death.

The defence of domesticity is not that it is always happy, or even that it is always harmless. It is rather that it does involve, like all heroic things, the possibilities of calamity and even of crime. Old Mother Hubbard may find that the cupboard is bare; she may even find a skeleton in the cupboard. All that is involved here is the insistence on the true case for this intimate type of association; that in itself it is certainly not commonplace and most certainly is not conventional. The conventions belong rather to those wider worldly organisations which are now set up as rivals to it; to the club, to the school and above all to the State. You cannot have a successful club without rules; but a family will really do without any rules exactly in proportion as it is a successful family. What somebody said about the songs of a people could be said much more truly about the jokes of a household. And a joke is in its nature a wild and spontaneous thing; even the modern fanaticism for organisation has never really attempted to organise laughter like a chorus. Therefore, we may truly say that these external emblems or examples of something grotesque and extravagant about our private possessions are not mere artistic exercises in the incongruous; they are not, as the phrase goes, mere paradoxes. They are really related to the aboriginal nature of the institution itself and the idea that is behind it. The real family is something as wild and elemental as a cabbage.

ON ABOLISHING SUNDAY

THE report that the Bolshevist Government had abolished Sunday might be read in several ways. Some of the Bolshevists were of the race which might be expected to substitute Saturday. Others have a marked intellectual affinity to the great religion which, oddly enough, selects Friday. The Moslem day of rest is Friday; and, when I was in Jerusalem, very quaint results sometimes followed from the three religious festivals coming on the three successive days. It was complained that the Jews took an unfair advantage of the fact that their Sabbath ceases at sunset; but, anyhow, it was highly significant of a universal human need that the three great cosmopolitan communions, which all disagreed about the choice of a sacred day, all agreed in having one. They had fought and persecuted and oppressed and exploited each other in all sorts of ways. But they all had the profound human instinct of a Truce of God, in which men should, if possible, leave off fighting, and even (if the thought be conceivable) leave off exploiting.

If the Bolshevists have really declared war on the intrinsic idea of a common Day of Rest, it is not perhaps the first point in which they have proved themselves much stupider than Jews, Turks, infidels and heretics. We all tend to talk naturally about antiquated pedantry. But the most pedantic sort of pedant is he who is too limited to be anti-quated. He is cut off from antiquity and therefore from humanity; he will learn nothing from things, but only from theories; and, in the very act of claiming to teach by experiment, refuses to learn by experience. There could hardly be a stronger example of this sort of deaf and dull impatience than a merely destructive attitude towards Sabbaths and special days. The fact that men have always felt them necessary only makes this sort of prig more certain that they are unnecessary. Their universality, even in variety, ought to warn him that he is dealing with something deep and delicate--something at once subtle and stubborn. I do not say that he is bound to consider them right; but he is bound to consider them. And he never does consider them, because he finds it the line of least resistance to condemn them. It is almost enough for him that mankind has always desired something; he will instantly set to work to deliver mankind from anything that it has always desired. Sooner or later, we shall doubt less see a movement for freeing men from the old and barbarous custom of eating food. We have already, for that matter, seen something like a movement for delivering them from the fantastic habit of drinking drinks. We shall have revolutionists denouncing the degrading necessity of going to bed at night. Alter all, the prostrate posture might be considered servile or touched with the superstitions of the suppliant. The true active, alert, and self-respecting citizen may reasonably be expected to stand upright for twenty-four hours on end. The progressive philosopher may be required to walk in his sleep, and even to talk in his sleep; and, considering what he says and where he walks to, it seems likely enough. Anyhow, the same sort of dehumanized philosophy which destroys the recurrence of one day in seven may well disregard the recurrence of six hours in twenty-four. We may see a vast intellectual revolt against the Slavery of Sleep. I can vividly imagine the pamphlets and the posters; the elaborate statistics showing that, if people never stopped working, they would produce more than they do at present; the lucid diagrams setting forth the loss to labour by the fact that few men axe actually at work in their factor while they are asleep in their beds. These scientific demonstrations are always so close and cogent. I can almost see the rows of figures showing successively in the case of coal, cotton, butter, boot-laces, pork and pig-iron, that in every single example more work would be done if every body could only go on working. It is true that this sort of argument is generally of most ultimate use to Capitalism. But so is Bolshevism.

But these true friends of Capitalism, who still call themselves Communists, do not, of course, mean that nobody should have any leisure, any more than that nobody should have any sleep. The Communists would say that there should be shifts of labour, and frequent recurrences of leisure; but so would the capitalists. They would say that the labour should be organized for all, and the leisure given in turn to each individual; but so would the Capitalists. There is really not much difference in the general plan of the factory system presided over by the collectivism of Moscow and the individualism of Detroit. It is only fair to say that Mr. Ford has forgotten what anybody ever meant by Individualism, quite as completely as the Bolshevist leaders have forgotten what they themselves originally meant by Bolshevism. The holiday is given to the individual, but there is nothing individual about it. It is given by an impersonal power by a mechanical rotation, over which the individual himself has no power. It is not given to him on his birthday, or the day of his patron saint, or even on the day that he would personally prefer; God forbid!-- or, rather (as the Bolshevists would say), Godlessness forbid!

But, even apart from the failure of the solitary holiday to be a personal holiday, there is a deeper objection to the disappearance of a social holiday. It lies deep in the mysteries of human nature, the one thing which the pedantic revolutionist is always too impatient to understand. He will study mathematics in a week and metaphysics in a fortnight; and as for economics, he has picked up the whole truth about them by looking at a little pamphlet in the lunch-hour. But he will not study Man; he dodges that science by simply dismissing all the elements he cannot understand as superstitions. Now one thing that is essential to man is rhythm; and not merely a rhythm in his own life, but to some extent in the living world around him. I will even remark, chiefly for the pleasure of annoying the scientific sociologist, that the most profound and practical truth of the matter is found in the statement that God made the world in six days and rested on the seventh day. In other words, there is a rhythm at the back of things, and in the beginning and nature of the universe; and there must be something of the same kind in the social and secular manifestations of the world. Men are not happy if things always look the same; it is recognized in practice in the common medical case for what is called 'a change'. The mere fact that a man has not got to do any work himself on Tuesday is a very small part of the general sense of release or refreshment that existed in an institution like Sunday. I once ventured to use the expression (though I put it into the mouth of a bull- terrier), 'the smell of Sunday morning'. And I am prepared to say that there is such a thing, though my own sense of smell is very deficient compared with a bull-terrier's. There is something in the very light and air of a world in which most people are not working, or not working as much or in the same way as usual, which satisfied the subconscious craving for crisis and fulfilment. If men have nothing but an endless series of days which look alike, it would matter little whether they were days of leisure or labour. They would not give that particular sense of something achieved, or, at least, of something measured; of the image of God resting on the seventh day. it is a psychological fact that such monotony would take on a character as of mathematical insanity. It would be like the endless corridors of a nightmare. Men have always known this by instinct, Pagans as well as Christians. And when nil humanity has agreed on the necessity for some thing, we may be perfectly certain that some sort of humanitarian will want to destroy it.

HOW NOT TO DO IT

There are two recognised ways of arguing with a Communist; and they are both wrong. There is also a third way which is right but which is not recognised. Now I have a notion that, for one reason or another, a considerable part of our time will be taken up soon by arguing with Communists. And I should like to sketch very roughly this notion of mine about the right way to do it. Curiously enough, the two commonest ways of contradicting Communism also contradict each other. The first consists of convicting the Bolshevist of all vices. The second, curiously enough, consists of convicting him of all the virtues. It actually consists of pitting all our vices against his virtues; or his supposed virtues.

This is very much the more dangerous and even suicidal trick of the two; but its nature needs a little explanation. The first common or conventional method is at least simple enough. The Capitalist says to the Communist, "You shall not enter my house, for I know you would burn it down; you shall not speak to my family, for I know you would blow them up; you are a common thief and murderer and I am a highly respectable and moral person; and not as this Russian." Now I do not like talking like that to a Bolshevist; because I should not like talking like that to a burglar. It is Pharisaical; and the Pharisee is a more ancient enemy of the Christian than the Marxian.

But I rather prefer it to the other method, which I find extremely common, among those who profess to defend property or individualism against the Marxian heresy. It really consists of telling the Communist that he is an idealist, or, in other words, that he must be wrong because he has ideals. In this second case, the Capitalist says to the Communist, "You believe in a lot of nonsense about the brotherhood of men; but I tell you, as a practical man, that every man wants to get as much as he can for himself, and will beat his own brother in business if he can. Every man must obey his acquisitive instinct." (I read these very words recently in an attack on the Bolshevist theory.) "You cannot keep things humming and hustling without private enterprise; and you cannot produce private enterprise unless you bribe or reward it with the glittering prizes of private property." People use these arguments against Communism, as if they were the only arguments against Communism; and then they are surprised that a number of more generous and spirited young people become Communists.

They do not seem to see that, to such young people, the Capitalist in question only seems to be saying, "I am a greedy old scoundrel, and I forbid you to be anything else."

Now the true, full and final argument against Communism is that private property is much more important than private enterprise. A pickpocket represents private enterprise, but we should hardly say that he supports private property. Private property is not a bribe that exists for the sake of private enterprise. On the contrary, private enterprise is only a tool or weapon, that may sometimes be useful to preserve private property. And it is necessary to preserve private property; simply because the other name of it is liberty. On the one hand, it is not merely a conventional respectability; on the contrary, it is only the man with some property and privacy who can live his own life freely. On the other hand, it is not a mere licence to trade, still less a mere licence to cheat; on the contrary, the whole point of property is that in that alone can be naturally nourished the sentiment of honour. It would need some space to expound it here and might take some time to expound it to the Communist. But the Communist would listen at least longer than he would to a man merely boasting of self-righteousness or a man merely boasting of avarice.

TWO KINDS OF PARADOX

There is nothing that needs more fastidious care than our choice of nonsense. Sense is like daylight or daily air, and may come from any quarter or in any quantity. But nonsense is an art. Like an art, it is rarely successful, and yet entirely simple when it is successful. Like an art, it depends on the smallest word, and a misprint can spoil it. And like an art, when it is not in the service of heaven it is almost always in the service of hell. Numberless imitators of Lewis Carroll or of Edward Lear have tried to write nonsense and failed; falling back (one may hope) upon writing sense. But certainly, as the great Gilbert said, wherever there has been nonsense it has been precious nonsense. Les Précieuses Ridicules might be translated, perhaps, in two ways. No one doubts that serious artists are absurd; but it might also be maintained that absurdity is always a serious art.

I have suffered as much as any man from the public insult of the misprint. I have seen my love of books described as a love of boots. I have seen the word "cosmic" invariably printed as "comic"; and have merely reflected that the two are much the same. As to Nationalists and Rationalists, I have come to the conclusion that no human handwriting or typewriting can clearly distinguish them; and I now placidly permit them to be interchanged, though the first represents everything I love and the second everything I loathe. But there is one kind of misprint I should still find it hard to forgive. I could not pardon a blunder in the printing of "Jabberwock." I insist on absolute literalism in that really fine poem of Lear,--"TheDong with the Luminous Nose." To spoil these new nonsense words would be like shooting a great musician improvising on the piano. The sounds could never be recovered again. "And as in uffish thought he stood." If the printer had printed it "affish" I doubt if the first edition would have sold. "Over the Great Gromboolian Plain." Suppose I had seen it printed "Gromhoolian." Perhaps I should never have known, as I know now, that Edward Lear was a yet greater man than Lewis Carroll.

The first principle, then, may be considered clear. Let mistakes be made in ordinary books--that is, in scientific works, established biographies, histories, and so on. Do not let us be hard on misprints when they occur merely in time-tables or atlases or works of science. In works like those of Professor Haeckel, for example, it is sometimes quite difficult to discover which are the misprints and which are the intentional assertions. But in anything artistic, anything which avowedly strays beyond reason, there we must demand the exactitude of art. If a thing is admittedly not possible, then the next best thing it can do is to be beautiful. If a thing is nonsensical, it ought to be perfectly nonsensical.

This, which applies to the nonsensical borderland of words, as in Lear and Carroll, applies also to the nonsensical borderland of thoughts, as in Oscar Wilde or Bernard Shaw. There also the difficulty is not to find nonsense, but to find any precious nonsense. Many accuse Mr. Shaw and others of merely saying anything opposite to the current view. But if these critics have detected such a scheme of success, why do they not merely profit by it? If they have got the key, let them use it. If they know the trick, let them do it. If a man can achieve prominence and prosperity merely by saying that the sun shines at night and the stars by day, that every man has four legs and every horse two--surely the path to success is open, for there must be many such things to say. But the truth is that, while we can all wallow in commonplaces (a thoroughly healthy thing, like a mud bath), we must all be particular in our selection of paradoxes. Here, for once, taste is really important.

For there are two kinds of paradoxes. They are not so much the good and the bad, nor even the true and the false. Rather they are the fruitful and the barren; the paradoxes which produce life and the paradoxes that merely announce death. Nearly all modern paradoxes merely announce death. I see everywhere among the young men who have imitated Mr. Shaw a strange tendency to utter epigrams which deny the possibility of further life and thought. A paradox may be a thing unusual, menacing, even ugly-- like a rhinoceros. But, as a live rhinoceros ought to produce more rhinoceri, so a live paradox ought to produce more paradoxes. Nonsense ought to be suggestive; but nowadays it is abortive. The new epigrams are not even fantastic finger-posts on the wild road: they are tablets, each set into a brick wall at the end of a blind alley. So far as they concern thought at all, they cry to men, "Think no more," as the voice said "Sleep no more" to Macbeth. These rhetoricians never speak except to move the closure. Even when they are really witty (as in the case of Mr. Shaw), they commonly commit the one crime that cannot be forgiven among free men. They say the last word.

I will give such instances as happen to lie before me. I see on my table a book of aphorisms by a young Socialist writer, Mr. Holbrook Jackson; it is called "Platitudes in the Making," and curiously illustrates this difference between the paradox that starts thought and the paradox that prevents thought. Of course, the writer has read too much Nietzsche and Shaw, and too little of less groping and more gripping thinkers. But he says many really good things of his own, and they illustrate perfectly what I mean here about the suggestive and the destructive nonsense.

Thus in one place he says. "Suffer fools gladly: they may be right." That strikes me as good; but here I mean specially that it strikes me as fruitful and free. You can do something with the idea, it opens an avenue. One can go searching among one´s more solid acquaintances and relatives for the fires of a concealed infallibility. One may fancy one sees the star of immortal youth in the somewhat empty eye of Uncle George; one may faintly follow some deep rhythm of nature in the endless repetitions with which Miss Bootle tells a story; and in the grunts and gasps of the Major next door may hear, as it were, the cry of a strangled god. It can never narrow our minds, it can never arrest our life, to suppose that a particular fool is not such a fool as he looks. It must be all to the increase of charity, and charity is the imagination of the heart.

I turn the next page, and come on what I call the barren paradox. Under the head of "Advices," Mr. Jackson writes, "Don't think--do." This is exactly like saying "Don't eat--digest." All doing that is not mechanical or accidental involves thinking; only the modern world seems to have forgotten that there can be such a thing as decisive and dramatic thinking. Everything that comes from the will must pass through the mind, though it may pass quickly. The only sort of thing the strong man can "do" without thinking is something like falling over a doormat. This is not even making the mind jump; it is simply making it stop. I take another couple of cases at random. "The object of life is life." That affects me as ultimately true; always presuming the author is liberal enough to include eternal life. But even if it is nonsense, it is thoughtful nonsense.

On another page I read, "Truth is one's own conception of things." That is thoughtless nonsense. A man would never have had any conception of things at all unless he had thought they were things and there was some truth about them. Here we have the black nonsense, like black magic, that shuts down the brain. "A lie is that which you do not believe." That is a lie; so perhaps Mr. Jackson does not believe it.

THE ROOTS OF THE WORLD

Once upon a time a little boy lived in a garden in which he was permitted to pick the flowers but forbidden to pull them up by the roots. There was, however, one particular plant, insignificant, somewhat thorny, with a small, star-like flower, which he very much wanted to pull up by the roots. His tutors and guardians, who lived in the house with him, were worthy, formal people, and they gave him reasons why he should not pull it up. They were silly reasons as a rule. But none of the reasons against doing the thing were quite so silly as the little boy's reason for wanting to do it; for his reason was that Truth demanded that he should pull the thing up by the roots to see how it was growing. Still it was a sleepy, thoughtless kind of house, and nobody gave him the real answer to his argument, which was that it would kill the plant, and that there is no more Truth about a dead plant than about a live one. So one dark night, when clouds sealed the moon like a secret too good or too bad to be told, the little boy came down the old creaking stairs of his farmhouse and crept into the garden in his nightgown. He told himself repeatedly that there was no more reason against his pulling this plant off the garden than against his knocking off a thistle top idly in a lane. Yet the darkness which he had chosen contradicted

him, and also his own throbbing pulse, for he told himself continually that next morning he might be crucified as the blasphemer who
had tom up the sacred tree.

Perhaps he might have been so crucified if he had so torn it up. I
cannot say. But he did not tear it up; and it was not for want of trying.
For when he laid hold of the little plant in the garden he tugged and
tugged, and found the thing held as if clamped to the earth with iron.
And when he strained himself a third time there came a frightful
noise behind him, and either nerves or (which he would have denied)
conscience made him leap back and stagger and stare around. The
house he lived in was a mere bulk of blackness against a sky almost
as black. Yet after staring long he saw that the very outline had grown
unfamiliar, for the great chimney of the kitchen had fallen crooked
and calamitous. Desperately he gave another pull at the plant, and
heard far off the roof of the stables fall in and the horses shriek and
plunge. Then he ran into the house and rolled himself in the
bedclothes. Next morning found the kitchen ruined, the day's food
destroyed, two horses dead, and three broken loose and lost. But the
boy still kept a furious curiosity, and a little while after, when a fog
from the sea had hidden home and garden, he dragged again at the
roots of the indestructible plant. He hung on to it like a boy on the
rope of a tug of war, but it did not give. Only through the grey sea-fog
came choking and panic-stricken cries; they cried that the King's
castle had fallen, that the towers guarding the coast were gone; that
half the great sea-city had split away and slid into the sea. Then the
boy was frightened for a little while, and said no more about the
plant, but when he had come to a strong and careless manhood, and
the destruction in the district had been slowly repaired, he said
openly before the people, "Let us have done with the riddle of this
irrational weed. In the name of Truth let us drag it up." And he gathered a great company of strong men, like an army to meet invaders,
and they all laid hold of the little plant and they tugged night and
day. And the Great Wall fell down in China for forty miles. And the
Pyramids were split up into jagged stones. And the Eiffel Tower in
Paris went over like a ninepin, killing half the Parisians; and the

Statue of Liberty in New York harbour fell forward suddenly and smashed the American fleet; and St. Paul's Cathedral killed all the journalists in Fleetstreet, and Japan had a record series of earth-quakes and then sank into the sea. Some have declared that these last two incidents were not calamities properly so called; but into that I will not enter. The point, was that when they had tugged for about twenty-four hours the strong men of that country had pulled down about half of the civilized world, but had not pulled up the plant. I will not weary the reader with the full facts of this realistic story, with how they used first elephants and then steam engines to tear up the flower, and how the only result was that the flower stuck fast, but that the moon began to be agitated and even the sun was a bit dicky. At last the human race interfered, as it always does at last, by means of a revolution. But long before that the boy, or man, who is the hero of this tale had thrown up the business, merely saying to his pastors and masters, "You gave me a number of elaborate and idle reasons why I should not pull up this shrub. Why did you not give me the two good reasons: first, that I can't; second, that I should damage everything else if I even tried it on?"

All those who have sought in the name of science to uproot reli-gion seem to me very like the little boy in the garden. Skeptics do not succeed in pulling up the roots of Christianity; but they do succeed in pulling up the roots of every man's ordinary vine and fig tree, of every man's garden and every man's kitchen garden. Secularists have not succeeded in wrecking divine things; but Secularists have succeeded in wrecking secular things. A religion cannot be shown to be monstrous at the last; a religion is monstrous from the beginning. It announces itself as extraordinary. It offers itself as extravagant. The sceptics at the most can only ask us to reject our creed as something wild. And we have accepted it as something wild. So far one would think there would be a mere impasse, a block between us and those who cannot feel as we do. But then follows the curious practical expe-rience which has ratified religion in our reason for ever. For the enemies of religion cannot leave it alone. They laboriously attempt to smash religion. They cannot smash religion; but they do smash everything else. With your queries and dilemmas you have made no havoc in faith,: from the first it was a transcendental conviction; it cannot be made any more transcendental than it was. But you have (if that is any comfort to you) made a certain havoc in common morals and common sense.

The opponents of our religion do not commit us to accepting their axioms; our axioms remain what they were before; but they do commit themselves to every doctrine of insanity and despair. They do not hit us, but they do plunge past us into the marsh and the abyss. Mr. Blatchford cannot commit us to the comment that man is not the image of his maker for that statement is as dogmatic as its denial. But he can and does commit himself to the statement, humanly ludicrous and intolerable, that I must not blame a bully or praise the man who knocks him down. Evolutionists cannot drive us, because of the nameless gradation in Nature, to deny the personality of God, for a personal God might as well work by gradations as in any other way; but they do drive themselves, through those gradations, to deny the existence of a personal Mr. Jones, because he is within the scope of evolution and his edges are rubbed away. The evolutionists uproot the world, but not the flowers. The Titans never scaled heaven, but they laid waste the earth.

CHRISTIANITY AND RATIONALISM

My friend, Mr. George Haw, has asked me to state, in one or two articles, my general belief on the subject of Christianity, to be inserted in the Clarion. I will not pretend to any particlular reluctance to do so; but I ought not to do it without first of all offering to Mr. Blatchford our gratitude, and something which is better than gratitude, our congratulations, upon the very magnanimous action which he has taken in thus putting this paper into the hands of the religious opponents. In doing so he has scored, in a generous unconsciousness, a real point.

Most of the awful revelations of Christian evil and ignorance do not, I am afraid, affect me in quite so serious a manner as they ought to. When I hear that a German professor has found the four-hundreth accurate origin of protoplasm, I try in vain to feel excitement; when I read that savages paint their faces green to please the ghosts (or what not), I have no feeling beyond a vague pleasure and sympathy. Both the German professor and the green-faced savage seem to me to be doing the same thing--that is, falling under the influence of that starry impulse which leads men to take a vast deal of trouble about quite useless things.

But such things do not make much difference to my view of

Christianity. In the whole of this controversy I have felt the force of one thing, which has really hit practical Christianity; I think it is a good argument; I think it is a terrible argument. It is not that this controversy is being conducted in a non-Christian paper. It certainly is a fair point scored against a religion that the people who seem to be most interested in it are those who believe it to be a fraud. I think, therefore, that Mr. Blatchford's magnanimity, like all magnanimity, is profoundly philosophical and wise.

Nor do I blame him, as some have done, for having discussed it at great length; as the subject is the nature of the Universe, it is necessarily as large as the Universe, and as rich as the Universe, and I may add, as amusing as the Universe.

In fact, I fancy there must be such a thing as Immortality, merely that Mr. Blatchford and I may have time to discuss whether it is true.

Before I give an outline of my view, there is one other thing to be said in which I cannot avoid the personal note. I have begun to realise that there are a good many people to whom my way of speaking about these things appears like an indication that I am flippant or imperfectly sincere. Since, as a matter of fact, I am more certain of myself in this affair than I am of the existence of the moon, this naturally causes me some considerable regret; but I think I see the naturalness of the mistake and how it arose in people for removed from the Christian atmosphere. Christianity is itself so jolly a thing that it fills the possessor of it with a certain silly exuberance, which sad and high-minded Rationalists might reasonably mistake for mere buffoonery and blasphemy; just as their prototypes, the sad and high-minded Stoics of old Rome, did mistake the Christian joyousness for buffoonery and blasphemy.

This difference holds good everywhere, in the cold Pagan architectrure and the grinning gargoyles of Christendom, in the preposterous motley of the Middle Ages and the dingy dress of this Rationlistic century. And if Mr. Blatchford wishes to know why we should be surprised if the Duke of Devonshire walked about with one leg red and the other yellow (as a nobleman might have done in the thirteenth century), I can obligingly inform him that it is because of the decay of our faith. Nowhere in history has there ever been any popular brightness and gaiety without religion.

The first of all the difficulties that I have in controverting Mr. Blatchford is simply this, that I shall be very largely going over his own ground. My favourite text-book of theology is God and my Neighbour but I cannot repeat it in detail. If I gave each of my reasons for being a Christian, a vast number of them would be Mr. Blachford's reasons for not being one.

For instance, Mr. Blatchford and his school point out that there are many myths parallel to the Christian story; that there were Pagan Christs, and Red Indian Incarnations, and Patagonian Crucifixions, for all I know or care. But does not Mr. Blatchford see the other side of this fact? If the Christian God really made the human race, would not the human race tend to rumours and perversions of the Christian God? If the center of our life is a certain fact, would not people far from the center have a muddled version of that fact? If we are so made that a Son of God must deliver us, is it odd that Patagonians should dream of a Son of God?

The Blatchfordian position really amounts to this--that because a certain thing has impressed millions of different people as likely or necessary therefore is connot be true. And then this bashful being, veiling his own talents, convicts the wretched G.K.C. of paradox! I like paradox, but I am not prepared to dance and dazzle to the extent of Nunquam, who points to humanity crying out to a thing, and pointing to it from immemorial ages, as a proof that it cannot be there.

The story of a Christ is very common in legend and literature. So is the story of two lovers parted by Fate. So is the story of two friends killing each other for a woman. But will it seriously be maintained that, because these two stories are common as legends, therefore not two friends were ever separated by love or no two lovers by circumstances? It is tolerably plain, surely, that these two stories are common because the situation is an intensely probable and human one, because our nature is so built as to make them almost inevitable.

Why should it not be that our nature is so built as to make certain spiritual events inevitable? In any case, it is clearly ridiculous to attempt to disprove Christianity by the number and variety of Pagan Christs. You might as well take the number and variety of ideal schemes of society, from Plato's Republic to Morris' News from Nowhere, from More's Utopia to Blatchford's Merrie England, and then try and prove from them that mankind cannot ever reach a better social condition. If anything, of course, they prove the opposite; they suggest a human tendency towards a better condition.

Thus, in this first instance, when learned skeptics come to me and say, "Are you aware that the Kaffirs have a story of Incarnation?" I should reply: "Speaking as an unlearned person, I don't know. But speaking as a Christian, I should be very much astonished if they hadn't."

Take a second instance. The Secularist says that Christianity has been a gloomy and ascetic thing, and points to the procession of austere or ferocious saints who have given up home and happiness and macerated health and sex. But it never seems to occur to him that the very oddity and completeness of the men's surrender make it look very much as if there were really something actual and solid in the thing for which they sold themselves. They gave up all human experiences for the sake on one superhuman experience. They may have been wicked, but it looks as if there were such an experience.

It is perfectly tenable that this experience is as dangerous and selfish a thing as drink. A man who goes ragged and homeless in order to see visions may be as repellent and immoral as a man who goes ragged and homeless in order to drink brandy. That is a quite reasonable position. But what is manifestly not a reasonable position what would be, in fact not far from being an insane position, would be to say that the raggedness of the man, and the homelessness of the man, and the stupefied degradation of the man proved that there was no such thing as brandy.

That is precisely what the Secularist tries to say. He tries to prove that there is no such think as supernatural experience by pointing at the people who have given up everything for it. He tries to prove that there is no such thing by proving that there are people who live on nothing else.

Again I may submissively ask: "Whose is the paradox?" The frantic severity of these men may, of course, show that they were eccentric people who loved unhappiness for its own sake. But is seems more in accordance with commonsense to suppose that they had really found the secret of some actual power or experience which was, like wine, a terrible consolation and a lonely joy.

Thus, then, in the second instance, when the learned sceptic says to me: "Christian saints gave up love and liberty for this one rapture of Christianity, I should have been surprised if they hadn't."

Take a third instance. The Secularist says that Christianity produced tumult and cruelty. He seems to suppose that this proves it to be bad. But it might prove it to be very good. For men commit crimes not only for bad things, far more often for good things. For no bad things can be desired quite so passionately and persistently as good things can be desired and only very exceptional men desire very bad and unnatural things.

Most crime is committed because, owing to some peculiar complication, very beautiful or necessary things are in some danger. For instance, if we wanted to abolish thieving and swindling at one blow, the best thing to do would be to abolish babies. Babies, the most beautiful things on earth, have been the excuse and origin of almost all the business of brutality and financial infamy on earth.

If we could abolish monogamic or romantic love, again the country would be dotted with Maiden Assizes. And if anywhere in history masses of common and kindly men become cruel it almost certainly does not mean that they are serving something in itself tyrannical (for why should they?). It almost certainly does mean that something that they rightly value is in peril such as the food of their children, the chasity of their women, or the independence of their country. And when something is set before them that is not only enormously valuable, but also quite new, the sudden vision, the chance of winning it, the chance of losing it, drive them mad. It has the same effect in the moral world that the finding of gold has in the economic world. It upsets values, and creates a kind of cruel rush.

We need not go far for instances quite apart from the instances of religion. When the modern doctrines of brotherhood and liberty were preached in France in the eighteenth century the time was ripe for them, the educated classes everywhere had been growing towards them, the world to a very considerable extend welcomed them. And yet all that preparation and openness were unable to prevent the burst of anger and agony which greets anything good. And if the slow and polite preaching of rational fraternity in a rational age ended in the massacres of September, what an a fortiori is here! What would be likely to be the effect of the sudden dropping into a dreadfully evil century of a dreadfully perfect truth? What would happen if a world baser than the world of Sade were confronted with a gospel purer than the gospel of Rousseau?

The mere flinging of the polished pebble of Republican Indealism into the artificial lake of eighteenth century Europe produced a splash that seemed to splash the heavens, and a storm that drowned ten thousand men. What would happen if a star from heaven really fell into the slimy and bloody pool of a hopeless and decaying humanity? Men swept a city with the guillotine, a continent with the sabre, because Liberty, Equality, and Fraternity were too precious to be lost. How if Christianity was yet more maddening because it was yet more precious?

But why should we labour the point when One who knew human nature as it can really be learnt, from fishermen and women and natural people, saw from his quiet village the track of this truth across history, and, in saying that He came to bring not peace but a sword, set up eternally His colossal realism against the eternal sentimentality of the Secularist?

Thus, then, in the third instance, when the learned sceptic says: "Christianiaity produced wars and persecutions," we shall reply: "Naturally."

And, lastly, let me take an example which leads me on directly to the general matter I wish to discuss for the remining space of the articles at my command. The Secularist constantly points out that the Hebrew and Christian religions began as local things; that their god was a tribal god; that they gave him material form, and attached him to particular places.

This is an excellent example of one of the things that if I were conducting a detailed campaign I should use as an argument for the validity of Biblical experience. For if there really are some other and higher beings than ourselves, and if they in some strange ways, at some emotional crisis, really revealed themselves to rude poets or dreamers in very simple times, that the rude people should regard the revelation as local, and connect it with the particular hill or river where it happened, seems to me exactly what any reasonable human being would expect. It has a far more credible look than if they had talked cosmic philosophy from the beginning. If they had, I should have suspected "priestcraft" and forgeries and third-century Gnosticism

If there be such a being as God, and He can speak to a child, and if God spoke to a child in the garden the child would, of course, say that God lived in the garden. I should not think it any less likely to be true for that. If the child said: "God is everywhere: an impalpable essence pervading and supporting all constituents of the Cosmos alike"--if, I say, the infant addressed me in the above terms, I should think he was mouch more likely to have been with the governess than with God.

So if Moses had said God was an Infinite Energy, I should be certain he had seen nothing extraordinary. As he said He was a Burning Bush, I think it very likely that he did see something extraordinary. For whatever be the Divine Secret, and whether or no it has (as all people have believed) sometimes broken bounds and surged into our work, at least it lies on the side furthest away from pedants and their definitions, and nearest to the silver souls of quiet people, to the beauty of bushes, and the love of one's native place.

Thus, then in our last instance (out of hundreds that might be taken), we conclude in the same way. When the learned sceptic says:

"The visions of the Old Testament were local, and rustic, and grotesque," we shall answer: "Of course. They were genuine."

Thus, as I said at the beginning, I find myself, to start with, face to face with the difficulty that to mention the reasons that I have for believing in Christianity is, in very many cases, to repeat those arguments which Mr. Blatchford, in some strange way, seems to regard as arguments against it. His book is really rich and powerful. He has undoubtedly set up these four great guns of which I have spoken. I have nothing to say against the size and ammunition of the guns. I only say that by some accident of arrangement he has set up those four pieces of artillery with the tails pointing at me and the mouths pointing at himself. If I were not so humane, I should say: "Gentlemen of the Secularist Guard, fire first."

But there is more to be said. Mr. Blatchford, for some reason or other (possibly want of space), has neglected to urge all the arguments for Christianity. And, oddly enough, the two or three arguments he has omitted to state are the really vital and essential ones. Without them, even the excellent four facts which he and I have respectively explained may apprear superficially unitelligible.

Why will many of you not accept my four explanations? Obviously, in mere logic, they are as logical as Mr. Blatchford's. It is as reasonable, in the abstract, that a truth should be distorted as that a lie should be distorted; it is as reasonable, in the abstract, that men should starve and sin for a real benefit as for an unreal one. You will not believe it because you are armed to the teeth, and buttoned up to the chin with the great Agnostic Orthodoxy, perhaps the most placid and perfect of all the orthodoxies of mean. You could sooner believe that Socrates was a Government spy than believe that he heard a voice from his God. You could more easily think that Christ murdered His mother, than that He had a psychic energy of which we know nothing. I approach you with the reverence and the courage due to a bench of bishops.

FRENCH AND ENGLISH

It is obvious that there is a great deal of difference between being international and being cosmopolitan. All good men are international. Nearly all bad men are cosmopolitan. If we are to be international we must be national. And it is largely because those who call themselves the friends of peace have not dwelt sufficiently on this distinction that they do not impress the bulk of any of the nations to which they belong. International peace means a peace between nations, not a peace after the destruction of nations, like the Buddhist peace after the destruction of personality. The golden age of the good European is like the heaven of the Christian: it is a place where people will love each other; not like the heaven of the Hindu, a place where they will be each other. And in the case of national character this can be seen in a curious way. It will generally be found, I think, that the more a man really appreciates and admires the soul of another people the less he will attempt to imitate it; he will be conscious that there is something in it too deep and too unmanageable to imitate. The Englishman who has a fancy for France will try to be French; the Englishman who admires France will remain obstinately English. This is to be particularly noticed in the case of our relations with the French, because it is one of the outstanding peculiarities of the French that their vices are all on the surface, and their extraordinary virtues concealed. One might almost say that their vices are the flower of their virtues.

Thus their obscenity is the expression of their passionate love of dragging all things into the light. The avarice of their peasants means the independence of their peasants. What the English call their rudeness in the streets is a phase of their social equality. The worried look of their women is connected with the responsibility of their women; and a certain unconscious brutality of hurry and gesture in the men is related to their inexhaustible and extraordinary military courage. Of all countries, therefore, France is the worst country for a superficial fool to admire. Let a fool hate France: if the fool loves it he will soon be a knave. He will certainly admire it, not only for the things that are not creditable, but actually for the things that are not there. He will admire the grace and indolence of the most industrious people in the world. He will admire the romance and fantasy of the most determinedly respectable and common-place people in the world. This mistake the Englishman will make if he admires France too hastily; but the mistake that he makes about France will be slight compared with the mistake that he makes about himself. An Englishman who professes really to like French realistic novels, really to be at home in a French modern theatre, really to experience no shock on first seeing the savage French caricatures, is making a mistake very dangerous for his own sincerity. He is admiring something he does not understand. He is reaping where he has not sown, and taking up where he has not laid down; he is trying to taste the fruit when he has never toiled over the tree. He is trying to pluck the exquisite fruit of French cynicism, when he has never tilled the rude but rich soil of French virtue.

The thing can only be made clear to Englishmen by turning it round. Suppose a Frenchman came out of democratic France to live in England, where the shadow of the great houses still falls everywhere, and where even freedom was, in its origin, aristocratic. If the Frenchman saw our aristocracy and liked it, if he saw our snobbishness and liked it, if he set himself to imitate it, we all know what we should feel. We all know that we should feel that that particular Frenchman was a repulsive little gnat. He would be imitating English aristocracy; he would be imitating the English vice. But he would not even understand the vice he plagiarised: especially he would not understand that the vice is partly a virtue. He would not understand those elements in the English which balance snobbishness and make it human: the great kindness of the English, their hospitality, their unconscious poetry, their sentimental conservatism, which really admires the gentry. The French Royalist sees that the English like their King. But he does not grasp that while it is base to worship a King, it is almost noble to worship a powerless King. The impotence of the Hanoverian Sovereigns has raised the English loyal subject almost to the chivalry and dignity of a Jacobite. The Frenchman sees that the English servant is respectful: he does not realise that he is also disrespectful; that there is an English legend of the humorous and faithful servant, who is as much a personality as his master; the Caleb Balderstone, the Sam Weller. He sees that the English do admire a nobleman; he does not allow for the fact that they admire a nobleman most when he does not behave like one. They like a noble to be unconscious and amiable: the slave may be humble, but the master must not be proud. The master is Life, as they would like to enjoy it; and among the joys they desire in him there is none which they desire more sincerely than that of generosity, of throwing money about among mankind, or, to use the noble mediaeval word, largesse - the joy of largeness. That is why a cabman tells you you are no gentleman if you give him his correct fare. Not only his pocket, but his soul is hurt. You have wounded his ideal. You have defaced his vision of the perfect aristocrat. All this is really very subtle and elusive; it is very difficult to separate what is mere slavishness from what is a sort of vicarious nobility in the English love of a lord. And no Frenchman could easily grasp it at all. He would think it was mere slavishness; and if he liked it, he would be a slave. So every Englishman must (at first) feel French candour to be mere brutality. And if he likes it, he is a brute. These national merits must not be understood so easily. It requires long years of plentitude and quiet, the slow growth of great parks, the seasoning of oaken beams, the dark enrichment of red wine in cellars and in inns, all the leisure and the life of England through many centuries, to produce at last the generous and genial fruit of English snobbishness. And it requires battery and barricade, songs in the streets, and ragged men dead for an idea, to produce and justify the terrible flower of French indecency.

When I was in Paris a short time ago, I went with an English friend of mine to an extremely brilliant and rapid succession of French plays, each occupying about twenty minutes. They were all astonishingly effective; but there was one of them which was so effective that my friend and I fought about it outside, and had almost to be separated by the police. It was intended to indicate how men really behaved in a wreck or naval disaster, how they break down, how they scream, how they fight each other without object and in a mere hatred of everything. And then there was added, with all that horrible irony which Voltaire began, a scene in which a great statesman made a speech over their bodies, saying that they were all heroes and had died in a fraternal embrace. My friend and I came out of this theatre, and as he had lived long in Paris, he said, like a Frenchman: "What admirable artistic arrangement! Is it not exquisite?" "No," I replied, assuming as far as possible the traditional attitude of John Bull in the pictures in Punch - "No, it is not exquisite. Perhaps it is unmeaning; if it is unmeaning I do not mind. But if it has a meaning I know what the meaning is; it is that under all their pageant of chivalry men are not only beasts, but even hunted beasts. I do not know much of humanity, especially when humanity talks in French. But I know when a thing is meant to uplift the human soul, and when it is meant to depress it. I know that Cyrano de Bergerac (where the actors talked even quicker) was meant to encourage man. And I know that this was meant to discourage him." "These sentimental and moral views of art," began my friend, but I broke into his words as a light broke into my mind. "Let me say to you," I said, "what Jaurès said to Liebknecht at the Socialist Conference: `You have not died on the barricades.' You are an Englishman, as I am, and you ought to be as amiable as I am. These people have some right to be terrible in art, for they have been terrible in politics. They may endure mock tortures on the stage; they have seen real tortures in the streets. They have been hurt for the idea of Democracy. They have been hurt for the idea of Catholicism. It is not so utterly unnatural to them that they should be hurt for the idea of literature. But, by blazes, it is altogether unnatural to me! And the worst thing of all is that I, who am an Englishman, loving comfort, should find comfort in such things as this. The French do not seek comfort here, but rather unrest. This restless people seeks to keep itself in a perpetual agony of the revolutionary mood. Frenchmen, seeking revolution, may find the humiliation of humanity inspiring. But God forbid that two plea-sure-seeking Englishmen should ever find it pleasant!"

DIVORCE VERSUS DEMOCRACY

PREFACE

I have been asked to put forward in pamphlet form this rather hasty essay as it appeared in "Nash's Magazine"; and I do so by the kind permission of the editor. The rather chaotic quality of its journalism it is now impossible to alter. The convictions upon which it is based are unaltered and unalterable. Indeed, in so far as circumstances have since affected them, they are greatly strengthened. In so far as there was something sporadic and seemingly irrelevant in the writing, it was partly because I was contending against an evil that was diffused and indefinable, at once tentative and ubiquitous. Since then that disease has come to a head and burst; primarily in the North of Europe. By that historic habit which generally makes one European people the standard bearer of a social tendency, which made the Empire a Roman Empire and the Revolution a French Revolution, the North Germans have become the peculiar champions of that modern change which would make the State infinitely superior to the Family. It is even asserted that Prussian political authority is now encouraging the abandonment of common morality for the support of population; and even if this horrible thing be untrue, it is highly significant that it can be plausibly said of Prussia and certainly of no other Christian State. And in the new light of action it is possible to trace more clearly the trend towards divorce, as also that trend towards the other pagan institution of slavery, which would certainly have accompanied it. But the enslaving force in Europe struck too early; and the whole movement has been brought to a standstill.

The same circumstances have given an importance to a formula of my own which I still think rather important. It may be summarised as the patriotism of the household. In the experience of nationality we do not admit that any excess of despair can come into the same logical world as desertion. No amount of tragedy need amount to treason. The Christian view of marriage conceives of the home as self-governing in a manner analogous to an independent state; that is, that it may include internal reform and even internal rebellion; but because of the bond, not against it. In this way it is itself a sort of standing reformer of the State; for the State is judged by whether its arrangements bear helpfully or bear hardly on the human fullness and fertility of the free family. Thus the Wicked Ten in Rome were condemned and cast down because their public powers permitted a wrong against the purity of a private family. Thus the mediaeval revolt against the Poll Tax began by the authority of an official insulting the authority of a father. Men do not now, any more than then, become sinless by receiving a post in a bureaucracy; and if the domestic affairs of the poor were once put into the hands of mere lawyers and inspectors, the poor would soon find themselves in positions from which there is no exit save by the sword of Virginius and the hammer of Wat Tyler. As for the section of the rich who are still seeking a servile solution, they, of course, are still seeking the extension of divorce. It is only "'divide et impera"; and they want the division of sex for the division of labour. The very same economic calculation which makes them encourage tyranny in the shop makes them encourage licence in the family. But now the free families of five great nations have risen against them; and their plot has failed.

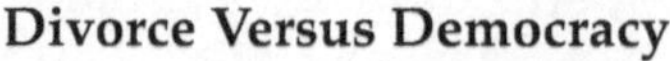

Divorce Versus Democracy

On this question of divorce I do not profess to be impartial, for I have never perceived any intelligent meaning in the word. I merely (and most modestly) profess to be right. I also profess to be representative: that is, democratic. Now, one may believe in democracy or disbelieve in it. It would be grossly unfair to conceal the fact that there are difficulties on both sides. The difficulty of believing in democracy is that it is so hard to believe-- like God and most other good things. The difficulty of disbelieving in democracy is that there is nothing else to believe in. I mean there is nothing else on earth or in earthly politics. Unless an aristocracy is selected by gods, it must be selected by men. It may be negatively and passively permitted, but either heaven or humanity must permit it; otherwise it has no more moral authority than a lucky pickpocket. It is babytalk to talk about "Supermen" or "Nature's Aristocracy" or "The Wise Few." "The Wise Few" must be either those whom others think wise--who are often fools; or those who think themselves wise--who are always fools.

Well, if one happens to believe in democracy as I do, as a large trust in the active and passive judgment of the human conscience, one can have no hesitation, no "impartiality," about one's view of divorce; and especially about one's view of the extension of divorce among the democracy. A democrat in any sense must regard that extension as the last and vilest of the insults offered by the modern rich to the modern poor. The rich do largely believe in divorce; the poor do mainly believe in fidelity. But the modern rich are powerful and the modern poor are powerless. Therefore for years and decades past the rich have been preaching their own virtues. Now that they have begun to preach their vices too, I think it is time to kick.

There is one enormous and elementary objection to the popularising of divorce, which comes before any consideration of the nature of marriage. It is like an alphabet in letters too large to be seen. It is this: That even if the democracy approved of divorce as strongly and deeply as the democracy does (in fact--disapprove of it--any man of common sense must know that nowadays the thing will be worked probably against the democracy, but quite certainly by the plutocracy. People seem to forget that in a society where power goes with wealth and where wealth is in an extreme state of inequality, extending the powers of the law means something entirely different from extending the powers of the public. They seem to forget that there is a great deal of difference between what laws define and what laws do. A poor woman in a poor public-house was broken with a ruinous fine for giving a child a sip of shandy-gaff. Nobody supposed that the law verbally stigmatised the action for being done by a poor person in a poor public-house. But most certainly nobody will dare to pretend that a rich man giving a boy a sip of champagne would have been punished so heavily--or punished at all. I have seen the thing done frequently in country houses; and my host and hostess would have been very much surprised if I had gone outside and telephoned for the police. The law theoretically condemns any one who tries to frustrate the police or even fails to assist them. Yet the rich motorists are allowed to keep up an organised service of anti-police detectives-- wearing a conspicuous uniform-- for the avowed purpose of showing motorists how to avoid capture. No one supposes again that the law says in so many words that the right to organise for the evasion of laws is a privilege of the rich but not of the poor. But take the same practical test. What would the police say, what would the world say, if men stood about the streets in green and yellow uniforms, notoriously for the purpose of warning pickpockets of the presence of a plain-clothes officer? What would the world say if recognised officials in peaked caps watched by night to warn a burglar that the police were waiting for him? Yet there is no distinction of principle between the evasion of that police-trap and the other police-trap--the police-trap which prevents a motorist from killing a child like a chicken; which prevents the most frivolous kind of murder, the most piteous kind of sudden death.

Well, the Poor Man's Divorce Law will be applied exactly as all these others are applied. Everybody must know that it would mean in practice that well-dressed men, doctors, magistrates, and inspectors, would have rnore power over the family lives of the ill-dressed men, navvies, plumbers, and potmen. Nobody can have the impudence to pretend that it would mean that navvies, plumbers, and pot men would (either individually or collectively) have more power over the family lives of doctors, magistrates, and inspectors. Nobody dare assert that because divorce is a State affair, therefore the poor citizen will have any power, direct or indirect, to divorce a duchess from a duke or a banker from a banker's wife. But no one will call it inconceivable that the power of rich families over poor families, which is already great, the power of the duke as landlord, the power of the banker as money-lender, might be considerably increased by arming magistrates with more powers of interference in private life. For the dukes and bankers often are magistrates, always the friends and relatives of magistrates. The navvies are not. The navvy will be the subject of the new experiments; certainly never the experimentalist. It is the poor man who will show to the imaginative eye of science all those horrors which, according to newspaper correspondents, cry aloud for divorce--drunkenness, madness, cruelty, incurable disease. If he is slow in working for his master, he will be "defective." If he is worn out by working for his master, he will be "degenerate." If he, at some particular opportunity, prefers to work for himself to working for his master, he will be obviously insane. If he never has any opportunity of working for any master he will be "unemployable." All the bitter embarrassments and entanglements incidental to extreme poverty will be used to break conjugal happiness, as they are already used to break parental authority. Marriage will be called a failure wherever it is a struggle, just as parents in modern England are sent to prison for neglecting the children whom they cannot afford to feed.

I will take but one instance of the enormity and silliness which is really implied in these proposals for the extension of divorce. Take the case quoted by many contributors to the discussion in the papers-

- the case of what is called "cruelty." Now what is the real meaning of this as regards the prosperous and as regards the struggling classes of the community? Let us take the prosperous classes first. Every one knows that those who are really to be described as gentlemen all profess a particular tradition, partly chivalrous, partly merely modern and refined--a tradition against "laying hands upon a woman, save in a way of kindness." I do not mean that a gentleman hates the cowing of a woman by brute force: any one must hate that. I mean he has a ritual, taboo kind of feeling about the laying on of a finger. If a gentle man (real or imitation) has struck his wife ever so lightly, he feels he has done one of those things that thrill the thoughts with the notion of a border-line, something like saying the Lord's Prayer backwards, touching a hot kettle, reversing the crucifix, or "breaking the pledge." The wife may forgive the husband more easily for this than for many things; but the husband will find it hard to forgive himself. It is a purely class sentiment, like the poor folks' dislike of hospitals. What is the effect of this class sentiment on divorce among the higher classes?

The first effect, of course, is greatly to assist those faked divorces so common among the fashionable. I mean that where there is a collusion, a small pat or push can be remembered, exaggerated, or invented; and yet seem to the solemn judges a very solemn thing in people of their own social class. But outside these cases, the test is not wholly inappropriate as applied to the richer classes. For all Gentlemen feeling or affecting this special horror, it does really look bad if a gentleman has broken through it, it does look like madness or a personal hatred and persecution. It may even look like worse things. If a man with luxurious habits, in artistic surroundings, is cruel to his wife, it may be connected with some perversion of sex cruelty, such as was alleged (I know not how truly) in the case of the millionaire Thaw. We need not deny that such cases are cases for separation, if not for divorce.

But this test of technical cruelty, which is rough and ready as applied to the rich, is absolutely mad and meaningless as applied to the poor. A poor woman does not judge her husband as a bully by whether he has ever hit out. One might as well say that a school-boy judges whether another schoolboy is a bully by whether he has ever hit out. The poor wife, like the schoolboy, judges him as a bully by whether he is a bully. She knows that while wife-beating may really be a crime, wife-hitting is sometimes very like just self-defence. No one knows better than she does that her husband often has a great deal to put up with; sometimes she means him to; sometimes she is justified. She comes and tells this to magistrates again and again; in police court after police court women with black eyes try to explain the thing to judges with no eyes. In street after street women turn in anger on the hapless knight-errant who has interrupted an instantaneous misunderstanding. In these people's lives the rooms are crowded, the tempers are torn to rags, the natural exits are forbidden. In such societies it is as abominable to punish or divorce people for a blow as it would be to punish or divorce a gentleman for slamming a door. Yet who can doubt, if ever divorce is applied to the populace, it would be applied in the spirit which takes the blow quite seriously? If any one doubts it, he does not know what world he is living in. It is common to meet nowadays men who talk of what they call Free Love as if it were something like Free Silver--a new and ingenious political scheme. They seem to forget that it is as easy to judge what it would be like as to judge of what legal marriage would be like. "Free Love" has been going on in every town and village since the beginning of the world; and the first fact that every man of the world knows about it is plain enough. It never does produce any of the wild purity and perfect freedom its friends attribute to it. If any paper had the pluck to head a column "Is Concubinage a Failure?" instead of "Is Marriage a Failure?" the answer "Yes" would be given by the personal memory of all. Modern people perpetually quote some wild expression of monks in the wilderness (when a whole civilisation was maddened by remorse) about the perilous quality of Woman, about how she was a spectre and a serpent and a destroying fire. Probably the establishment of nuns, situated a few miles off, described Man also as a serpent and a spectre; but their works have not come down to us.

Now all this old-world wit against Benedick the married man was sensible enough. But so was the bachelorhood of the old monks, who said it, sensible enough. It is perfectly true that to entangle yourself with another soul in the most tender and tragic degree is to make, in all rational possibility, a martyr or a fool of yourself. Most of the modern denunciations of marriage might have been copied direct from the maddest of the monkish diaries. The attack on marriage is an argument for celibacy. It is not an argument for divorce. For that entanglement which celibacy avowedly avoids, divorce merely reduplicates and repeats. It may have been a sort of solemn comfort to a gentleman of Africa to reflect that he had no wife. It cannot be anything but a discomfort to a gentleman of America to wonder which wife he really has. If progress means, as in the ludicrous definition of Herbert Spencer, "an advance from the simple to the complex," then certainly divorce is a part of progress. Nothing can be conceived more complex than the condition of a man who has settled down finally four or five times. Nothing can be conceived more complex than the position of a profligate who has not only had ten liaisons, but ten legal liaisons. There is a real sense in which free love might free men. But freer divorce would catch them in the most complicated net ever woven in this wicked world.

The tragedy of love is in love, not in marriage. There is not unhappy marriage that might not be an equally unhappy concubinage, or a far more unhappy seduction. Whether the tie be legal or no, matters something to the faithless party; it matters nothing to the faithful one. The pathos reposes upon the perfectly simple fact that if any one deliberately provokes either passions or affections, he is responsible for them as long as they go on, as the man is responsible for letting loose a flood or setting fire to a city. His remedy is not to provoke them, like the hermit. His punishment, when he deserves punishment, is to spend the rest of his life in trying to undo any ill he has done. His escape is despair--which is called, in this connection, divorce. For every healthy man feels one fundamental fact in his soul. He feels that he must have a life, and not a series of lives. He would rather the human drama were a tragedy than that it were a series of Music-hall Turns and Potted Plays. A man wishes to save the souls of all the men he has been: of the dirty little schoolboy; of the doubtful and morbid youth; of the lover; of the husband. Re-incarnation has always seemed to me a cold creed; because each incarnation must forget the other. It would be worse still if this short human life were broken up into yet shorter lives, each of which was in its turn forgotten.

If you are a democrat who likes also to be an honest man-- if (in other words) you want to know what the people want and not merely what you can somehow induce them to ask for-- then there is no doubt at all that this is what they want. You can only realise it by looking for human nature elsewhere than in election reports, but when you have once looked for it you see it and you never forget it. From the fact that every one thinks it natural that young men and women should carve names on trees, to the fact that every one thinks it unnatural that old men and women should be separated in work houses, millions and millions of daily details prove that people do regard the relation as normally permanent; not a vision, but as a vow.

Now for the exceptions, true or false. I would note a strange and even silly oversight in the discussion of such exceptions, which has haunted most arguments for further divorce. The ordinary emancipated prig or poet who urges this side of the question always talks to one tune. "Marriage may be the best for most men," he says, "but there are exceptional natures that demand a more undulating experience; constancy will do for the common herd, but there are complex natures and complex cases where no one could recommend constancy. I do not ask (at the present Stage of Progress) for the abolition of marriage; I hereby ask that it may be remitted in such individual and extreme examples."

Now it is perfectly astounding to me that any one who has walked about this world should make such a blunder about the breed we call mankind. Surely it is plain enough that if you ask for dreadful exceptions, you will get them--too many of them. Let me take once again a rough parable. Suppose I advertised in the papers that I had a place for any one who was too stupid to be a clerk. Probably I should receive no replies; possibly one. Possibly also (nay, probably) it would be from the one man who was not stupid at all. But suppose I had advertised that I had a place for any one who was too clever to be a clerk. My office would be instantly besieged by all the most hopeless fools in the four kingdoms. To advertise for exceptions is simply to advertise for egoists. To advertise for egoists is to advertise for idiots. It is exactly the bore who does think that his case is interesting. It is precisely the really common person who does think that his case is uncommon. It is always the dull man who does think himself rather wild. To ask solely for strange experiences of the soul is simply to let loose all the imbecile asylums about one's ears. Whatever other theory is right, this theory of the exceptions is obviously wrong--or (what matters more to our modern atheists) is obviously unbusinesslike. It is, moreover, to any one with popular political sympathies, a very deep and subtle sort of treason. By thus putting a premium on the exceptional we grossly deceive the unconsciousness of the normal. It seems strangely forgotten that the indifference of a nation is sacred as well as its differences. Even public apathy is a kind of public opinion--and in many cases a very sensible kind. If I ask every body to vote about Mineral Meals and do not get a single ballot-paper returned, I may say that the citizens have not voted. But they have.

The principle held by the populace, against which this plutocratic conspiracy is being engineered, is simply the principle expressed in the Prayer Book in the words "for better, for worse." It is the principle that all noble things have to be paid for, even if you only pay for them with a promise. One does not take one's interest out of England as one takes it out of Consols. A man is not an Englishman unless he can endure even the decay and death of England. And just as every citizen is a potential soldier, so every wife or husband is a potential hospital nurse-- or even asylum attendant. For though we should all approve of certain tragedies being mitigated by a celibate separation-- yet the more real love and honour there has been in the marriage, the less real mitigation there will be in the parting. But this sound public instinct both about patriotism and marriage also insists that the first vow or obligation shall be mitigated, not merely erased and forgotten.

Many a good woman has loved and refused a doubtful man, with the proviso that she would marry no one else; the old institution of marriage has the same feeling about the tragedy that is post-matrimonial. The thing remains real; it binds one to something. If I am exiled from England I will go and live on an island somewhere and be as jolly as I can. I will not become a patriot of any other land.

WHAT IS AMERICA?

I have never managed to lose my old conviction that travel narrows the mind. At least a man must make a double effort of moral humility and imaginative energy to prevent it from narrowing his mind. Indeed there is something touching and even tragic about the thought of the thoughtless tourist, who might have stayed at home loving Laplanders, embracing Chinamen, and clasping Patagonians to his heart in Hampstead or Surbiton, but for his blind and suicidal impulse to go and see what they looked like. This is not meant for nonsense; still less is it meant for the silliest sort of nonsense, which is cynicism. The human bond that he feels at home is not an illusion. On the contrary, it is rather an inner reality. Man is inside all men. In a real sense any man may be inside any men. But to travel is to leave the inside and draw dangerously near the outside. So long as he thought of men in the abstract, like naked toiling figures in some classic frieze, merely as those who labor and love their children and die, he was thinking the fundamental truth about them. By going to look at their unfamiliar manners and customs he is inviting them to disguise themselves in fantastic masks and costumes. Many modern internationalists talk as if men of different nationalities had only to meet and mix and understand each other. In reality that is the moment of supreme danger--the moment when they meet. We might shiver, as at the old euphemism by which a meeting meant a duel.

Travel ought to combine amusement with instruction; but most travelers are so much amused that they refuse to be instructed. I do not blame them for being amused; it is perfectly natural to be amused at a Dutchman for being Dutch or a Chinaman for being Chinese. Where they are wrong is that they take their own amusement seriously. They base on it their serious ideas of international instruction. It was said that the Englishman takes his pleasures sadly; and the pleasure of despising foreigners is one which he takes most sadly of all. He comes to scoff and does not remain to pray, but rather to excommunicate. Hence in international relations there is far too little laughing, and far too much sneering. But I believe that there is a better way which largely consists of laughter; a form of friendship between nations which is actually founded on differences.

Let me begin my American impressions with two impressions I had before I went to America. One was an incident and the other an idea; and when taken together they illustrate the attitude I mean. The first principle is that nobody should be ashamed of thinking a thing funny because it is foreign; the second is that he should be ashamed of thinking it wrong because it is funny. The reaction of his senses and superficial habits of mind against something new, and to him abnormal, is a perfectly healthy reaction. But the mind which imagines that mere unfamiliarity can possibly prove anything about inferiority is a very inadequate mind. It is inadequate even in criticizing things that may really be inferior to the things involved here. It is far better to laugh at a Negro for having a black face than to sneer at him for having a sloping skull. It is proportionally even more preferable to laugh rather than judge in dealing with highly civilized peoples. Therefore I put at the beginning two working examples of what I felt about America before I saw it; the sort of thing that a man has a right to enjoy as a joke, and the sort of thing he has a duty to understand and respect, because it is the explanation of the joke.

When I went to the American consulate to regularize my passports, I was capable of expecting the American consulate to be American. Embassies and consulates are by tradition like islands of the soil for which they stand; and I have often found the tradition corresponding to a truth. I have seen the unmistakable French official living on omelettes and a little wine and serving his sacred abstractions under the last palm-trees frying in a desert. In the heat and noise of quarreling Turks and Egyptians, I have come suddenly, as with the cool shock of his own shower-bath, on the listless amiability of the English gentleman. The officials I interviewed were very American, especially in being very polite; for whatever may have been the mood or meaning of Martin Chuzzlewit, I have always found Americans by far the politest people in the world. They put in my hands a form to be filled up, to all appearances like other forms I had filled up in other passport offices. But in reality it was very different from any form I had ever filled up in my life. At least it was a little like a freer form of the game called "Confessions" which my friends and I invented in our youth; an examination paper containing questions like, "If you saw a rhinoceros in the front garden, what would you do?" One of my friends, I remember, wrote, "Take the pledge." But that is another story, and might bring Mr. Pussyfoot Johnson on the scene before his time.

One of the questions on the paper was, "Are you an anarchist?" To which a detached philosopher would naturally feel inclined to answer, "What the devil has that to do with you? Are you an atheist" along with some playful efforts to cross-examine the official about what constitutes atheist. Then there was the question, "Are you in favor of subverting the government of the United States by force?" Against this I should write, "I prefer to answer that question at the end of my tour and not the beginning." The inquisitor, in his more than morbid curiosity, had then written down, "Are you a polygamist?" The answer to this is, "No such luck" or "Not such a fool," according to our experience of the other sex. But perhaps a better answer would be that given to W. T. Stead when he circulated the rhetorical question, "Shall I slay my brother Boer"--the answer that ran, "Never interfere in family matters." But among many things that amused me almost to the point of treating the form thus disrespectfully, the most amusing was the thought of the ruthless outlaw who should feel compelled to treat it respectfully. I like to think of the foreign desperado, seeking to slip into America with official papers under official protection, and sitting down to write with a beautiful gravity, "I am an anarchist. I hate you all and wish to destroy you." Or, "I intend to subvert by force the government of the United States as soon as possible, sticking the long sheath-knife in my left trouser-pocket into your President at the earliest opportunity." Or again, "Yes, I am a polygamist all right, and my forty-seven wives are accompanying me on the voyage disguised as secretaries." There seems to be a certain simplicity of mind about these answers; and it is reassuring to know that anarchists and polygamists are so pure and good that the police have only to ask them questions and they are certain to tell no lies.

Now that is the model of the sort of foreign practice, founded on foreign problems, at which a man's first impulse is naturally to laugh. Nor have I any intention of apologizing for my laughter. A man is perfectly entitled to laugh at a thing because he happens to find it incomprehensible. What he has no right to do is to laugh at it as incomprehensible, and then criticise it as if he comprehended it. The very fact of its unfamiliarity and mystery ought to set him thinking about the deeper causes that make people so different from himself, and that without merely assuming that they must be inferior to himself.

Superficially this is rather a queer business. It would be easy enough to suggest that in this America has introduced a quite abnormal spirit of inquisition; an interference with liberty unknown among all the ancient despotisms and aristocracies. About that there will be something to be said later; but superficially it is true that this degree of officialism is comparatively unique. In a journey which I took only the year before I had occasion to have my papers passed by governments which many worthy people in the West would vaguely identify with corsairs and assassins; I have stood on the other side of Jordan, in the land ruled by a rude Arab chief, where the police looked so like brigands that one wondered what the brigands looked like. But they did not ask me whether I had come to subvert the power of the Shereef; and they did not exhibit the faintest curiosity about my personal views on the ethical basis of civil authority. These ministers of ancient Moslem despotism did not care about whether I was an anarchist; and naturally would not have minded if I had been a polygamist. The Arab chief was probably a polygamist himself. These slaves of Asiatic autocracy were content, in the old liberal fashion, to judge me by my actions; they did not inquire into my thoughts. They held their power as limited to the limitation of practice; they did not forbid me to hold a theory. It would be easy to argue here that Western democracy persecutes where even Eastern despotism tolerates or emancipates. It would be easy to develop the fancy that, as compared with the sultans of Turkey or Egypt, the American Constitution is a thing like the Spanish Inquisition.

Only the traveler who stops at that point is totally wrong; and the traveler only too often does stop at that point. He has found something to make him laugh, and he will not suffer it to make him think. And the remedy is not to unsay what he has said, not even, so to speak, to unlaugh what he has laughed, not to deny that there is something unique and curious about this American inquisition into our abstract opinions, but rather to continue the train of thought, and follow the admirable advice of Mr. H. G. Wells, who said, "It is not much good thinking of a thing unless you think it out." It is not to deny that American officialism is rather peculiar on this point, but to inquire what it really is which makes America peculiar, or which is peculiar to America. In short, it is to get some ultimate idea of what America is; and the answer to that question will reveal something much deeper and grander and more worthy of our intelligent interest.

It may have seemed something less than a compliment to compare the American Constitution to the Spanish Inquisition. But oddly enough, it does involve a truth, and still more oddly perhaps, it does involve a compliment. The American Constitution does resemble the Spanish Inquisition in this: that it is founded on a creed. America is the only nation in the world that is founded on creed. That creed is set forth with dogmatic and even theological lucidity in the Declaration of Independence; perhaps the only piece of practical politics that is also theoretical politics and also great literature. It enunciates that all men are equal in their claim to justice, that governments exist to give them that justice, and that their authority is for that reason just. It certainly does condemn anarchism. and it does also by inference condemn atheism, since it clearly names the Creator as the ultimate authority from whom these equal rights are derived. Nobody expects a modern political system to proceed logically in the application of such dogmas, and in the matter of God and Government it is naturally God whose claim is taken more lightly. The point is that there is a creed, if not about divine, at least about human things.

Now a creed is at once the broadest and the narrowest thing in the world. In its nature it is as broad as its scheme for a brotherhood of all men. In its nature it is limited by its definition of the nature of all men. This was true of the Christian Church, which was truly said to exclude neither Jew nor Greek, but which did definitely substitute something else for Jewish religion or Greek philosophy. It was truly said to be a net drawing in of all kinds; but a net of a certain pattern, the pattern of Peter the Fisherman. And this is true even of the most disastrous distortions or degradations of that creed; and true among others of the Spanish Inquisition. It may have been narrow about theology, it could not confess to being narrow about nationality or ethnology. The Spanish Inquisition might be admittedly Inquisitorial; but the Spanish Inquisition could not be merely Spanish. Such a Spaniard, even when he was narrower than his own creed, had to be broader than his own empire. He might burn a philosopher because he was heterodox; but he must accept a barbarian because he was orthodox. And we see, even in modern times, that the same Church which is blamed for making sages heretics is also blamed for making savages priests. Now in a much vaguer and more evolutionary fashion, there is something of the same idea at the back of the great American experiment; the experiment of a democracy of diverse races which has been compared to a melting-pot. But even that metaphor implies that the pot itself is of a certain shape and a certain substance; a pretty solid substance. The melting-pot must not melt. The original shape was traced on the lines of Jeffersonian democracy; and it will remain in that shape until it becomes shapeless. America invites all men to become citizens; but it implies the dogma that there is such a thing as citizenship. Only, so far as its primary ideal is concerned, its exclusiveness is religious because it is not racial. The missionary can condemn a cannibal, precisely because he cannot condemn a Sandwich Islander. And in something of the same spirit the American may exclude a polygamist, precisely because he cannot exclude a Turk.

Now in America this is no idle theory. It may have been theoretical, though it was thoroughly sincere, when that great Virginian gentleman declared it in surroundings that still had something of the character of an English countryside. It is not merely theoretical now. There is nothing to prevent America being literally invaded by Turks, as she is invaded by Jews or Bulgars. In the most exquisitely inconsequent of the Bab Ballads, we are told concerning Pasha Bailey Ben:

One morning knocked at half-past eight A tall Red Indian at his gate. In Turkey, as you'r' p'raps aware, Red Indians are extremely rare.

But the converse need by no means be true. There is nothing in the nature of things to prevent an emigration of Turks increasing and multiplying on the plains where the Red Indians wandered; there is nothing to necessitate the Turks being extremely rare. The Red Indians, alas, are likely to be rarer. And as I much prefer Red Indians to Turks, I speak without prejudice; but the point here is that America, partly by original theory and partly by historical accident, does lie open to racial admixtures which most countries would think incongruous or comic. That is why it is only fair to read any American definitions or rules in a certain light, and relatively to a rather unique position. It is not fair to compare the position of those who may meet Turks in the back street with that of those who have never met Turks except in the Bab Ballads. It is not fair simply to compare America with England in its regulations about the Turk. In short, it is not fair to do what almost every Englishman probably does; to look at the American international examination paper, and laugh and be satisfied with saying, "We don't have any of that nonsense in England."

We do not have any of that nonsense in England because we have never attempted to have any of that philosophy in England. And, above all, because we have the enormous advantage of feeling it natural to be national, because there is nothing else to be. England in these days is not well governed; England is not well educated; England suffers from wealth and poverty that are not well distributed. But England is English--esto perpetua. England is English as France is French or Ireland is Irish; the great mass of men taking certain national traditions for granted. Now this gives us a totally different and a very much easier task. We have not got an inquisition, because we have not got a creed; but it is arguable that we do not need a creed, because we have got a character. In any of the old nations the national unity is preserved by the national type. Because we have a type we do not need to have a test.

Take that innocent question, "Are you an anarchist?" which is intrinsically quite as impudent as "Are you an optimist?" or "Are you a philanthropist" I am not discussing here whether these things are right, but whether most of us are in a position to know them rightly. Now it is quite true that most Englishmen do not find it necessary to go about all day asking each other whether they are anarchists. It is quite true that the phrase occurs on no British forms that I have seen. But this is not only because most of the Englishmen are not anarchists. It is even more because even the anarchists are Englishmen. For instance, it would be easy to make fun of the American formula by noting that the cap would fit all sorts of bald academic heads. It might well be maintained that Herbert Spencer was an anarchist. It is practically certain that Auberon Herbert was an anarchist. But Herbert Spencer was an extraordinary typical Englishman of the Nonconformist middle class. And Auberon Herbert was an extraordinarily typical English aristocrat of the old and genuine aristocracy.

Everyone knew in his head that the squire would not throw a bomb at the Queen, and the Nonconformist would not throw a bomb at anybody. Every one knew that there was something subconscious in a man like Auberon Herbert, which would have come out only in throwing bombs at the enemies of England; as it did come out in his son and namesake, the generous and unforgotten. who fell flinging bombs from the sky far beyond the German line. Every one knows that normally, in the last resort, the English gentleman is patriotic. Every one knows that the English Nonconformist is national even when he denies that he is patriotic. Nothing is more notable indeed than the fact that nobody is more stamped with the mark of his own nation than the man who says that there ought to be no nations. Somebody called Cobden the International Man; but no man could be more English than Cobden. Everybody recognises Tolstoy as the iconoclast of all patriotism; but nobody could be more Russian than Tolstoy. In the old countries where there are these national types, the types may be allowed to hold any theories. Even if they hold certain theories they are unlikely to do certain things. So the conscientious objector, in the English sense, may be and is one of the peculiar by-products of England. But the conscientious objector will probably have a conscientious objection to throwing bombs.

Now I am very far from intending to imply that these American tests are good tests or that there is no danger of tyranny becoming the temptation of America. I shall have something to say later on about that temptation or tendency. Nor do I say that they apply consistently this conception of a nation with the soul of a church, protected by religious and not racial selection. If they did apply that principle consistently, they would have to exclude pessimists and rich cynics who deny the democratic ideal; an excellent thing but a rather improbable one. What I say is that when we realise that this principle exists at all, we see the whole position in a totally different perspective. We say that the Americans are doing something heroic or doing something insane, or doing it in an unworkable or unworthy fashion, instead of simply wondering what the devil they are doing.

A SOMEWHAT IMPROBABLE STORY

I cannot remember whether this tale is true or not. If I read it through very carefully I have a suspicion that I should come to the conclusion that it is not. But, unfortunately, I cannot read it through very carefully, because, you see, it is not written yet. The image and the idea of it clung to me through a great part of my boyhood; I may have dreamt it before I could talk; or told it to myself before I could read; or read it before I could remember. On the whole, however, I am certain that I did not read it, for children have very clear memories about things like that; and of the books which I was really fond I can still remember, not only the shape and bulk and binding, but even the position of the printed words on many of the pages. On the whole, I incline to the opinion that it happened to me before I was born.

At any rate, let us tell the story now with all the advantages of the atmosphere that has clung to it. You may suppose me, for the sake of argument, sitting at lunch in one of those quick-lunch restaurants in the City where men take their food so fast that it has none of the quality of food, and take their half-hour's vacation so fast that it has none of the qualities of leisure; to hurry through one's leisure is the most unbusiness-like of actions. They all wore tall shiny hats as if they could not lose an instant even to hang them on a peg, and they all had one eye a little off, hypnotized by the huge eye of the clock. In short, they were the slaves of the modern bondage, you could hear their fetters clanking. Each was, in fact, bound by a chain; the heaviest chain ever tied to a man -- it is called a watch-chain.

Now, among these there entered and sat down opposite to me a man who almost immediately opened an uninterrupted monologue. He was like all the other men in dress, yet he was startlingly opposite to them in all manner. He wore a high shiny hat and a long frock coat, but he wore them as such solemn things were meant to be worn; he wore the silk hat as if it were a mitre, and the frock coat as if it were the ephod of a high priest. He not only hung his hat up on the peg, but he seemed (such was his stateliness) almost to ask permission of the hat for doing so, and to apologize to the peg for making use of it. When he had sat down on a wooden chair with the air of one considering its feelings and given a sort of slight stoop or bow to the wooden table itself, as if it were an altar, I could not help some comment springing to my lips. For the man was a big, sanguine-faced, prosperous-looking man, and yet he treated everything with a care that almost amounted to nervousness.

For the sake of saying something to express my interest I said, "This furniture is fairly solid; but, of course, people do treat it much too carelessly."

As I looked up doubtfully my eye caught his, and was fixed as his was fixed in an apocalyptic stare. I had thought him ordinary as he entered, save for his strange, cautious manner; but if the other people had seen him then they would have screamed and emptied the room. They did not see him, and they went on making a clatter with their forks, and a murmur with their conversation. But the man's face was the face of a maniac.

"Did you mean anything particular by that remark?" he asked at least, and the blood crawled back slowly into his face.

"Nothing whatever," I answered. "one does not mean anything here; it spoils people's digestions."

He limped back and wiped his broad forehead with a big handkerchief; and yet there seemed to be a sort of regret in his relief.

"I though perhaps," he said in a low voice, "that another of them had gone wrong."

"If you mean another digestion gone wrong," I said, "I never heard of one here that went right. This is the heart of the Empire, and the other organs are in an equally bad way."

"No, I mean another street gone wrong," and he said heavily and quietly, "but as I suppose that doesn't explain much to you, I think I shall have to tell you the story. I do so with all the less responsibility, because I know you won't believe it. For forty years of my life I invariably left my office, which is in Leadenhall Street, at half-past five in the afternoon, taking with me an umbrella in the right hand an a bag in the left hand. For forty years two months and four days I passed out of the side office door, walked down the street on the left-hand side, took the first turning to the left and the third to the right, from where I bought and evening paper, followed the road on the right-hand side round two obtuse angles, and came out just outside a Metropolitan station, where I took a train home. For forty years two months and four days I fulfilled this course by accumulated habit: it was not a long street that I traversed, and it took me about four and a half minutes to do it. After forty years two months and four days, on the fifth day I went out in the same manner, with my umbrella in the right hand and my bag in the left, and I began to notice that walking along the familiar street tired me somewhat more than usual; and when I turned it I was convinced that I had turned down the wrong one. For now the street shot up quite a steep slant, such as one only sees in the hilly parts of London, and in this part there were no hills at all. yet it was not the wrong street; the name written on it was the same; the shuttered shops were the same; the lamp-posts and the whole look of the perspective was the same; only it was tilted upwards like a lit. Forgetting any trouble about breathlessness or fatigue I ran furiously forward, and reached the second of my accustomed turnings, which ought to bring me almost within sight of the station. And as I turned that corner I nearly fell on the pavement. For now the street went up straight in front of my face like a steep staircase or the side of a pyramid. There was not for miles round that place so much as a slope like that of Ludgate Hill. And this was a slope like that of the Matterhorn. The whole street had lifted itself like a single wave, and yet every speck and detail of it was the same, and I saw in the high distance, as at the top of an Alpine pass, picked out in pink letters the name over my paper shop.

"I ran on and on blindly now, passing all the shops and coming to a part of the road where there was a long grey row of private houses. I had, I know not why, and irrational feeling that I was a long iron bridge in empty space. An impulse seized me, and I pulled up the iron trap of a coal-hole. Looking down through it I saw empty space and the stairs.

"When I looked up again a man was standing in his front garden, having apparently come out of his house; he was leaning over the railings and gazing at me. We were all alone on that nightmare road; his face was in shadow; his dress was dark and ordinary; but when I saw him standing so perfectly still I knew somehow that he was not of this world. And the stars behind his head were larger and fiercer than ought to be endured by the eyes of men.

"`If you are a kind angel,' I said, `or a wise devil, or have anything in common with mankind, tell me what is this street possessed of devils.'

"After a long silence he said, `What do you say that it is?'

"`It is Bumpton Street, of course,' I snapped. `It goes to Oldgate Station.'

"`Yes, he admitted gravely; `it goes there sometimes. Just now, however, it is going to heaven.'

"`To heaven?' I said. `Why?'

"`It is going to heaven for justice,' he replied. `You must have treated it badly. Remember always that there is one thing that cannot be endured by anybody or anything. That one unendurable thing is to be overworked and also neglected. For instance, you can overwork women -- everybody does. But you can't neglect women -- I defy you to. At the same time, you can neglect tramps and gypsies and all the apparent refuse of the State so long as you do not overwork it. But no beast of the field, no horse, no dog can endure long to be asked to do more than his work and yet have less than his honour. It is the same with streets. You have worked this street to death, and yet you have never remembered its existence. If you had a healthy democracy, even of pagans, they would have hung this street with garlands and given it the name of a god. Then it would have gone quietly. but at least the street has grown tired of your tireless insolence; and it is bucking and rearing its head to heaven. Have you never sat on a bucking horse?'

"I looked at the long grey street, and for a moment it seemed to me to be exactly like the long grey neck of a horse flung up to heaven. But in a moment my sanity returned, and I said, `But this is all nonsense. Streets go to the place they have to go. A street must always go to its end.'

"`Why do you think so of a street?' he asked, standing very still.

"`Because I have always seen it do the same thing,' I replied, in reasonable anger. `Day after day, year after year, it has always gone to Oldgate Station; day after ...'

"I stopped, for he had flung up his head with the fury of the road in revolt.

"`And you?' he cried terribly. `What do you think the road thinks of you? Does the road think you are alive? Are you alive? Day after day, year after year, *you* have gone to Oldgate Station ...' Since then I have respected the things called inanimate."

And bowing slightly to the mustard-pot, the man in the restaurant withdrew.

THE RUNAWAY ABBOT

Some miles from the monastery of Monte Cassino stood a great crag or cliff, standing up like a pillar of the Apennines. It was crowned with a castle that bore the name of The Dry Rock, and was the eyrie in which the eaglets of the Aquino branch of the Imperial family were nursed to fly. Here lived Count Landulf of Aquino, who was the father of Thomas Aquinas and some seven other sons. In military affairs he doubtless rode with his family, in the feudal manner; and apparently had something to do with the destruction of the monastery. But it was typical of the tangle of the time, that Count Landulf seems afterwards to have thought that it would be a tactful and delicate act to put in his son Thomas as Abbot of the monastery. This would be of the nature of a graceful apology to the Church, and also, it would appear, the solution of a family difficulty.

For it had been long apparent to Count Landulf that nothing could be done with his seventh son Thomas, except to make him an Abbot or something of that kind. Born in 1226, he had from childhood a mysterious objection to becoming a predatory eagle, or even to taking an ordinary interest in falconry or tilting or any other gentlemanly pursuits. He was a large and heavy and quiet boy, and phenomenally silent, scarcely opening his mouth except to say suddenly to his schoolmaster in an explosive manner, "What is God?" The answer is not recorded but it is probable that the asker went on worrying out answers for himself. The only place for a person of this kind was the Church and presumably the cloister; and so far as that went, there was no particular difficulty. It was easy enough for a man in Count Landulf's position to arrange with some monastery for his son to be received there; and in this particular case he thought it would be a good idea if he were received in some official capacity, that would be worthy of his worldly rank. So everything was smoothly arranged for Thomas Aquinas becoming a monk, which would seem to be what he himself wanted; and sooner or later becoming Abbot of Monte Cassino. And then the curious thing happened.

In so far as we may follow rather dim and disputed events, it would seem that the young Thomas Aquinas walked into his father's castle one day and calmly announced that he had become one of the Begging Friars, of the new order founded by Dominic the Spaniard; much as the eldest son of the squire might go home and airily inform the family that he had married a gypsy; or the heir of a Tory Duke state that he was walking tomorrow with the Hunger Marchers organised by alleged Communists. By this, as has been noted already, we may pretty well measure the abyss between the old monasticism and the new, and the earthquake of the Dominican and Franciscan revolution. Thomas had appeared to wish to be a Monk; and the gates were silently opened to him and the long avenues of the abbey, the very carpet, so to speak, laid for him up to the throne of the mitred abbot. He said he wished to be a Friar, and his family flew at him like wild beasts; his brothers pursued him along the public roads, half-rent his friar's frock from his back and finally locked him up in a tower like a lunatic.

It is not very easy to trace the course of this furious family quarrel, and how it eventually spent itself against the tenacity of the young Friar; according to some stories, his mother's disapproval was short-lived and she went over to his side; but it was not only his relatives that were embroiled. We might say that the central governing class of Europe, which partly consisted of his family, were in a turmoil over the deplorable youth; even the Pope was asked for tactful intervention, and it was at one time proposed that Thomas should be allowed to wear the Dominican habit while acting as Abbot in the Benedictine Abbey. To many this would seem a tactful compromise; but it did not commend itself to the narrow medieval mind of Thomas Aquinas. He indicated sharply that he wished to be a Dominican in the Dominican Order, and not at a fancy-dress ball; and the diplomatic proposal appears to have been dropped.

Thomas of Aquino wanted to be a Friar. It was a staggering fact to his contemporaries; and it is rather an intriguing fact even to us; for this desire, limited literally and strictly to this statement, was the one practical thing to which his will was clamped with adamantine obstinacy till his death. He would not be an Abbot; he would not be a Monk; he would not even be a Prior or ruler in his own fraternity; he would not be a prominent or important Friar; he would be a Friar. It is as if Napoleon had insisted on remaining a private soldier all his life. Something in this heavy, quiet, cultivated, rather academic gentleman would not be satisfied till he was, by fixed authoritative proclamation and official pronouncement, established and appointed to be a Beggar. It is all the more interesting because, while he did more than his duty a thousand times over, he was not at all like a Beggar; nor at all likely to be a good Beggar. He had nothing of the native vagabond about him, as had his great precursors; he was not born with something of the wondering minstrel, like St. Francis; or something of the tramping missionary, like St. Dominic. But he insisted upon putting himself under military orders, to do these things at the will of another, if required. He may be compared with some of the more magnanimous aristocrats who have enrolled themselves in revolutionary armies; or some of the best of the poets and scholars who volunteered as private soldiers in the Great War. Something in the courage and consistency of Dominic and Francis had challenged his deep sense of justice; and while remaining a very reasonable person, and even a diplomatic one, he never let anything shake the iron immobility of this one decision of his youth; nor was he to be turned from his tall and towering ambition to take the lowest place.

The first effect of his decision, as we have seen, was much more stimulating and even startling. The General of the Dominicans, under whom Thomas had enrolled himself, was probably well aware of the diplomatic attempts to dislodge him and the worldly difficulties of resisting them. His expedient was to take his young follower out of Italy altogether; bidding him proceed with a few other friars to Paris. There was something prophetic even about this first progress of the travelling teacher of the nations; for Paris was indeed destined to be in some sense the goal of his spiritual journey; since it was there that he was to deliver both his great defence of the Friars and his great defiance to the antagonists of Aristotle. But this his first journey to Paris was destined to be broken off very short indeed. The friars had reached a turn of the road by a wayside fountain, a little way north of Rome, when they were overtaken by a wild cavalcade of captors, who seized on Thomas like brigands, but who were in fact only rather needlessly agitated brothers. He had a large number of brothers: perhaps only two were here involved. Indeed he was the seventh; and friends of Birth Control may lament that this philosopher was needlessly added to the noble line of ruffians who kidnapped him. It was an odd affair altogether. There is something quaint and picturesque in the idea of kidnapping a begging friar, who might in a sense be called a runaway abbot. There is a comic and tragic tangle in the motives and purposes of such a trio of strange kinsmen. There is a sort of Christian cross-purposes in the contrast between the feverish illusion of the importance of things, always marking men who are called practical; and the much more practical pertinacity of the man who is called theoretical.

Thus at least did those three strange brethren stagger or trail along their tragic road, tied together, as it were, like criminal and constable; only that the criminals were making the arrest. So their figures are seen for an instant against the horizon of history; brothers as sinister as any since Cain and Abel. For this queer outrage in the great family of Aquino does really stand out symbolically, as representing something that will forever make the Middle Ages a mystery and a bewilderment; capable of sharply contrasted interpretations like darkness and light. For in two of those men there raged, we might say screamed, a savage pride of blood and blazonry of arms, though they were princes of the most refined world of their time, which would seem more suitable to a tribe dancing round a totem. For the moment they had forgotten everything except the name of a family, that is narrower than a tribe, and far narrower than a nation. And the third figure of that trio, born of the same mother and perhaps visibly one with the others in face or form, had a conception of brotherhood broader than most modern democracy, for it was not national but international; a faith in mercy and modesty far deeper than any mere mildness of manners in the modern world; and a drastic oath of poverty, which would now be counted quite a mad exaggeration of the revolt against plutocracy and pride. Out of the same Italian castle came two savages and one sage; or one saint more pacific than most modern sages. That is the double aspect confusing a hundred controversies. That is what makes the riddle of the medieval age; that it was not one age but two ages. We look into the moods of some men, and it might be the Stone Age; we look into the minds of other men, and they might be living in the Golden Age; in the most modern sort of Utopia. There were always good men and bad men; but in this time good men who were subtle lived with bad men who were simple. They lived in the same family; they were brought up in the same nursery; and they came out to struggle, as the brothers of Aquino struggled by the wayside, when they dragged the new friar along the road and shut him up in the castle on the hill.

When his relations tried to despoil him of his friar's frock he seems to have laid about them in the fighting manner of his fathers, and it would seem successfully, since this attempt was abandoned. He accepted the imprisonment itself with his customary composure, and probably did not mind very much whether he was left to philosophise in a dungeon or in a cell. Indeed there is something in the way the whole tale is told, which suggests that through a great part of that strange abduction, he had been carried about like a lumbering stone statue. Only one tale told of his captivity shows him merely in anger; and that shows him angrier than he ever was before or after. It struck the imagination of his own time for more important reasons; but it has an interest that is psychological as well as moral. For once in his life, for the first time and the last, Thomas of Aquino was really *hors de lui*; riding a storm outside that tower of intellect and contemplation in which he commonly lived. And that was when his brothers introduced into his room some specially gorgeous and painted courtesan, with the idea of surprising him by a sudden temptation, or at least involving him in a scandal. His anger was justified, even by less strict moral standards than his own; for the meanness was even worse than the foulness of the expedient. Even on the lowest grounds, he knew his brothers knew, and they knew that he knew, that it was an insult to him as a gentleman to suppose that he would break his pledge upon so base a provocation; and he had behind him a far more terrible sensibility; all that huge ambition of humility which was to him the voice of God out of heaven. In this one flash alone we see that huge unwieldy figure in an attitude of activity, or even animation; and he was very animated indeed. He sprang from his seat and snatched a brand out of the fire, and stood brandishing it like a flaming sword. The woman not unnaturally shrieked and fled, which was all that he wanted; but it is quaint to think of what she must have thought of that madman of monstrous stature juggling with flames and apparently threatening to burn down the house. All he did, however, was to stride after her to the door and bang and bar it behind her; and then, with a sort of impulse of violent ritual, he rammed the burning brand into the door, blackening and blistering it with one big black sign of the cross. Then he returned, and dropped it again into the fire; and sat down on that seat of sedentary scholarship, that chair of philosophy, that secret throne of contemplation, from which he never rose again....

A DEFENCE OF RASH VOWS

I f a prosperous modern man, with a high hat and a frock-coat, were to solemnly pledge himself before all his clerks and friends to count the leaves on every third tree in Holland Walk, to hop up to the City on one leg every Thursday, to repeat the whole of Mill's `Liberty' seventy-six times, to collect 300 dandelions in fields belonging to anyone of the name of Brown, to remain for thirty-one hours holding his left ear in his right hand, to sing the names of all his aunts in order of age on the top of an omnibus, or make any such unusual undertaking, we should immediately conclude that the man was mad, or, as it is sometimes expressed, was `an artist in life.' Yet these vows are not more extraordinary than the vows which in the Middle Ages and in similar periods were made, not by fanatics merely, but by the greatest figures in civic and national civilization -- by kings, judges, poets, and priests. One man swore to chain two mountains together, and the great chain hung there, it was said, for ages as a monument of that mystical folly. Another swore that he would find his way to Jerusalem with a patch over his eyes, and died looking for it. It is not easy to see that these two exploits, judged from a strictly rational standpoint, are any saner than the acts above suggested. A mountain is commonly a stationary and reliable object which it is not necessary to chain up at night like a dog. And it is not easy at first sight to see that a man pays a very high compliment to the Holy City by setting out for it under conditions which render it to the last degree improbable that he will ever get there.

But about this there is one striking thing to be noticed. If men behaved in that way in our time, we should, as we have said, regard them as symbols of the `decadence.' But the men who did these things were not decadent; they belonged generally to the most robust classes of what is generally regarded as a robust age. Again, it will be urged that if men essentially sane performed such insanities, it was under the capricious direction of a superstitious religious system. This, again, will not hold water; for in the purely terrestrial and even sensual departments of life, such as love and lust, the medieval princes show the same mad promises and performances, the same misshapen imagination and the same monstrous self-sacrifice. Here we have a contradiction, to explain which it is necessary to think of the whole nature of vows from the beginning. And if we consider seriously and correctly the nature of vows, we shall, unless I am much mistaken, come to the conclusion that it is perfectly sane, and even sensible, to swear to chain mountains together, and that, if insanity is involved at all, it is a little insane not to do so.

The man who makes a vow makes an appointment with himself at some distant time or place. The danger of it is that himself should not keep the appointment. And in modern times this terror of one's self, of the weakness and mutability of one's self, has perilously increased, and is the real basis of the objection to vows of any kind. A modern man refrains from swearing to count the leaves on every third tree in Holland Walk, not because it is silly to do so (he does many sillier things), but because he has a profound conviction that before he had got to the three hundred and seventy-ninth leaf on the first tree he would be excessively tired of the subject and want to go home to tea. In other words, we fear that by that time he will be, in the common but hideously significant phrase, another man. Now, it is this horrible fairy tale of a man constantly changing into other men that is the soul of the decadence. That John Paterson should, with apparent calm, look forward to being a certain General Barker on Monday, Dr. Macgregor on Tuesday, Sir Walter Carstairs on Wednesday, and Sam Slugg on Thursday, may seem a nightmare; but to that nightmare we give the name of modern culture. One great decadent, who is now dead, published a poem some time ago, in which he powerfully summed up the whole spirit of the movement by declaring that he could stand in the prison yard and entirely comprehend the feelings of a man about to be hanged.

> `For he that lives more lives than one*
> *More deaths than one must die.'*

And the end of all this is that maddening horror of unreality which descends upon the decadents, and compared with which physical pain itself would have the freshness of a youthful thing. The one hell which imagination must conceive as most hellish is to be eternally acting a play without even the narrowest and dirtiest greenroom in which to be human. And this is the condition of the decadent, of the aesthete, of the free-lover. To be everlastingly passing through dangers which we know cannot scare us, to be taking oaths which we know cannot bind us, to defying enemies who we know cannot conquer us -- this is the grinning tyranny of decadence which is called freedom.

Let us turn, on the other hand, to the maker of vows. The man who made a vow, however wild, gave a healthy and natural expression to the greatness of a great moment. He vowed, for example, to chain two mountains together, perhaps a symbol of some great relief of love, or aspiration. Short as the moment of his resolve might be, it was, like all great moments, a moment of immortality, and the desire to say of it *exegi monumentum aere perennius* was the only sentiment that would satisfy his mind. The modern aesthetic man would, of course, easily see the emotional opportunity; he would vow to chain two mountains together. But, then, he would quite as cheerfully vow to chain the earth to the moon. And the withering consciousness that he did not mean what he said, that he was, in truth, saying nothing of any great import, would take from him exactly that sense of daring actuality which is the excitement of a vow.

The revolt against vows has been carried in our day even to the extent of a revolt against the typical vow of marriage. It is most amusing to listen to the opponents of marriage on this subject. They appear to imagine that the ideal of constancy was a yoke mysteriously imposed on mankind by the devil, instead of being, as it is, a yoke consistently imposed by all lovers on themselves. They have invented a phrase, a phrase that is a black and white contradiction in two words -- `free-love' -- as if a lover ever had been, or ever could be, free. It is the nature of love to bind itself, and the institution of marriage merely paid the average man the compliment of taking him at his word. Modern sages offer to the lover, with an ill-favoured grin, the largest liberties and the fullest irresponsibility; but they do not respect him as the old Church respected him; they do not write his oath upon the heavens, as the record of his highest moment. They give him every liberty except the liberty to sell his liberty, which is the only one that he wants.

It is exactly this backdoor, this sense of having a retreat behind us, that is, to our minds, the sterlizing spirit in modern pleasure. Everywhere there is the persistent and insane attempt to obtain pleasure without paying for it. Thus, in politics the modern Jingoes practically say, `Let us have the pleasure of conquerors without the pains of soldiers: let us sit on sofas and be a hardy race.' Thus, in religion and morals, the decadent mystics say: `Let us have the fragrance of sacred purity without the sorrows of self-restraint; let us sing hymns alternately to the Virgin and Priapus.' Thus in love the free-lovers say: `Let us have the splendour of offering ourselves without the peril of committing ourselves; let us see whether one cannot commit suicide an unlimited number of times.'

Emphatically it will not work. There are thrilling moments, doubtless, for the spectator, the amateur, and the aesthete; but there is one thrill that is known only to the soldier who fights for his own flag, to the aesthetic who starves himself for his own illumination, to the lover who makes finally his own choice. And it is this transfiguring self-discipline that makes the vow a truly sane thing. It must have satisfied even the giant hunger of the soul of a lover or a poet to know that in consequence of some one instant of decision that strange chain would hang for centuries in the Alps among the silences of stars and snows. All around us is the city of small sins, abounding in backways and retreats, but surely, sooner or later, the towering flame will rise from the harbour announcing that the reign of the cowards is over and a man is burning his ships.

CHILD PSYCHOLOGY AND NONSENSE

In this age of child-psychology nobody pays any attention to the actual psychology of the child. All that seems to matter is the psychology of the psychologist and the particular theory or train of thought that he is maintaining against another psychologist. Most of the art and literature now magnificently manufactured for children is not even honestly meant to please children. The artist would hardly condescend to make a baby laugh if nobody else laughed, or even listened. These things are not meant to please the child. At best they are meant to please the child-lover. At the worst they are experiments in scientific educational method. Beautiful, wise, and witty lyrics like those of Stevenson's "Child's Garden of Verses" will always remain as a pure lively fountain of pleasure--for grown up people. But the point of many of them is not only such that a child could not see it, it is such that a child ought not to be allowed to see it--

> *The child that is not clean and neat,*
> *With lots of toys and things to eat,*
> *He is a naughty child, I'm sure,*
> *Or else his dear papa is poor.*

No child ought to understand the appalling abyss of that after-thought. No child could understand, without being a snob or a social reformer or something hideous, the irony of that illusion to the inequalities and iniquities with which this wicked world has insulted the sacred dignity of fatherhood. The child who could really smile at that line would be capable of sitting down immediately to write a Gissing novel, and then hanging himself on the nursery bed-post. But neither Stevenson or any Stevensonian (and I will claim to be a good Stevensonian) ever really dreamed of expecting a child to smile at the poem. It was the poet who smiled at the child, which is quite a different thing, though possibly quite as beautiful in its way. And that is the character of all this new nursery literature. It has the legitimate and even honourable object of educating the adult in the appreciation of babies. It is an excellent thing to teach men and women to take pleasure in children, but it is a totally different thing from giving children pleasure.

Now the old nursery rhymes were honestly directed to give children pleasure. Many of them have genuine elements of poetry, but they are not primarily meant to be poetry, because they are simply meant to be pleasure. In this sense "Hey Diddle Diddle" is something much more than an idyll. It is a masterpiece of psychology, a classic and perfect model of education. The lilt and jingle of it is exactly the sort that a baby can feel to be a tune and can turn into a dance. The imagery of it is exactly what is wanted for the first movements of imagination when it experiments in incongruity. For it is full of familiar objects in fantastic conjunction. The child has seen a cow and he has seen the moon. But the notion of the one jumping over the other is probably new to him and is, in the noblest word, nonsensical. Cats and dogs and dishes and spoons are all his daily companions and even his friends, but it gives him a sort of fresh surprise and happiness to think of their going on such a singular holiday. He would simply learn nothing at all from our attempts to find a fine shade of humour in the political economy of the poor papa, even if the poor papa were romantically occupied, not in jumping over the moon, but at least in shooting it.

Of course there is much more than this in "Hey Diddle Diddle." The cow jumping over the moon is not only a fancy very suitable to children, it is a theme very worthy of poets. The lunar adventure may appear to some a lunatic adventure, but it is one round which the imagination of man has always revolved, especially the imagination of romantic figures like Ariosto, and Cyrano de Bergerac. The notion that cattle might fly has received sublime imaginative treatment. The winged bull not only walks, as if shaking the earth, amid the ruins of Assyrian sculpture, but even wheeled and flamed in heaven as the Apocalyptic symbol of St. Luke. That which combines imaginations so instinctive and ancient, in a single fancy so simple and so clear, is certainly not without the raw material of poetry. And the general idea, which is that of a sort of cosmic Saturnalia or season when anything may happen, is itself an idea that has haunted humanity in a hundred forms, some of them exquisitely artistic forms.

It would be easy to justify a vast number of the other nursery rhymes, in the same vein of a more serious art criticism. If I were asked to quote four lines which sufficed to illustrate what has been called the imaginative reason, when it rises almost to touch an unimaginative unreason (for that point of contact is poetry), I should be content to quote four lines that were in a picture book in my own nursery--

> *The man in the wilderness asked of me,*
> *How many strawberries grow in the sea?*
> *I answered him, as I thought good:*
> *"As many red herrings as grow in the wood."*

Everything in that is poetical; from the dark unearthly figure of the man of the desert, with his mysterious riddles, to the perfect blend of logic and vision which makes beautiful pictures even in proving them impossible. But this artistic quality, though present, is not primary; the primary purpose is the amusement of children. And we are not amusing children; we are amusing ourselves with children.

Our fathers added a touch of beauty to all practical things, so they introduced fine fantastic figures and capering and dancing rhythms, which might be admired even by grown men, into what they primarily and practically designed to be enjoyed by children. But they did not always do this and they never thought mainly of doing it. What they always did was to make fun fitted for the young; and what they never did was turn it into irony only intelligible to the old. A nursery rhyme was like a nursery table or a nursery cupboard--a thing constructed for a particular human purpose. They saw their aim clearly and they achieved it. They wrote utter nonsense and took care to make it utterly nonsensical.

For there are two ways of dealing with nonsense in this world. One way is to put nonsense in the right place; as when people put nonsense into nursery rhymes. The other is to put nonsense in the wrong place; as when they put it into educational addresses, psychological criticisms, and complaints against nursery rhymes or other normal amusements of mankind.

THE ANTIQUITY OF CIVILISATION

The modern man looking at the most ancient origins has been like a man watching for daybreak in a strange land; and expecting to see that dawn breaking behind bare uplands or solitary peaks. But that dawn is breaking behind the black bulk of great cities long builded and lost for us in the original night; colossal cities like the houses of giants, in which even the carved ornamental animals are taller than the palm-trees; in which the painted portrait can be twelve times the size of the man; with tombs like mountains of man set four-square and pointing to the stars; with winged and bearded bulls standing and staring enormous at the gates of temples; standing still eternally as if a stamp would shake the world. The dawn of history reveals a humanity already civilized. Perhaps it reveals a civilisation already old. And among other more important things, it reveals the folly of most of the generalisations about the previous and unknown period when it was really young. The two first human societies of which we have any reliable and detailed record are Babylon and Egypt. It so happens that these two vast and splendid achievements of the genius of the ancients bear witness against two of the commonest and crudest assumptions of the culture of the moderns. If we want to get rid of half the nonsense about nomads and cave-men and the old man of the forest, we need only look steadily at the two solid and stupendous facts called Egypt and Babylon.

Of course most of these speculators who are talking about primitive men are thinking about modern savages. They prove their progressive evolution by assuming that a great part of the human race has not progressed or evolved; or even changed in any way at all. I do not agree with their theory of change; nor do I agree with their dogma of things unchangeable. I may not believe that civilised man has had so rapid and recent a progress; but I cannot quite understand why uncivilised man should be so mystically immortal and immutable. A somewhat simpler mode of thought and speech seems to me to be needed throughout this inquiry. Modern savages cannot be exactly like primitive man, because they are not primitive. Modern savages are not ancient because they are modern. Something has happened to their race as much as to ours, during the thousands of years of our existence and endurance on the earth. They have had some experiences, and have presumably acted on them if not profited by them. Like the rest of us. They have had some environment, and even some change of environment, and have presumably adapted themselves to it in a proper and decorous evolutionary manner. This would be true even if the experiences were mild or the environment dreary; for there is an effect in mere time when it takes the moral form of monotony. But it has appeared to a good many intelligent and well-informed people quite as probable that the experience of the savages has been that of a decline from civilisation. Most of those who criticise this view do not seem to have any very clear notion of what a decline from civilisation would be like. Heaven help them, it is likely enough that they will soon find out. They seem to be content if cave-men and cannibal islanders have some things in common, such as certain particular implements. But it is obvious on the face of it that any peoples reduced for any reason to a ruder life would have some things in common. If we lost all our firearms we should make bows and arrows; but we should not necessarily resemble in every way the first men who made bows and arrows. It is said that the

Russians in their great retreat were so short of armament that they fought with clubs cut in the wood. But a professor of the future would err in supposing that the Russian army of 1916 was a naked Scythian tribe that had never been out of the wood. It is like saying that a man in his second childhood must exactly copy his first. A baby is bald like an old man; but it would be an error for one ignorant of infancy to infer that the baby had a long white beard. Both a baby and an old man walk with difficulty; but he who shall expect the old gentleman to lie on his back, and kick joyfully instead, will be disappointed.

It is therefore absurd to argue that the first pioneers of humanity must have been identical with some of the last and most stagnant leavings of it. There were almost certainly some things, there were probably many things, in which the two were widely different or flatly contrary. An example of the way in which this distinction works, and an example essential to our argument here, is that of the nature and origin of government I have already alluded to Mr. H. G. Wells and the Old Man, with whom he appears to be on such intimate terms. If we considered the cold facts of prehistoric evidence for this portrait of the prehistoric chief of the tribe, we could only excuse it by saying that its brilliant and versatile author simply forgot for a moment that he was supposed to be writing a history, and dreamed he was writing one of his own very wonderful and imaginative romances. At least I cannot imagine how he can possibly know that the prehistoric ruler was called the Old Man or that court etiquette requires it to be spelt with capital letters. He says of the same potentate, 'No one was allowed to touch his spear or to sit in his seat.' I have difficulty in believing that anybody has dug up a prehistoric spear with a prehistoric label, 'Visitors are Requested not to Touch,' or a complete throne with the inscription, 'Reserved for the Old Man.' But it may be presumed that the writer, who can hardly be supposed to be merely making up things out of his own head, was merely taking for granted this very dubious parallel between the prehistoric and the decivilised man. It may be that in certain savage tribes the chief is called the Old Man and nobody is allowed to touch his spear or sit on his seat. It may be that in those cases he is surrounded with superstitious and traditional terrors; and it may be that in those cases, for all I know, he is despotic and tyrannical. But there is not a grain of evidence that primitive government was despotic and tyrannical. It may have been, of course, for it may have been anything or even nothing; it may not have existed at all. But the despotism in certain dingy and decayed tribes in the twentieth century does not prove that the first men were ruled despotically. It does not even suggest it; it does not even begin to hint at it. If there is one fact we really can prove, from the history that we really do know, it is that despotism can be a development, often a late development and very often indeed the end of societies that have been highly democratic. A despotism may almost be defined as a tired democracy. As fatigue falls on a community, the citizens are less inclined for that eternal vigilance which has truly been called the price of liberty; and they prefer to arm only one single sentinel to watch the city while they sleep. It is also true that they sometimes needed him for some sudden and militant act of reform; it is equally true that he often took advantage of being the strong man armed to be a tyrant like some of the Sultans of the East. But I cannot see why the Sultan should have appeared any earlier in history than many other human figures. On the contrary, the strong man armed obviously depends upon the superiority of his armour, and armament of that sort comes with more complex civilisation. One man may kill twenty with a machine-gum; it is obviously less likely that he could do it with a piece of flint. As for the current cant about the strongest man ruling by force and fear, it is simply a nursery fairy-tale about a giant with a hundred hands. Twenty men could hold down the strongest strong man in any society, ancient or modern. Undoubtedly they might admire, in a romantic and poetical sense, the man who was really the strongest; but that is quite a different thing, and is as purely moral and even mystical as the admiration for the purest or the wisest. But the spirit that endures the mere cruelties and caprices of an established despot is the spirit of an ancient and settled and probably stiffened society, not the spirit of a new one. As his name implies, the Old Man is the ruler of an old humanity.

It is far more probable that a primitive society was something like a pure democracy. To this day the comparatively simple agricultural communities are by far the purest democracies. Democracy is a thing which is always breaking down through the complexity of civilisation. Anyone who likes may state it by saying that democracy is the foe of civilisation. But he must remember that some of us really prefer democracy to civilisation, in the sense of preferring democracy to complexity. Anyhow, peasants tilling patches of their own land in a rough equality, and meeting to vote directly under a village tree, are the most truly self-governing of men. It is surely as likely as not that such a simple idea was found in the first condition of even simpler men. Indeed the despotic vision is exaggerated, even if we do not regard the men as men. Even on an evolutionary assumption of the most materialistic sort, there is really no reason why men should not have had at least as much camaraderie as rats or rooks. Leadership of some sort they doubtless had, as have the gregarious animals; but leadership implies no such irrational servility as that attributed to the superstitious subjects of the Old Man. There was doubtless some body corresponding, to use Tennyson's expression, to the many-wintered crow that leads the clanging rookery home. But I fancy that if that venerable fowl began to act after the fashion of some Sultans in ancient and decayed Asia, it would become a very clanging rookery and the many-wintered crow would not see many more winters. It may be remarked, in this connection, but even among animals it would seem that something else is respected more than bestial violence, if it be only the familiarity which in men is called tradition or the experience which in men is called wisdom. I do not know if crows really follow the oldest crow, but if they do they are certainly not following the strongest crow. And I do know, in the human case, that if some ritual of seniority keeps savages reverencing somebody called Old Man, then at least they have not our own servile sentimental weakness for worshipping the Strong Man.

It may be said then that primitive government, like primitive art and religion and everything else, is very imperfectly known or rather guessed at; but that it is at least as good a guess to suggest that it was as popular as a Balkan or Pyrenean village as that it was as capricious and secret as a Turkish divan. Both the mountain democracy and the oriental palace are modern in the sense that they are still there, or are some sort of growth of history; but of the two the palace has much more the look of being an accumulation and a corruption, the village much more the look of being a really unchanged and primitive thing. But my suggestions at this point do not go beyond expressing a wholesome doubt about the current assumption. I think it interesting, for instance, that liberal institutions have been traced even by moderns back to barbarians or undeveloped states, when it happened to be convenient for the support of some race or nation or philosophy. So the Socialists profess that their ideal of communal property existed in very early times. So the Jews are proud of the Jubilees or juster redistributions under their ancient law . So the Teutonists boasted of tracing parliaments and juries and various popular things among the Germanic tribes of the north. So the Celtophiles and those testifying to the wrongs of Ireland have pleaded the more equal justice of the clan system, to which the Irish chiefs bore witness before Strongbow. The strength of the case varies in the different cases; but as there is some case for all of them, I suspect there is some case for the general proposition that popular institutions of some sort were by no means uncommon in early and simple societies. Each of these separate schools were making the admission to prove a particular modern thesis; but taken together they suggest a more ancient and general truth, that there was something more in prehistoric councils than ferocity and fear. Each of these separate theorists had his own axe to grind, but he was willing to use a stone axe; and he manages to suggest that the stone axe might have been as republican as the guillotine.

But the truth is that the curtain rises upon the play already in progress In one sense it is a true paradox that there was history before history. But it is not the irrational paradox implied in prehistoric history; for it is a history we do not know. Very probably it was exceedingly like the history we do know, except in the one detail that we do not know it. It is thus the very opposite of the pretentious prehistoric history, which professes to trace everything in a consistent course from the amoeba to the anthropoid and from the anthropoid to the agnostic. So far from being a question of our knowing all about queer creatures very different from ourselves, they were very probably people very like ourselves, except that we know nothing about them. In other words, our most ancient records only reach back to a time when humanity had long been human, and even long been civilised. The most ancient records we have not only mention but take for granted things like kings and priests and princes and assemblies of the people; they describe communities that are roughly recognisable as communities in our own sense. Some of them are despotic; but we cannot tell that they have always been despotic. Some of them may be already decadent and nearly all are mentioned as if they were old. We do not know what really happened in the world before those records; but the little we do know would leave us anything but astonished if we learnt that it was very much like what happens in this world now. There would be nothing inconsistent or confounding about the discovery that those unknown ages were full of republics collapsing under monarchies and rising again as republics, empires expanding and finding colonies and then losing colonies. Kingdoms combining again into world states and breaking up again into small nationalities, classes selling themselves into slavery and marching out once more into liberty; all that procession of humanity which may or may not be a progress but most assuredly a romance. But the first chapters of the romance have been torn out of the book; and we shall never read them.

It is so also with the more special fancy about evolution and social stability. According to the real records available, barbarism and civilisation were not successive states in the progress of the world. They were conditions that existed side by side, as they still exist side by side. There were civilisations then as there are civilisations now; there are savages now as there were savages then. It is suggested that all men passed through a nomadic stage; but it is certain that there are some who have never passed out of it, and it seems not unlikely that there were some who never passed into it. It is probable that from very primitive times the static tiller of the soil and the wandering shepherd were two distinct types of men; and the chronological rearrangement of them is but a mark of that mania for progressive stages that has largely falsified history. It is suggested that there was a communist stage, in which private property was everywhere unknown, a whole humanity living on the negation of property; but the evidences of this negation are themselves rather negative. Redistributions of property, jubilees, and agrarian laws, occur at various intervals and in various forms; but that humanity inevitably passed through a communist stage seems as doubtful as the parallel proposition that humanity will inevitably return to it. It is chiefly interesting as evidence that the boldest plans for the future invoke the authority of the past; and that even a revolutionary seeks to satisfy himself that he is also a reactionary. There is an amusing parallel example in the case of what is called feminism. In spite of all the pseudo-scientific gossip about marriage by capture and the cave-man beating the cave-woman with a club, it may be noted that as soon as feminism became a fashionable cry, it was insisted that human civilisation in its first stage had been a matriarchy. Apparently it was the cave-woman who carried the club. Anyhow all these ideas are little better than guesses; they have a curious way of following the fortune of modern theories and fads. In any case they are not history in the sense of record; and we may repeat that when it comes to record, the broad truth is that barbarism and civilisation have always dwelt side by side in the world, the civilisation sometimes spreading to absorb the barbarians, sometimes decaying into relative barbarism, and in almost all cases possessing in a more finished form certain ideas and institutions which the barbarians possess in a ruder form; such as government or social authority, the arts and especially the decorative arts, mysteries and taboos of various kinds especially surrounding the matter of sex, and some form of that fundamental thing which is the chief concern of this enquiry; the thing that we call religion.

Now Egypt and Babylon, those two primeval monsters, might in this matter have been specially provided as models. They might almost be called working models to show how these modern theories do not work. The two great truths we know about these two great cultures happen to contradict flatly the two current fallacies which have just been considered. The story of Egypt might have been invented to point the moral that man does not necessarily begin with despotism because he is barbarous, but very often finds his way to despotism because he is civilised. He finds it because he is experienced; or, what is often much the same thing, because he is exhausted And the story of Babylon might have been invented to point the moral that man need not be a nomad or a communist before he becomes a peasant or a citizen, and that such cultures are not always in successive stages but often in contemporary states. Even touching these great civilisations with which our written history begins there is a temptation of course to be too ingenious or too cocksure. We can read the bricks of Babylon in a very different sense from that in which we guess about the Cup and Ring stones; and we do definitely know what is meant by the animals in the Egyptian hieroglyphic as we know nothing of the animal in the neolithic cave. But even here the admirable archeologists who have deciphered line after line of miles of hieroglyphics may be tempted to read too much between the lines; even the real authority on Babylon may forget how fragmentary is his hard-won knowledge; may forget that Babylon has only heaved half a brick at him, though half a brick is better than no cuneiform. But some truths, historic and not prehistoric, dogmatic and not evolutionary, facts and not fancies, do indeed emerge from Egypt and Babylon; and these two truths are among them.

Egypt is a green ribbon along the river edging the dark red desolation of the desert. It is a proverb, and one of vast antiquity, that it is created by the mysterious bounty and almost sinister benevolence of the Nile. When we first hear of Egyptians they are living as in a string of river-side villages, in small and separate but co-operative communities along the bank of the Nile. Where the river branched into the broad Delta there was traditionally the beginning of a somewhat different district or people; but this need not complicate the main truth. These more or less independent though interdependent peoples were considerably civilised already. They had a sort of heraldry; that is, decorative art used for symbolic and social purposes; each sailing the Nile under its own ensign representing some bird or animal. Heraldry involves two things of enormous importance to normal humanity; the combination of the two making that noble thing called co-operation; on which rest all peasantries and peoples that are free. The art of heraldry means independence; an image chosen by the imagination to express the individuality. The science of heraldry means interdependence; an agreement between different bodies to recognise different images; a science of imagery. We have here therefore exactly that compromise of co-operation between free families or groups which is the most normal mode of life for humanity and is particularly apparent wherever men own their own land and live on it. With the very mention of the image of bird and beast the student of mythology will murmur the word 'totem' almost in his sleep. But to my mind much of the trouble arises from his habit of saying such words as if in his sleep. Throughout this rough outline I have made a necessarily inadequate attempt to keep on the inside rather than the outside of such things; to consider them where possible in terms of thought and not merely in terms of terminology. There is very little value in talking about totems unless we have some feeling of what it really felt like to have a totem. Granted that they had totems and we have no totems; was it because they had more fear of animals or more familiarity with animals? Did a man whose totem was a wolf feel like a were-wolf or like a man running away from a were-wolf? Did he feel like Uncle Remus about Brer Wolf or like St. Francis about his brother the wolf, or like Mowgli about his brothers the wolves? Was a totem a thing like the British lion or a thing like the British bull-dog? Was the worship of a totem like the feeling of niggers about Mumbo Jumbo, or of children about Jumbo? I have never read any book of folk-lore, however learned, that gave me any light upon this question, which I think by far the most important one. I will confine myself to repeating that the earliest Egyptian communities had a common understanding about the images that stood for their individual states; and that this amount of communication is prehistoric in the sense that it is already there at the beginning of history. But as history unfolds itself, this question of communication is clearly the main question of these riverside communities. With the need of communication comes the need of a common government and the growing greatness and spreading shadow of the king. The other binding force besides the king, and perhaps older than the king, is the priesthood; and the priesthood has presumably even more to do with these ritual symbols and signals by which men can communicate. And here in Egypt arose probably the primary and certainly the typical invention to which we owe all history, and the whole difference between the historic and the prehistoric: the archetypal script, the art of writing.

The popular pictures of these primeval empires are not half so popular as they might be. There is shed over them the shadow of an exaggerated gloom, more than the normal and even healthy sadness of heathen men. It is part of the same sort of secret pessimism that loves to make primitive man a crawling creature, whose body is filth and whose soul is fear. It comes of course from the fact that men are moved most by their religion; especially when it is irreligion. For them anything primary and elemental must be evil. But it is the curious consequence that while we have been deluged with the wildest experiments in primitive romance, they have all missed the real romance of being primitive. They have described scenes that are wholly imaginary, in which the men of the Stone Age are men of stone like walking statues; in which the Assyrians or Egyptians are as stiff or as painted as their own most archaic art. But none of these makers of imaginary scenes have tried to imagine what it must really have been like to see those things as fresh which we see as familiar. They have not seen a man discovering fire like a child discovering fireworks. They have not seen a man playing with the wonderful invention called the wheel, like a boy playing at putting up a wireless station. They have never put the spirit of youth into their descriptions of the youth of the world. It follows that amid all their primitive or prehistoric fancies there are no jokes. There are not even practical jokes, in connection with the practical inventions. And this is very sharply defined in the particular case of hieroglyphics; for there seems to be serious indication that the whole high human art of scripture or writing began with a joke.

There are some who will learn with regret that it seems to have begun with a pun. The king or the priests or some responsible persons, wishing to send a message up the river in that inconveniently long and narrow territory, hit on the idea of sending it in picture writing, like that of the Red Indian. Like most people who have written picture-writing for fun, he found the words did not always fit. But when the word for taxes sounded rather like the word for pig, he boldly put down a pig as a bad pun and chanced it. So a modern hieroglyphist might represent 'at once' by unscrupulously drawing a hat followed by a series of upright numerals. It was good enough for the Pharaohs and ought to be good enough for him. But it must have been great fun to write or even to read these messages, when writing and reading were really a new thing. And if people must write romances about ancient Egypt (and it seems that neither prayers nor tears nor curses can withhold them from the habit), I suggest that scenes like this would really remind us that the ancient Egyptians were human beings. I suggest that somebody should describe the scene of the great monarch sitting among his priests, and all of them roaring with laughter and bubbling over with suggestions as the royal puns grew more and more wild and indefensible. There might be another scene of almost equal excitement about the decoding of this cipher; the guesses and clues and discoveries having all the popular thrill of a detective story. That is how primitive romance and primitive history really ought to be written. For whatever was the quality of the religious or moral life of remote times, and it was probably much more human than is conventionally supposed, the scientific interest of such a time must have been intense. Words must have been more wonderful than wireless telegraphy; and experiments with common things a series of electric shocks. We are still waiting for somebody to write a lively story of primitive life. The point is in some sense a parenthesis here; but it is connected with the general matter of political development, by the institution which was most active in these first and most fascinating of all the fairy-tales of science.

It is admitted that we owe most of this science to the priests. Modern writers like Mr. Wells cannot be accused of any weakness of sympathy with a pontifical hierarchy; but they agree at least in recognising what pagan priesthoods did for the arts and sciences. Among the more ignorant of the enlightened there was indeed a convention of saying that priests had obstructed progress in all ages; and a politician once told me in a debate that I was resisting modern reforms exactly as some ancient priest probably resisted the discovery of wheels. I pointed out, in reply, that it was far more likely that the ancient priest made the discovery of the wheels. It is overwhelmingly probable that the ancient priest had a great deal to do with the discovery of the art of writing. It is obvious enough in the fact that the very word hieroglyphic is akin to the word hierarchy. The religion of these priests was apparently a more or less tangled polytheism of a type that is more particularly described elsewhere. It passed through a period when it cooperated with the king, another period when it was temporarily destroyed by the king, who happened to be a prince with a private theism of his own, and a third period when it practically destroyed the king and ruled in his stead. But the world has to thank it for many things which it considers common and necessary: and the creators of those common things ought really to have a place among the heroes of humanity. If we were at rest in a real paganism, instead of being restless in a rather irrational reaction from Christianity, we might pay some sort of pagan honour to these nameless makers of mankind. We might have veiled statues of the man who first found fire or the man who first made a boat or the man who first tamed a horse. And if we brought them garlands or sacrifices, there would be more sense in it than in disfiguring our cities with cockney statues of stale politicians and philanthropists. But one of the strange marks of the strength of Christianity is that, since it came, no pagan in our civilisation has been able to be really human.

The point is here, however, that the Egyptian government, whether pontifical or royal, found it more and more necessary to establish communication; and there always went with communication a certain element of coercion. It is not necessarily an indefensible thing that the state grew more despotic as it grew more civilised; it is arguable that it had to grow more despotic in order to grow more civilised. That is the argument for autocracy in every age; and the interest lies in seeing it illustrated in the earliest age. But it is emphatically not true that it was most despotic in the earliest age and grew more liberal in a later age; the practical process of history is exactly the reverse. It is not true that the tribe began in the extreme of terror of the Old Man and his seat and spear; it is probable, at least in Egypt, that the Old Man was rather a New Man armed to attack new conditions. His spear grew longer and longer and his throne rose higher and higher, as Egypt rose into a complex and complete civilisation. That is what I mean by saying that the history of the Egyptian territory is in this the history of the earth; and directly denies the vulgar assumption that terrorism can only come at the beginning and cannot come at the end. We do not know what was the very first condition of the more or less feudal amalgam of land owners, peasants and slaves in the little commonwealths beside the Nile; but it may have been a peasantry of an even more popular sort. What we do know is that it was by experience and education that little commonwealths lose their liberty; that absolute sovereignty is something not merely ancient but rather relatively modern; and it is at the end of the path called progress that men return to the king.

Egypt exhibits, in that brief record of its remotest beginnings, the primary problem of liberty and civilisation. It is the fact that men actually lose variety by complexity. We have not solved the problem properly any more than they did; but it vulgarises the human dignity of the problem itself to suggest that even tyranny has no motive save in tribal terror. And just as the Egyptian example refutes the fallacy about despotism and civilisation, so does the Babylonian example refute the fallacy about civilisation and barbarism. Babylon also we first hear of when it is already civilised; for the simple reason that we cannot hear of anything until it is educated enough to talk. It talks to us in what is called cuneiform; that strange and stiff triangular symbolism that contrasts with the picturesque alphabet of Egypt. However relatively rigid Egyptian art may be, there is always something different from the Babylonian spirit which was too rigid to have any art. There is always a living grace in the lines of the lotus and something of rapidity as well as rigidity in the movement of the arrows and the birds. Perhaps there is something of the restrained but living curve of the river, which makes us in talking of the serpent of old Nile almost think of the Nile as a serpent. Babylon was a civilisation of diagrams rather than of drawings. Mr. W. B. Yeats who has a historical imagination to match his mythological imagination (and indeed the former is impossible without the latter) wrote truly of the men who watched the stars 'from their pedantic Babylon.' The cuneiform was cut upon bricks, of which all their architecture was built up; the bricks were of baked mud and perhaps the material had something in it forbidding the sense of form to develop in sculpture or relief. Theirs was a static but a scientific civilisation, far advanced in the machinery of life and in some ways highly modern. It is said that they had much of the modern cult of the higher spinsterhood and recognised an official class of independent working women. There is perhaps something in that mighty stronghold of hardened mud that suggests the utilitarian activity of a huge hive. But though it was huge it was human; we see many of the same social problems as in ancient Egypt or modern England; and whatever its evils this also was one of the earliest masterpieces of man. It stood, of course, in the triangle formed by the almost legendary rivers of Tigris and Euphrates, and the vast agriculture of its empire, on which its towns depended, was perfected by a highly scientific system of canals. It had by tradition a high intellectual life, though rather philosophic than artistic; and there preside over its primal foundation those figures who have come to stand for the star-gazing wisdom of antiquity; the teachers of Abraham; the Chaldees.

Against this solid society, as against some vast bare wall of brick, there surged age after age the nameless armies of the Nomads. They came out of the deserts where the nomadic life had been lived from the beginning and where it is still lived to-day. It is needless to dwell on the nature of that life; it was obvious enough and even easy enough to follow a herd or a flock which generally found its own grazing-ground and to live on the milk or meat it provided. Nor is there any reason to doubt that this habit of life could give almost every human thing except a home. Many such shepherds or herdsmen may have talked in the earliest time of all the truths and enigmas of the Book of Job; and of these were Abraham and his children, who have given to the modern world for an endless enigma the almost mono-maniac monotheism of the Jews. But they were a wild people without comprehension of complex social organisation; and a spirit like the wind within them made them wage war on it again and again. The history of Babylonia is largely the history of its defence against the desert hordes; who came on at intervals of a century or two and generally retreated as they came. Some say that an admixture of nomad invasion built at Nineveh the arrogant kingdom of the Assyrians, who carved great monsters upon their temples, bearded bulls with wings like cherubim, and who sent forth many military conquerors who stamped the world as if with such colossal hooves. Assyria was an imperial interlude; but it was an interlude. The main story of all that land is the war between the wandering peoples and the state that was truly static. Presumably in prehistoric times, and certainly in historic times, those wanderers went westward to waste whatever they could find. The last time they came they found Babylon vanished; but that was in historic times and the name of their leader was Mahomet.

Now it is worth while to pause upon that story because, as has been suggested, it directly contradicts the impression still current that nomadism is merely a prehistoric thing and social settlement a comparatively recent thing. There is nothing to show that the Babylonians had ever wandered; there is very little to show that the tribes of the desert ever settled down. Indeed it is probable that this notion of a nomadic stage followed by a static stage has already been abandoned by the sincere and genuine scholars to whose researches we all owe so much. But I am not at issue in this book with sincere and genuine scholars, but with a vast and vague public opinion which has been prematurely spread from certain imperfect investigations, and which has made fashionable a false notion of the whole history of humanity. It is the whole vague notion that a monkey evolved into a man and in the same way a barbarian evolved into a civilised man and therefore at every stage we have to look back to barbarism and forward to civilisation. Unfortunately this notion is in a double sense entirely in the air. It is an atmosphere in which men live rather than a thesis which they defend. Men in that mood are more easily answered by objects than by theories; and it will be well if anyone tempted to make that assumption, in some trivial turn of talk or writing, can be checked for a moment by shutting his eyes and seeing for an instant, vast and vaguely crowded, like a populous precipice, the wonder of the Babylonian wall.

One fact does certainly fall across us like its shadow. Our glimpses of both these early empires show that the first domestic relation had been complicated by something which was less human, but was often regarded as equally domestic. The dark giant called Slavery had been called up like a genii and was labouring on gigantic works of brick and stone. Here again we must not too easily assume that what was backward was barbaric; in the matter of manumission the earlier servitude seems in some ways more liberal than the later; perhaps more liberal than the servitude of the future. To insure food for humanity by forcing part of it to work was after all a very human expedient; which is why it will probably be tried again. But in one sense there is a significance in the old slavery. It stands for one fundamental fact about all antiquity before Christ; something to be assumed from first to last. It is the insignificance of the individual before the State. It was as true of the most democratic City State in Hellas as of any despotism in Babylon. It is one of the signs of this spirit that a whole class of individuals could be insignificant or even invisible. It must be normal because it was needed for what would now be called 'social service.' Somebody said, 'The Man is nothing and the Work is all,' meaning it for a breezy Carlylean commonplace. It was the sinister motto of the heathen Servile State. In that sense there is truth in the traditional vision of vast pillars and pyramids going up under those everlasting skies for ever by the labour of numberless and nameless men, toiling like ants and dying like flies, wiped out by the work of their own hands.

But there are two other reasons for beginning with the two fixed points of Egypt and Babylon. For one thing they are fixed in tradition as the types of antiquity; and history without tradition is dead. Babylon is still the burden of a nursery rhyme, and Egypt (with its enormous population of princesses awaiting reincarnation) is still the topic of an unnecessary number of novels. But a tradition is generally a truth; so long as the tradition is sufficiently popular; even if it is almost vulgar. And there is a significance in this Babylonian and Egyptian element in nursery rhymes and novels; even the news papers, normally so much behind the times, have already got as far as the reign of Tutankhamen. The first reason is full of the common sense of popular legend; it is the simple fact that we do know more of these traditional things than of other contemporary things; and that we always did. All travellers from Herodotus to Lord Carnarvon follow this route. Scientific speculations of to-day do indeed spread out a map of the whole primitive world, with streams of racial emigration or admixture marked in dotted lines everywhere; over spaces which the unscientific medieval map-maker would have been content to call 'Terra incognita,' if he did not fill the inviting blank with a picture of a dragon, to indicate the probable reception given to pilgrims. But these speculations are only speculations at the best; and at the worst the dotted lines can be far more fabulous than the dragon.

There is unfortunately one fallacy here into which it is very easy for men to fall, even those who are most intelligent and perhaps especially those who are most imaginative. It is the fallacy of suppositing that because an idea is greater in the sense of larger, therefore it is greater in the sense of more fundamental and fixed and certain. If a man lives alone in a straw hut in the middle of Thibet, he may be told that he is living in the Chinese Empire; and the Chinese Empire is certainly a splendid and spacious and impressive thing. Or alternatively he may be told that he is living in the British Empire, and be duly impressed. But the curious thing is that in certain mental states he can feel much more certain about the Chinese Empire that he can not see than about the straw hut that he can see. He has some strange magical juggle in his mind, by which his argument begins with the empire though his experience begins with the hut. Sometimes he goes mad and appears to be proving that a straw hut cannot exist in the domains of the Dragon Throne; that it is impossible for such a civilisation as he enjoys to contain such a hovel as he inhabits. But his insanity arises from the intellectual slip of supposing that because China is a large and all-embracing hypothesis, therefore it is something more than a hypothesis. Now modern people are perpetually arguing in this way; and they extend it to things much less real and certain than the Chinese Empire. They seem to forget, for instance, that a man is not even certain of the Solar System as he is certain of the South Downs. The Solar System is a deduction, and doubtless a true deduction; but the point is that it is a very vast and far-reaching deduction and therefore he forgets that it is a deduction at all and treats it as a first principle. He might discover that the whole calculation is a mis-calculation; and the sun and stars and street-lamps would look exactly the same. But he has forgotten that it is a calculation, and is almost ready to contradict the sun if it does not fit into the solar system. If this is a fallacy even in the case of facts pretty well ascertained, such as the Solar System and the Chinese Empire, it is an even more devastating fallacy in connection with theories and other things that are not really ascertained at all. Thus history, especially prehistoric history, has a horrible habit of beginning with certain generalisations about races. I will not describe the disorder and misery this inversion has produced in modern politics. Because the race is vaguely supposed to have produced the nation, men talk as if the nation were something vaguer than the race. Because they have themselves invented a reason to explain a result, they almost deny the result in order to justify the reason. They first treat a Celt as an axiom and then treat an Irishman as an inference. And then they are surprised that a great fighting, roaring Irishman is angry at being treated as an inference. They cannot see that the Irish are Irish whether or no they are Celtic, whether or no there ever were any Celts. And what misleads them once more is the size of the theory; the sense that the fancy is bigger than the fact. A great scattered Celtic race is supposed to contain the Irish, so of course the Irish must depend for their very existence upon it. The same confusion, of course, has eliminated the English and the Germans by swamping them in the Teutonic race; and some tried to prove from the races being at one that the nations could not be at war. But I only give these vulgar and hackneyed examples in passing, as more familiar examples of the fallacy; the matter at issue here is not its application to these modern things but rather to the most ancient things. But the more remote and unrecorded was the racial problem, the more fixed was this curious inverted certainty in the Victorian man of science. To this day it gives a man of those scientific traditions the same sort of shock to question these things, which were only the last inferences when he turned them into first principles. He is still more certain that he is an Aryan even than that he is an Anglo-Saxon, just as he is more certain that he is an Anglo-Saxon than that he is an Englishman. He has never really discovered that he is a European. But he has never doubted that he is an Indo-European. These Victorian theories have shifted a great deal in their shape and scope; but this habit of a rapid hardening of a hypothesis into a theory, and of a theory into an assumption, has hardly yet gone out of fashion. People cannot easily get rid of the mental confusion of feeling that the foundations of history must surely be secure; that the first steps must be safe; that the biggest generalisation must be obvious. But though the contradiction may seem to them a paradox, this is the very contrary of the truth. It is the large thing that is secret and invisible; it is the small thing that is evident and enormous.

Every race on the face of the earth has been the subject of these speculations, and it is impossible even to suggest an outline of the subject. But if we take the European race alone, its history, or rather its prehistory, has undergone many retrospective revolutions in the short period of my own lifetime. It used to be called the Caucasian race; and I read in childhood an account of its collision with the

Mongolian race; it was written by Bret Harte and opened with the query 'Or is the Caucasian played out?' Apparently the Caucasian was played out, for in a very short time he had been turned into the Indo-European man; sometimes, I regret to say, proudly presented as the Indo-Germanic man. It seems that the Hindu and the German have similar words for mother or father; there were other similarities between Sanskrit and various Western tongues; and with that all superficial differences between a Hindu and a German seemed suddenly to disappear. Generally this composite person was more conveniently described as the Aryan, and the really important point was that he had marched westward out of those high lands of India where fragments of his language could still be found. When I read this as a child, I had the fancy that after all the Aryan need not have marched westward and left his language behind him; he might also have marched eastward and taken his language with him. If I were to read it now, I should content myself with confessing my ignorance of the whole matter. But as a matter of fact I have great difficulty in reading it now, because it is not being written now. It looks as if the Aryan is also played out. Anyhow he has not merely changed his name but changed his address; his starting-place and his route of travel. One new theory maintains that our race did not come to its present home from the East but from the South. Some say the Europeans did not come from Asia but from Africa. Some have even had the wild idea that the Europeans came from Europe; or rather that they never left it.

Then there is a certain amount of evidence of a more or less prehistoric pressure from the North, such as that which seems to have brought the Greeks to inherit the Cretan culture and so often brought the Gauls over the hills into the fields in Italy. But I merely mention this example of European ethnology to point out that the learned have pretty well boxed the compass by this time; and that I, who am not one of the learned, cannot pretend for a moment to decide where such doctors disagree. But I can use my own common sense, and I sometimes fancy that theirs is a little rusty from want of use. The first act of common sense is to recognise the difference between a cloud and a mountain. And I will affirm that nobody knows any of these things, in the sense that we all know of the existence of the Pyramids of Egypt.

The truth, it may be repeated, is that what we really see, as distinct from what we may reasonably guess, in this earliest phase of history is darkness covering the earth and great darkness the peoples, with a light or two gleaming here and there on chance patches of humanity; and that two of these flames do burn upon two of these tall primeval towns; upon the high terraces of Babylon and the huge pyramids of the Nile. There are indeed other ancient lights, or lights that may be conjectured to be very ancient, in very remote parts of that vast wilderness of night. Far away to the east there is a high civilisation of vast antiquity in China; there are the remains of civilisations in Mexico and South America and other places, some of them apparently so high in civilisation as to have reached the most refined forms of devil-worship. But the difference lies in the element of tradition; the tradition of these lost cultures has been broken off, and though the tradition of China still lives, it is doubtful whether we know anything about it. Moreover, a man trying to measure the Chinese antiquity has to use Chinese traditions of measurement; and he has a strange sensation of having passed into another world under other laws of time and space. Time is telescoped outwards and centuries assume the slow and stiff movement of aeons; the white man trying to see it as the yellow man sees, feels as if his head were turning round and wonders wildly whether it is growing a pigtail. Any how he cannot take in a scientific sense that queer perspective that leads up to the primeval pagoda of the first of the Sons of Heaven. He is the real antipodes; the only true alternative world to Christendom; and he is after a fashion walking upside down. I have spoken of the medieval map-maker and his dragon; but what medieval traveller, however much interested in monsters, would expect to find a country where a dragon is a benevolent and amiable being? Of the more serious side of Chinese tradition something will be said in another connection; but I am only talking of tradition and the test of antiquity. And I only mention China as an antiquity that is not for us reached by a bridge of tradition; and Babylon and Egypt as antiquities that are. Herodotus is a human being, in a sense in which a Chinaman in a billy-cock hat, sitting opposite to us in a London tea shop, is hardly human. We feel as if we knew what David and Isaiah felt like, in a way in which we never were quite certain what Li Hung Chang felt like. The very sins that snatched away Helen or Bathsheba have passed into a proverb of private human weakness, of pathos and even of pardon. The very virtues of the Chinaman have about them something terrifying. This is the difference made by the destruction or preservation of a continuous historical inheritance; as from ancient Egypt to modern Europe. But when we ask what was that world that we inherit, and why those particular people and places seem to belong to it, we are led to the central fact of civilised history.

That centre was the Mediterranean; which was not so much a piece of water as a world. But it was a world with something of the character of such a water; for it became more and more a place of unification in which the streams of strange and very diverse cultures met. The Nile and the Tiber alike flow into the Mediterranean; so did the Egyptian and the Etrurian alike contribute to a Mediterranean civilisation. The glamour of the great sea spread indeed very far in land and the unity was felt among the Arabs alone in the deserts and the Gauls beyond the northern hills. But the gradual building up of a common culture running round all the coasts of this inner sea is the main business of antiquity. As will be seen, it was sometimes a bad business as well as a good business. In that *orbis terrarum* or circle of lands there were the extremes of evil and of piety, there were contrasted races and still more contrasted religions. It was the scene of an endless struggle between Asia and Europe from the night of the Persian ships at Salamis to the flight of the Turkish ships at Lepanto. It was the scene, as will be more especially suggested later, of a supreme spiritual struggle between the two types of paganism, confronting each other in the Latin and the Phoenician cities; in the Roman forum and the Punic mart. It was the world of war and peace, the world of good and evil, the world of all that matters most, with all respect to the Aztecs and the Mongols of the Far East, they did not matter as the Mediterranean tradition mattered and still matters. Between it and the Far East there were, of course, interesting cults and conquests of various kinds, more or less in touch with it, and in proportion as they were so intelligible also to us. The Persians came riding in to make an end of Babylon; and we are told in a Greek story how these barbarians learned to draw the bow and tell the truth. Alexander the great Greek marched with his Macedonians into the sunrise and brought back strange birds coloured like the sunrise clouds and strange flowers and jewels from the gardens and treasuries of nameless kings. Islam went eastward into that world and made it partly imaginable to us; precisely because Islam itself was born in that circle of lands that fringed our own ancient and ancestral sea. In the Middle Ages the empire of the Moguls increased its majesty without losing its mystery; the Tartars conquered China and the Chinese apparently took very little notice of them. All these things are interesting in themselves; but it is impossible to shift the centre of gravity to the inland spaces of Asia from the in]and sea of Europe. When all is said, if there were nothing in the world but what was said and done and written and built in the lands lying round the Mediterranean, it would still be in all the most vital and valuable things the world in which we live. When that southern culture spread to the north-west it produced many very wonderful things; of which doubtless we ourselves are the most wonderful. When it spread thence to colonies and new countries, it was still the same culture so long as it was culture at all. But round that little sea like a lake were the things themselves, apart from all extensions and echoes and commentaries on the things, the Republic and the Church; the Bible and the heroic epics; Islam and Israel and the memories of the lost empires, Aristotle and the measure of all things. It is because the first light upon this world is really light, the daylight in which we are still walking to-day, and not merely the doubtful visitation of strange stars, that I have begun here with noting where that light first falls on the towered cities of the eastern Mediterranean.

But though Babylon and Egypt have thus a sort of first claim, in the very fact of being familiar and traditional, fascinating riddles to us but also fascinating riddles to our fathers, we must not imagine that they were the only old civilisations on the southern sea; or that all the civilisation was merely Sumerian or Semitic or Coptic, still less merely Asiatic or African. Real research is more and more exalting the ancient civilisation of Europe and especially of what we may still vaguely call the Greeks. It must be understood in the sense that there were Greeks before the Greeks, as in so many of their mythologies there were gods before the gods. The island of Crete was the centre of the civilisation now called Minoan, after the Minos who lingered in ancient legend and whose labyrinth was actually discovered by modern archeology. This elaborate European society, with its harbours and its drainage and its domestic machinery, seems to have gone down before some invasion of its northern neighbours, who made or inherited the Hellas we know in history. But that earlier period did not pass till it had given to the world gifts so great that the world has ever since been striving in vain to repay them, if only by plagiarism.

Somewhere along the Ionian coast opposite Crete and the islands was a town of some sort, probably of the sort that we should call a village or hamlet with a wall. It was called Ilion but it came to be called Troy, and the name will never perish from the earth. A poet who may have been a beggar and a ballad-monger, who may have been unable to read and write, and was described by tradition as a blind, composed a poem about the Greeks going to war with this town to recover the most beautiful woman in the world. That the most beautiful woman in the world lived in that one little town sounds like a legend; that the most beautiful poem in the world was written by somebody who knew of nothing larger than such little towns is a historical fact. It is said that the poem came at the end of the period; that the primitive culture brought it forth in its decay; in which case one would like to have seen that culture in its prime. But anyhow it is true that this, which is our first poem, might very well be our last poem too. It might well be the last word as well as the first word spoken by man about his mortal lot, as seen by merely mortal vision. If the world becomes pagan and perishes, the last man left alive would do well to quote the *Iliad* and die.

But in this one great human revelation of antiquity there is another element of great historical importance; which has hardly I think been given its proper place in history. The poet has so conceived the poem that his sympathies apparently, and those of his reader certainly, are on the side of the vanquished rather than of the victor. And this is a sentiment which increases in the poetical tradition even as the poetical origin itself recedes. Achilles had some status as a sort of demigod in pagan times; but he disappears altogether in late times. But Hector grows greater as the ages pass, and it is his name that is the name of a Knight of the Round Table and his sword that legend puts into the hand of Roland, laying about him with the weapon of the defeated Hector in the last ruin and splendour of his own defeat. The name anticipates all the defeats through which our race and religion were to pass; that survival of a hundred defeats that is its triumph.

The tale of the end of Troy shall have no ending, for it is lifted up forever into living echoes, immortal as our hopelessness and our hope. Troy standing was a small thing that may have stood nameless for ages. But Troy falling has been caught up in a flame and suspended in an immortal instant of annihilation; and because it was destroyed with fire the fire shall never be destroyed. And as with the city so with the hero; traced in archaic lines in that primeval twilight is found the first figure of the Knight. There is a prophetic coincidence in his title; we have spoken of the word chivalry and how it seems to mingle the horseman with the horse. It is almost anticipated ages before in the thunder of the Homeric hexameter, and that long leaping word with which the *Iliad* ends. It is that very unity for which we can find no name but the holy centaur of chivalry. But there are other reasons for giving in this glimpse of antiquity the name upon the sacred town. The sanctity of such towns ran like a fire round the coasts and islands of the northern Mediterranean, the high-fenced hamlet for which heroes died. From the smallness of the city came the greatness of the citizen. Hellas with her hundred statues produced nothing statelier than that walking statue; the ideal of the self-commanding man. Hellas of the hundred statues was one legend and literature; and all that labyrinth of little walled nations resounding with the lament of Troy.

A later legend, an afterthought but not an accident, said that stragglers from Troy founded a republic on the Italian shore. It was true in spirit that republican virtue had such a root. A mystery of honour, that was not born of Babylon or the Egyptian pride, there shone like the shield of Hector, defying Asia and Africa; till the light of a new day was loosened, with the rushing of the eagles and the coming of the name; the name that came like a thunderclap when the world woke to Rome.

THE FALLACY OF THE YOUNG NATION

To say that a man is an idealist is merely to say that he is a man; but, nevertheless, it might be possible to effect some valid distinction between one kind of idealist and another. One possible distinction, for instance, could be effected by saying that humanity is divided into conscious idealists and unconscious idealists. In a similar way, humanity is divided into conscious ritualists and unconscious ritualists. The curious thing is, in that example as in others, that it is the conscious ritualism which is comparatively simple, the unconscious ritual which is really heavy and complicated. The ritual which is comparatively rude and straightforward is the ritual which people call "ritualistic." It consists of plain things like bread and wine and fire, and men falling on their faces. But the ritual which is really complex, and many coloured, and elaborate, and needlessly formal, is the ritual which people enact without knowing it. It consists not of plain things like wine and fire, but of really peculiar, and local, and exceptional, and ingenious things—things like doormats, and doorknockers, and electric bells, and silk hats, and white ties, and shiny cards, and confetti. The truth is that the modern man scarcely ever gets back to very old and simple things except when he is performing some religious mummery. The modern man can hardly get away from ritual except by entering a ritualistic church. In the case of these old and mystical formalities we can at least say that the ritual is not mere ritual; that the symbols employed are in most cases symbols which belong to a primary human poetry. The most ferocious opponent of the Christian ceremonials must admit that if Catholicism had not instituted the bread and wine, somebody else would most probably have done so. Anyone with a poetical instinct will admit that to the ordinary human instinct bread symbolizes something which cannot very easily be symbolized other-wise; that wine, to the ordinary human instinct, symbolizes some-thing which cannot very easily be symbolized otherwise. But white ties in the evening are ritual, and nothing else but ritual. No one would pretend that white ties in the evening are primary and poeti-cal. Nobody would maintain that the ordinary human instinct would in any age or country tend to symbolize the idea of evening by a white necktie. Rather, the ordinary human instinct would, I imagine, tend to symbolize evening by cravats with some of the colours of the sunset, not white neckties, but tawny or crimson neckties—neckties of purple or olive, or some darkened gold. Mr. J. A. Kensit, for exam-ple, is under the impression that he is not a ritualist. But the daily life of Mr. J. A. Kensit, like that of any ordinary modern man, is, as a matter of fact, one continual and compressed catalogue of mystical mummery and flummery. To take one instance out of an inevitable hundred: I imagine that Mr. Kensit takes off his hat to a lady; and what can be more solemn and absurd, considered in the abstract, than, symbolizing the existence of the other sex by taking off a portion of your clothing and waving it in the air? This, I repeat, is not a natural and primitive symbol, like fire or food. A man might just as well have to take off his waistcoat to a lady; and if a man, by the social ritual of his civilization, had to take off his waistcoat to a lady, every chivalrous and sensible man would take off his waistcoat to a lady. In short, Mr. Kensit, and those who agree with him, may think, and quite sincerely think, that men give too much incense and ceremonial to their adoration of the other world. But nobody thinks that he can give too much incense and ceremonial to the adoration of this world. All men, then, are ritualists, but are either conscious or unconscious ritualists. The conscious ritualists are generally satisfied with a few very simple and elementary signs; the unconscious ritualists are not satisfied with anything short of the whole of human life, being almost insanely ritualistic. The first is called a ritualist because he invents and remembers one rite; the other is called an anti-ritualist because he obeys and forgets a thousand. And a somewhat similar distinction to this which I have drawn with some unavoidable length, between the conscious ritualist and the unconscious ritualist, exists between the conscious idealist and the unconscious idealist. It is idle to inveigh against cynics and materialists—there are no cynics, there are no materialists. Every man is idealistic; only it so often happens that he has the wrong ideal. Every man is incurably sentimental; but, unfortunately, it is so often a false sentiment. When we talk, for instance, of some unscrupulous commercial figure, and say that he would do anything for money, we use quite an inaccurate expression, and we slander him very much. He would not do anything for money. He would do some things for money; he would sell his soul for money, for instance; and, as Mirabeau humorously said, he would be quite wise "to take money for muck." He would oppress humanity for money; but then it happens that humanity and the soul are not things that he believes in; they are not his ideals. But he has his own dim and delicate ideals; and he would not violate these for money. He would not drink out of the soup-tureen, for money. He would not wear his coattails in front, for money. He would not spread a report that he had softening of the brain, for money. In the actual practice of life we find, in the matter of ideals, exactly what we have already found in the matter of ritual. We find that while there is a perfectly genuine danger of fanaticism from the men who have unworldly ideals, the permanent and urgent danger of fanaticism is from the men who have worldly ideals.

People who say that an ideal is a dangerous thing, that it deludes and intoxicates, are perfectly right. But the ideal which intoxicates most is the least idealistic kind of ideal. The ideal which intoxicates least is the very ideal ideal; that sobers us suddenly, as all heights and precipices and great distances do. Granted that it is a great evil to mistake a cloud for a cape; still, the cloud, which can be most easily mistaken for a cape, is the cloud that is nearest the earth. Similarly, we may grant that it may be dangerous to mistake an ideal for something practical. But we shall still point out that, in this respect, the most dangerous ideal of all is the ideal which looks a little practical. It is difficult to attain a high ideal; consequently, it is almost impossible to persuade ourselves that we have attained it. But it is easy to attain a low ideal; consequently, it is easier still to persuade ourselves that we have attained it when we have done nothing of the kind. To take a random example. It might be called a high ambition to wish to be an archangel; the man who entertained such an ideal would very possibly exhibit asceticism, or even frenzy, but not, I think, delusion. He would not think he was an archangel, and go about flapping his hands under the impression that they were wings. But suppose that a sane man had a low ideal; suppose he wished to be a gentleman. Anyone who knows the world knows that in nine weeks he would have persuaded himself that he was a gentleman; and this being manifestly not the case, the result will be very real and practical dislocations and calamities in social life. It is not the wild ideals which wreck the practical world; it is the tame ideals.

The matter may, perhaps, be illustrated by a parallel from our modern politics. When men tell us that the old Liberal politicians of the type of Gladstone cared only for ideals, of course, they are talking nonsense—they cared for a great many other things, including votes. And when men tell us that modern politicians of the type of Mr. Chamberlain or, in another way, Lord Rosebery, care only for votes or for material interest, then again they are talking nonsense— these men care for ideals like all other men. But the real distinction which may be drawn is this, that to the older politician the ideal was an ideal, and nothing else. To the new politician his dream is not only a good dream, it is a reality. The old politician would have said, "It would be a good thing if there were a Republican Federation dominating the world." But the modern politician does not say, "It would be a good thing if there were a British Imperialism dominating the world." He says, "It is a good thing that there is a British Imperialism dominating the world;" whereas clearly there is nothing of the kind. The old Liberal would say "There ought to be a good Irish government in Ireland." But the ordinary modern Unionist does not say, "There ought to be a good English government in Ireland." He says, "There is a good English government in Ireland;" which is absurd. In short, the modern politicians seem to think that a man becomes practical merely by making assertions entirely about practical things. Apparently, a delusion does not matter as long as it is a materialistic delusion. Instinctively most of us feel that, as a practical matter, even the contrary is true. I certainly would much rather share my apartments with a gentleman who thought he was God than with a gentleman who thought he was a grasshopper. To be continually haunted by practical images and practical problems, to be constantly thinking of things as actual, as urgent, as in process of completion—these things do not prove a man to be practical; these things, indeed, are among the most ordinary signs of a lunatic. That our modern statesmen are materialistic is nothing against their being also morbid. Seeing angels in a vision may make a man a supernaturalist to excess. But merely seeing snakes in delirium tremens does not make him a naturalist.

And when we come actually to examine the main stock notions of our modern practical politicians, we find that those main stock notions are mainly delusions. A great many instances might be given of the fact. We might take, for example, the case of that strange class of notions which underlie the word "union," and all the eulogies heaped upon it. Of course, union is no more a good thing in itself than separation is a good thing in itself. To have a party in favour of union and a party in favour of separation is as absurd as to have a party in favour of going upstairs and a party in favour of going downstairs. The question is not whether we go up or down stairs, but where we are going to, and what we are going for? Union is strength; union is also weakness. It is a good thing to harness two horses to a cart; but it is not a good thing to try and turn two hansom cabs into one four-wheeler. Turning ten nations into one empire may happen to be as feasible as turning ten shillings into one half-sovereign. Also it may happen to be as preposterous as turning ten terriers into one mastiff. The question in all cases is not a question of union or absence of union, but of identity or absence of identity. Owing to certain historical and moral causes, two nations may be so united as upon the whole to help each other. Thus England and Scotland pass their time in paying each other compliments; but their energies and atmospheres run distinct and parallel, and consequently do not clash. Scotland continues to be educated and Calvinistic; England continues to be uneducated and happy. But owing to certain other Moral and certain other political causes, two nations may be so united as only to hamper each other; their lines do clash and do not run parallel. Thus, for instance, England and Ireland are so united that the Irish can sometimes rule England, but can never rule Ireland. The educational systems, including the last Education Act, are here, as in the case of Scotland, a very good test of the matter. The overwhelming majority of Irishmen believe in a strict Catholicism; the overwhelming majority of Englishmen believe in a vague Protestantism. The Irish party in the Parliament of Union is just large enough to prevent the English education being indefinitely Protestant, and just small enough to prevent the Irish education being definitely Catholic. Here we have a state of things which no man in his senses would ever dream of wishing to continue if he had not been bewitched by the sentimentalism of the mere word "union."

This example of union, however, is not the example which I propose to take of the ingrained futility and deception underlying all the assumptions of the modern practical politician. I wish to speak especially of another and much more general delusion. It pervades the minds and speeches of all the practical men of all parties; and it is a childish blunder built upon a single false metaphor. I refer to the universal modern talk about young nations and new nations; about America being young, about New Zealand being new. The whole thing is a trick of words. America is not young, New Zealand is not new. It is a very discussable question whether they are not both much older than England or Ireland.

Of course we may use the metaphor of youth about America or the colonies, if we use it strictly as implying only a recent origin. But if we use it (as we do use it) as implying vigour, or vivacity, or crudity, or inexperience, or hope, or a long life before them or any of the romantic attributes of youth, then it is surely as clear as daylight that we are duped by a stale figure of speech. We can easily see the matter clearly by applying it to any other institution parallel to the institution of an independent nationality. If a club called "The Milk and Soda League" (let us say) was set up yesterday, as I have no doubt it was, then, of course, "The Milk and Soda League" is a young club in the sense that it was set up yesterday, but in no other sense. It may consist entirely of moribund old gentlemen. It may be moribund itself. We may call it a young club, in the light of the fact that it was founded yesterday. We may also call it a very old club in the light of the fact that it will most probably go bankrupt tomorrow. All this appears very obvious when we put it in this form. Anyone who adopted the young-community delusion with regard to a bank or a butcher's shop would be sent to an asylum. But the whole modern political notion that America and the colonies must be very vigorous because they are very new, rests upon no better foundation. That America was founded long after England does not make it even in the faintest degree more probable that America will not perish a long time before England. That England existed before her colonies does not make it any the less likely that she will exist after her colonies. And when we look at the actual history of the world, we find that great European nations almost invariably have survived the vitality of their colonies. When we look at the actual history of the world, we find that if there is a thing that is born old and dies young, it is a colony. The Greek colonies went to pieces long before the Greek civilization. The Spanish colonies have gone to pieces long before the nation of Spain—nor does there seem to be any reason to doubt the possibility or even the probability of the conclusion that the colonial civilization, which owes its origin to England, will be much briefer and much less vigorous than the civilization of England itself. The English nation will still be going the way of all European nations when the Anglo-Saxon race has gone the way of all fads. Now, of course, the interesting question is, have we, in the case of America and the colonies, any real evidence of a moral and intellectual youth as opposed to the indisputable triviality of a merely chronological youth? Consciously or unconsciously, we know that we have no such evidence, and consciously or unconsciously, therefore, we proceed to make it up. Of this pure and placid invention, a good example, for instance, can be found in a recent poem of Mr. Rudyard Kipling's. Speaking of the English people and the South African War Mr. Kipling says that "we fawned on the younger nations for the men that could shoot and ride." Some people considered this sentence insulting. All that I am concerned with at present is the evident fact that it is not true. The colonies provided very useful volunteer troops, but they did not provide the best troops, nor achieve the most successful exploits. The best work in the war on the English side was done, as might have been expected, by the best English regiments. The men who could shoot and ride were not the enthusiastic corn merchants from Melbourne, any more than they were the enthusiastic clerks from Cheapside. The men who could shoot and ride were the men who had been taught to shoot and ride in the discipline of the standing army of a great European power. Of course, the colonials are as brave and athletic as any other average white men. Of course, they acquitted themselves with reasonable credit. All I have here to indicate is that, for the purposes of this theory of the new nation, it is necessary to maintain that the colonial forces were more useful or more heroic than the gunners at Colenso or the Fighting Fifth. And of this contention there is not, and never has been, one stick or straw of evidence.

A similar attempt is made, and with even less success, to represent the literature of the colonies as something fresh and vigorous and important. The imperialist magazines are constantly springing upon us some genius from Queensland or Canada, through whom we are expected to smell the odours of the bush or the prairie. As a matter of fact, anyone who is even slightly interested in literature as such (and I, for one, confess that I am only slightly interested in literature as such), will freely admit that the stories of these geniuses smell of nothing but printer's ink, and that not of first-rate quality. By a great effort of Imperial imagination the generous English people reads into these works a force and a novelty. But the force and the novelty are not in the new writers; the force and the novelty are in the ancient heart of the English. Anybody who studies them impartially will know that the first-rate writers of the colonies are not even particularly novel in their note and atmosphere, are not only not producing a new kind of good literature, but are not even in any particular sense producing a new kind of bad literature. The first-rate writers of the new countries are really almost exactly like the second-rate writers of the old countries. Of course they do feel the mystery of the wilderness, the mystery of the bush, for all simple and honest men feel this in Melbourne, or Margate, or South St. Pancras. But when they write most sincerely and most successfully, it is not with a background of the mystery of the bush, but with a background, expressed or assumed, of our own romantic cockney civilization. What really moves their souls with a kindly terror is not the mystery of the wilderness, but the Mystery of a Hansom Cab.

Of course there are some exceptions to this generalization. The one really arresting exception is Olive Schreiner, and she is quite as certainly an exception that proves the rule. Olive Schreiner is a fierce, brilliant, and realistic novelist; but she is all this precisely because she is not English at all. Her tribal kinship is with the country of Teniers and Maarten Maartens—that is, with a country of realists. Her literary kinship is with the pessimistic fiction of the continent; with the novelists whose very pity is cruel. Olive Schreiner is the one English colonial who is not conventional, for the simple reason that South Africa is the one English colony which is not English, and probably never will be. And, of course, there are individual exceptions in a minor way. I remember in particular some Australian tales by Mr. McIlwain which were really able and effective, and which, for that reason, I suppose, are not presented to the public with blasts of a trumpet. But my general contention if put before anyone with a love of letters, will not be disputed if it is understood. It is not the truth that the colonial civilization as a whole is giving us, or shows any signs of giving us, a literature which will startle and renovate our own. It may be a very good thing for us to have an affectionate illusion in the matter; that is quite another affair. The colonies may have given England a new emotion; I only say that they have not given the world a new book.

Touching these English colonies, I do not wish to be misunderstood. I do not say of them or of America that they have not a future, or that they will not be great nations. I merely deny the whole established modern expression about them. I deny that they are "destined" to a future. I deny that they are "destined" to be great nations. I deny (of course) that any human thing is destined to be anything. All the absurd physical metaphors, such as youth and age, living and dying, are, when applied to nations, but pseudo-scientific attempts to conceal from men the awful liberty of their lonely souls.

In the case of America, indeed, a warning to this effect is instant and essential. America, of course, like every other human thing, can in spiritual sense live or die as much as it chooses. But at the present moment the matter which America has very seriously to consider is not how near it is to its birth and beginning, but how near it may be to its end. It is only a verbal question whether the American civilization is young; it may become a very practical and urgent question whether it is dying. When once we have cast aside, as we inevitably have after a moment's thought, the fanciful physical metaphor involved in the word "youth," what serious evidence have we that America is a fresh force and not a stale one? It has a great many people, like China; it has a great deal of money, like defeated Carthage or dying Venice. It is full of bustle and excitability, like Athens after its ruin, and all the Greek cities in their decline. It is fond of new things; but the old are always fond of new things. Young men read chronicles, but old men read newspapers. It admires strength and good looks; it admires a big and barbaric beauty in its women, for instance; but so did Rome when the Goth was at the gates. All these are things quite compatible with fundamental tedium and decay. There are three main shapes or symbols in which a nation can show itself essentially glad and great—by the heroic in government, by the heroic in arms, and by the heroic in art. Beyond government, which is, as it were, the very shape and body of a nation, the most significant thing about any citizen is his artistic attitude towards a holiday and his moral attitude towards a fight—that is, his way of accepting life and his way of accepting death.

Subjected to these eternal tests, America does not appear by any means as particularly fresh or untouched. She appears with all the weakness and weariness of modern England or of any other Western power. In her politics she has broken up exactly as England has broken up, into a bewildering opportunism and insincerity. In the matter of war and the national attitude towards war, her resemblance to England is even more manifest and melancholy. It may be said with rough accuracy that there are three stages in the life of a strong people. First, it is a small power, and fights small powers. Then it is a great power, and fights great powers. Then it is a great power, and fights small powers, but pretends that they are great powers, in order to rekindle the ashes of its ancient emotion and vanity. After that, the next step is to become a small power itself. England exhibited this symptom of decadence very badly in the war with the Transvaal; but America exhibited it worse in the war with Spain. There was exhibited more sharply and absurdly than anywhere else the ironic contrast between the very careless choice of a strong line and the very careful choice of a weak enemy. America added to all her other late Roman or Byzantine elements the element of the Caracallan triumph, the triumph over nobody.

But when we come to the last test of nationality, the test of art and letters, the case is almost terrible. The English colonies have produced no great artists; and that fact may prove that they are still full of silent possibilities and reserve force. But America has produced great artists. And that fact most certainly proves that she is full of a fine futility and the end of all things. Whatever the American men of genius are, they are not young gods making a young world. Is the art of Whistler a brave, barbaric art, happy and headlong? Does Mr. Henry James infect us with the spirit of a schoolboy? No; the colonies have not spoken, and they are safe. Their silence may be the silence of the unborn. But out of America has come a sweet and startling cry, as unmistakable as the cry of a dying man.

THE ETHICS OF ELFLAND

When the business man rebukes the idealism of his office-boy, it is commonly in some such speech as this: "Ah, yes, when one is young, one has these ideals in the abstract and these castles in the air; but in middle age they all break up like clouds, and one comes down to a belief in practical politics, to using the machinery one has and getting on with the world as it is." Thus, at least, venerable and philanthropic old men now in their honoured graves used to talk to me when I was a boy. But since then I have grown up and have discovered that these philanthropic old men were telling lies. What has really happened is exactly the opposite of what they said would happen. They said that I should lose my ideals and begin to believe in the methods of practical politicians. Now, I have not lost my ideals in the least; my faith in fundamentals is exactly what it always was. What I have lost is my old childlike faith in practical politics. I am still as much concerned as ever about the Battle of Armageddon; but I am not so much concerned about the General Election. As a babe I leapt up on my mother's knee at the mere mention of it. No; the vision is always solid and reliable. The vision is always a fact. It is the reality that is often a fraud. As much as

I ever did, more than I ever did, I believe in Liberalism. But there was a rosy time of innocence when I believed in Liberals.

I take this instance of one of the enduring faiths because, having now to trace the roots of my personal speculation, this may be counted, I think, as the only positive bias. I was brought up a Liberal, and have always believed in democracy, in the elementary liberal doctrine of a self-governing humanity. If anyone finds the phrase vague or threadbare, I can only pause for a moment to explain that the principle of democracy, as I mean it, can be stated in two propositions. The first is this: that the things common to all men are more important than the things peculiar to any men. Ordinary things are more valuable than extraordinary things; nay, they are more extraordinary. Man is something more awful than men; something more strange. The sense of the miracle of humanity itself should be always more vivid to us than any marvels of power, intellect, art, or civilization. The mere man on two legs, as such, should be felt as something more heartbreaking than any music and more startling than any caricature. Death is more tragic even than death by starvation. Having a nose is more comic even than having a Norman nose.

This is the first principle of democracy: that the essential things in men are the things they hold in common, not the things they hold separately. And the second principle is merely this: that the political instinct or desire is one of these things which they hold in common. Falling in love is more poetical than dropping into poetry. The democratic contention is that government (helping to rule the tribe) is a thing like falling in love, and not a thing like dropping into poetry. It is not something analogous to playing the church organ, painting on vellum, discovering the North Pole (that insidious habit), looping the loop, being Astronomer Royal, and so on. For these things we do not wish a man to do at all unless he does them well. It is, on the contrary, a thing analogous to writing one's own love-letters or blowing one's own nose. These things we want a man to do for himself, even if he does them badly. I am not here arguing the truth of any of these conceptions; I know that some moderns are asking to have their wives chosen by scientists, and they may soon be asking, for all I know, to have their noses blown by nurses. I merely say that mankind does recognize these universal human functions, and that democracy classes government among them. In short, the democratic faith is this: that the most terribly important things must be left to ordinary men themselves—the mating of the sexes, the rearing of the young, the laws of the state. This is democracy; and in this I have always believed.

But there is one thing that I have never from my youth up been able to understand. I have never been able to understand where people got the idea that democracy was in some way opposed to tradition. It is obvious that tradition is only democracy extended through time. It is trusting to a consensus of common human voices rather than to some isolated or arbitrary record. The man who quotes some German historian against the tradition of the Catholic Church, for instance, is strictly appealing to aristocracy. He is appealing to the superiority of one expert against the awful authority of a mob. It is quite easy to see why a legend is treated, and ought to be treated, more respectfully than a book of history. The legend is generally made by the majority of people in the village, who are sane. The book is generally written by the one man in the village who is mad. Those who urge against tradition that men in the past were ignorant may go and urge it at the Carlton Club, along with the statement that voters in the slums are ignorant. It will not do for us. If we attach great importance to the opinion of ordinary men in great unanimity when we are dealing with daily matters, there is no reason why we should disregard it when we are dealing with history or fable. Tradition may be defined as an extension of the franchise. Tradition means giving votes to the most obscure of all classes, our ancestors. It is the democracy of the dead. Tradition refuses to submit to the small and arrogant oligarchy of those who merely happen to be walking about. All democrats object to men being disqualified by the accident of birth; tradition objects to their being disqualified by the accident of death. Democracy tells us not to neglect a good man's opinion, even if he is our groom; tradition asks us not to neglect a good man's opinion, even if he is our father. I, at any rate, cannot separate the two ideas of democracy and tradition; it seems evident to me that they are the same idea. We will have the dead at our councils. The ancient Greeks voted by stones; these shall vote by tombstones. It is all quite regular and official, for most tombstones, like most ballot papers, are marked with a cross.

I have first to say, therefore, that if I have had a bias, it was always a bias in favour of democracy, and therefore of tradition. Before we come to any theoretic or logical beginnings I am content to allow for that personal equation; I have always been more inclined to believe the ruck of hardworking people than to believe that special and troublesome literary class to which I belong. I prefer even the fancies and prejudices of the people who see life from the inside to the clearest demonstrations of the people who see life from the outside. I would always trust the old wives' fables against the old maids' facts. As long as wit is mother wit it can be as wild as it pleases.

Now, I have to put together a general position, and I pretend to no training in such things. I propose to do it, therefore, by writing down one after another the three or four fundamental ideas which I have found for myself, pretty much in the way that I found them. Then I shall roughly synthesise them, summing up my personal philosophy or natural religion; then I shall describe my startling discovery that the whole thing had been discovered before. It had been discovered by Christianity. But of these profound persuasions which I have to recount in order, the earliest was concerned with this element of popular tradition. And without the foregoing explanation touching tradition and democracy I could hardly make my mental experience clear. As it is, I do not know whether I can make it clear, but I now propose to try.

My first and last philosophy, that which I believe in with unbroken certainty, I learnt in the nursery. I generally learnt it from a nurse; that is, from the solemn and star-appointed priestess at once of democracy and tradition. The things I believed most then, the things I believe most now, are the things called fairy tales. They seem to me to be the entirely reasonable things. They are not fantasies: compared with them other things are fantastic. Compared with them religion and rationalism are both abnormal, though religion is abnormally right and rationalism abnormally wrong. Fairyland is nothing but the sunny country of common sense. It is not earth that judges heaven, but heaven that judges earth; so for me at least it was not earth that criticised elfland, but elfland that criticised the earth. I knew the magic beanstalk before I had tasted beans; I was sure of the Man in the Moon before I was certain of the moon. This was at one with all popular tradition. Modern minor poets are naturalists, and talk about the bush or the brook; but the singers of the old epics and fables were supernaturalists, and talked about the gods of brook and bush. That is what the moderns mean when they say that the ancients did not "appreciate Nature," because they said that Nature was divine. Old nurses do not tell children about the grass, but about the fairies that dance on the grass; and the old Greeks could not see the trees for the dryads.

But I deal here with what ethic and philosophy come from being fed on fairy tales. If I were describing them in detail I could note many noble and healthy principles that arise from them. There is the chivalrous lesson of "Jack the Giant Killer"; that giants should be killed because they are gigantic. It is a manly mutiny against pride as such. For the rebel is older than all the kingdoms, and the Jacobin has more tradition than the Jacobite. There is the lesson of "Cinderella," which is the same as that of the Magnificat—*exaltavit humiles*. There is the great lesson of "Beauty and the Beast"; that a thing must be loved *before* it is loveable. There is the terrible allegory of the "Sleeping Beauty," which tells how the human creature was blessed with all birthday gifts, yet cursed with death; and how death also may perhaps be softened to a sleep. But I am not concerned with any of the separate statutes of elfland, but with the whole spirit of its law, which I learnt before I could speak, and shall retain when I cannot write. I am concerned with a certain way of looking at life, which was created in me by the fairy tales, but has since been meekly ratified by the mere facts.

It might be stated this way. There are certain sequences or developments (cases of one thing following another), which are, in the true sense of the word, reasonable. They are, in the true sense of the word, necessary. Such are mathematical and merely logical sequences. We in fairyland (who are the most reasonable of all creatures) admit that reason and that necessity. For instance, if the Ugly Sisters are older than Cinderella, it is (in an iron and awful sense) *necessary* that Cinderella is younger than the Ugly Sisters. There is no getting out of it. Haeckel may talk as much fatalism about that fact as he pleases: it really must be. If Jack is the son of a miller, a miller is the father of Jack. Cold reason decrees it from her awful throne: and we in fairyland submit. If the three brothers all ride horses, there are six animals and eighteen legs involved: that is true rationalism, and fairyland is full of it. But as I put my head over the hedge of the elves and began to take notice of the natural world, I observed an extraordinary thing. I observed that learned men in spectacles were talking of the actual things that happened—dawn and death and so on—as if *they* were rational and inevitable. They talked as if the fact that trees bear fruit were just as *necessary* as the fact that two and one trees make three. But it is not. There is an enormous difference by the test of fairyland; which is the test of the imagination. You cannot *imagine* two and one not making three. But you can easily imagine trees not growing fruit; you can imagine them growing golden candlesticks or tigers hanging on by the tail. These men in spectacles spoke much of a man named Newton, who was hit by an apple, and who discovered a law. But they could not be got to see the distinction between a true law, a law of reason, and the mere fact of apples falling. If the apple hit Newton's nose, Newton's nose hit the apple. That is a true necessity: because we cannot conceive the one occurring without the other. But we can quite well conceive the apple not falling on his nose; we can fancy it flying ardently through the air to hit some other nose, of which it had a more definite dislike. We have always in our fairy tales kept this sharp distinction between the science of mental relations, in which there really are laws, and the science of physical facts, in which there are no laws, but only weird repetitions. We believe in bodily miracles, but not in mental impossibilities. We believe that a Beanstalk climbed up to Heaven; but that does not at all confuse our convictions on the philosophical question of how many beans make five.

Here is the peculiar perfection of tone and truth in the nursery tales. The man of science says, "Cut the stalk, and the apple will fall"; but he says it calmly, as if the one idea really led up to the other. The witch in the fairy tale says, "Blow the horn, and the ogre's castle will fall"; but she does not say it as if it were something in which the effect obviously arose out of the cause. Doubtless she has given the advice to many champions, and has seen many castles fall, but she does not lose either her wonder or her reason. She does not muddle her head until it imagines a necessary mental connection between a horn and a falling tower. But the scientific men do muddle their heads, until they imagine a necessary mental connection between an apple leaving the tree and an apple reaching the ground. They do really talk as if they had found not only a set of marvellous facts, but a truth connecting those facts. They do talk as if the connection of two strange things physically connected them philosophically. They feel that because one incomprehensible thing constantly follows another incomprehensible thing the two together somehow make up a comprehensible thing. Two black riddles make a white answer.

In fairyland we avoid the word "law"; but in the land of science they are singularly fond of it. Thus they will call some interesting conjecture about how forgotten folks pronounced the alphabet, Grimm's Law. But Grimm's Law is far less intellectual than Grimm's Fairy Tales. The tales are, at any rate, certainly tales; while the law is not a law. A law implies that we know the nature of the generalisation and enactment; not merely that we have noticed some of the effects. If there is a law that pickpockets shall go to prison, it implies that there is an imaginable mental connection between the idea of prison and the idea of picking pockets. And we know what the idea is. We can say why we take liberty from a man who takes liberties. But we cannot say why an egg can turn into a chicken any more than we can say why a bear could turn into a fairy prince. As *ideas*, the egg and the chicken are further off each other than the bear and the prince; for no egg in itself suggests a chicken, whereas some princes do suggest bears. Granted, then, that certain transformations do happen, it is essential that we should regard them in the philosophic manner of fairy tales, not in the unphilosophic manner of science and the "Laws of Nature." When we are asked why eggs turn to birds or fruits fall in autumn, we must answer exactly as the fairy godmother would answer if Cinderella asked her why mice turned to horses or her clothes fell from her at twelve o'clock. We must answer that it is *magic*. It is not a "law," for we do not understand its general formula. It is not a necessity, for though we can count on it happening practically, we have no right to say that it must always happen. It is no argument for unalterable law (as Huxley fancied) that we count on the ordinary course of things. We do not count on it; we bet on it. We risk the remote possibility of a miracle as we do that of a poisoned pancake or a world-destroying comet. We leave it out of account, not because it is a miracle, and therefore an impossibility, but because it is a miracle, and therefore an exception. All the terms used in the science books, "law," "necessity," "order," "tendency," and so on, are really unintellectual, because they assume an inner synthesis which we do not possess. The only words that ever satisfied me as describing Nature are the terms used in the fairy books, "charm," "spell," "enchantment." They express the arbitrariness of the fact and its mystery. A tree grows fruit because it is a *magic* tree. Water runs downhill because it is bewitched. The sun shines because it is bewitched.

I deny altogether that this is fantastic or even mystical. We may have some mysticism later on; but this fairytale language about things is simply rational and agnostic. It is the only way I can express in words my clear and definite perception that one thing is quite distinct from another; that there is no logical connection between flying and laying eggs. It is the man who talks about "a law" that he has never seen who is the mystic. Nay, the ordinary scientific man is strictly a sentimentalist. He is a sentimentalist in this essential sense, that he is soaked and swept away by mere associations. He has so often seen birds fly and lay eggs that he feels as if there must be some dreamy, tender connection between the two ideas, whereas there is none. A forlorn lover might be unable to dissociate the moon from lost love; so the materialist is unable to dissociate the moon from the tide. In both cases there is no connection, except that one has seen them together. A sentimentalist might shed tears at the smell of apple-blossom, because, by a dark association of his own, it reminded him of his boyhood. So the materialist professor (though he conceals his tears) is yet a sentimentalist, because, by a dark association of his own, apple-blossoms remind him of apples. But the cool rationalist from fairyland does not see why, in the abstract, the apple tree should not grow crimson tulips; it sometimes does in his country.

This elementary wonder, however, is not a mere fancy derived from the fairy tales; on the contrary, all the fire of the fairy tales is derived from this. Just as we all like love tales because there is an instinct of sex, we all like astonishing tales because they touch the nerve of the ancient instinct of astonishment. This is proved by the fact that when we are very young children we do not need fairy tales: we only need tales. Mere life is interesting enough. A child of seven is excited by being told that Tommy opened a door and saw a dragon. But a child of three is excited by being told that Tommy opened a door. Boys like romantic tales; but babies like realistic tales—because they find them romantic. In fact, a baby is about the only person, I should think, to whom a modern realistic novel could be read without boring him. This proves that even nursery tales only echo an almost prenatal leap of interest and amazement. These tales say that apples were golden only to refresh the forgotten moment when we found that they were green. They make rivers run with wine only to make us remember, for one wild moment, that they run with water. I have said that this is wholly reasonable and even agnostic. And, indeed, on this point I am all for the higher agnosticism; its better name is Ignorance. We have all read in scientific books, and, indeed, in all romances, the story of the man who has forgotten his name. This man walks about the streets and can see and appreciate everything; only he cannot remember who he is. Well, every man is that man in the story. Every man has forgotten who he is. One may understand the cosmos, but never the ego; the self is more distant than any star. Thou shalt love the Lord thy God; but thou shalt not know thyself. We are all under the same mental calamity; we have all forgotten our names. We have all forgotten what we really are. All that we call common sense and rationality and practicality and positivism only means that for certain dead levels of our life we forget that we have forgotten. All that we call spirit and art and ecstacy only means that for one awful instant we remember that we forget.

But though (like the man without memory in the novel) we walk the streets with a sort of half-witted admiration, still it is admiration. It is admiration in English and not only admiration in Latin. The wonder has a positive element of praise. This is the next milestone to be definitely marked on our road through fairyland. I shall speak in the next chapter about optimists and pessimists in their intellectual aspect, so far as they have one. Here I am only trying to describe the enormous emotions which cannot be described. And the strongest emotion was that life was as precious as it was puzzling. It was an ecstacy because it was an adventure; it was an adventure because it was an opportunity. The goodness of the fairy tale was not affected by the fact that there might be more dragons than princesses; it was good to be in a fairy tale. The test of all happiness is gratitude; and I felt grateful, though I hardly knew to whom. Children are grateful when Santa Claus puts in their stockings gifts of toys or sweets. Could I not be grateful to Santa Claus when he put in my stockings the gift of two miraculous legs? We thank people for birthday presents of cigars and slippers. Can I thank no one for the birthday present of birth?

There were, then, these two first feelings, indefensible and indisputable. The world was a shock, but it was not merely shocking; existence was a surprise, but it was a pleasant surprise. In fact, all my first views were exactly uttered in a riddle that stuck in my brain from boyhood. The question was, "What did the first frog say?" And the answer was, "Lord, how you made me jump!" That says succinctly all that I am saying. God made the frog jump; but the frog prefers jumping. But when these things are settled there enters the second great principle of the fairy philosophy.

Anyone can see it who will simply read *Grimm's Fairy Tales* or the fine collections of Mr. Andrew Lang. For the pleasure of pedantry I will call it the Doctrine of Conditional Joy. Touchstone talked of much virtue in an "if"; according to elfin ethics all virtue is in an "if." The note of the fairy utterance always is, "You may live in a palace of gold and sapphire, *if* you do not say the word 'cow'"; or "You may live happily with the King's daughter, *if* you do not show her an onion." The vision always hangs upon a veto. All the dizzy and colossal things conceded depend upon one small thing withheld. All the wild and whirling things that are let loose depend upon one thing that is forbidden. Mr. W. B. Yeats, in his exquisite and piercing elfin poetry, describes the elves as lawless; they plunge in innocent anarchy on the unbridled horses of the air—

> "Ride on the crest of the dishevelled tide,
> And dance upon the mountains like a flame."

It is a dreadful thing to say that Mr. W. B. Yeats does not understand fairyland. But I do say it. He is an ironical Irishman, full of intellectual reactions. He is not stupid enough to understand fairyland. Fairies prefer people of the yokel type like myself; people who gape and grin and do as they are told. Mr. Yeats reads into elfland all the righteous insurrection of his own race. But the lawlessness of Ireland is a Christian lawlessness, founded on reason and justice. The Fenian is rebelling against something he understands only too well; but the true citizen of fairyland is obeying something that he does not understand at all. In the fairy tale an incomprehensible happiness rests upon an incomprehensible condition. A box is opened, and all evils fly out. A word is forgotten, and cities perish. A lamp is lit, and love flies away. A flower is plucked, and human lives are forfeited. An apple is eaten, and the hope of God is gone.

This is the tone of fairy tales, and it is certainly not lawlessness or even liberty, though men under a mean modern tyranny may think it liberty by comparison. People out of Portland Gaol might think Fleet Street free; but closer study will prove that both fairies and journalists are the slaves of duty. Fairy godmothers seem at least as strict as other godmothers. Cinderella received a coach out of Wonderland and a coachman out of nowhere, but she received a command— which might have come out of Brixton—that she should be back by twelve. Also, she had a glass slipper; and it cannot be a coincidence that glass is so common a substance in folklore. This princess lives in a glass castle, that princess on a glass hill; this one sees all things in a mirror; they may all live in glass houses if they will not throw stones. For this thin glitter of glass everywhere is the expression of the fact that the happiness is bright but brittle, like the substance most easily smashed by a housemaid or a cat. And this fairytale sentiment also sank into me and became my sentiment towards the whole world. I felt and feel that life itself is as bright as the diamond, but as brittle as the windowpane; and when the heavens were compared to the terrible crystal I can remember a shudder. I was afraid that God would drop the cosmos with a crash.

Remember, however, that to be breakable is not the same as to be perishable. Strike a glass, and it will not endure an instant; simply do not strike it, and it will endure a thousand years. Such, it seemed, was the joy of man, either in elfland or on earth; the happiness depended on *not doing something* which you could at any moment do and which, very often, it was not obvious why you should not do. Now, the point here is that to *me* this did not seem unjust. If the miller's third son said to the fairy, "Explain why I must not stand on my head in the fairy palace," the other might fairly reply, "Well, if it comes to that, explain the fairy palace." If Cinderella says, "How is it that I must leave the ball at twelve?" her godmother might answer, "How is it that you are going there till twelve?" If I leave a man in my will ten talking elephants and a hundred winged horses, he cannot complain if the conditions partake of the slight eccentricity of the gift. He must not look a winged horse in the mouth. And it seemed to me that existence was itself so very eccentric a legacy that I could not complain of not understanding the limitations of the vision when I did not understand the vision they limited. The frame was no stranger than the picture. The veto might well be as wild as the vision; it might be as startling as the sun, as elusive as the waters, as fantastic and terrible as the towering trees.

For this reason (we may call it the fairy godmother philosophy) I never could join the young men of my time in feeling what they called the general sentiment of *revolt*. I should have resisted, let us hope, any rules that were evil, and with these and their definition I shall deal in another chapter. But I did not feel disposed to resist any rule merely because it was mysterious. Estates are sometimes held by foolish forms, the breaking of a stick or the payment of a peppercorn: I was willing to hold the huge estate of earth and heaven by any such feudal fantasy. It could not well be wilder than the fact that I was allowed to hold it at all. At this stage I give only one ethical instance to show my meaning. I could never mix in the common murmur of that rising generation against monogamy, because no restriction on sex seemed so odd and unexpected as sex itself. To be allowed, like Endymion, to make love to the moon and then to complain that Jupiter kept his own moons in a harem seemed to me (bred on fairy tales like Endymion's) a vulgar anticlimax. Keeping to one woman is a small price for so much as seeing one woman. To complain that I could only be married once was like complaining that I had only been born once. It was incommensurate with the terrible excitement of which one was talking. It showed, not an exaggerated sensibility to sex, but a curious insensibility to it. A man is a fool who complains that he cannot enter Eden by five gates at once. Polygamy is a lack of the realization of sex; it is like a man plucking five pears in mere absence of mind. The aesthetes touched the last insane limits of language in their eulogy on lovely things. The thistledown made them weep; a burnished beetle brought them to their knees. Yet their emotion never impressed me for an instant, for this reason, that it never occurred to them to pay for their pleasure in any sort of symbolic sacrifice. Men (I felt) might fast forty days for the sake of hearing a blackbird sing. Men might go through fire to find a cowslip. Yet these lovers of beauty could not even keep sober for the black-bird. They would not go through common Christian marriage by way of recompense to the cowslip. Surely one might pay for extraordinary joy in ordinary morals. Oscar Wilde said that sunsets were not valued because we could not pay for sunsets. But Oscar Wilde was wrong; we can pay for sunsets. We can pay for them by not being Oscar Wilde.

Well, I left the fairy tales lying on the floor of the nursery, and I have not found any books so sensible since. I left the nurse guardian of tradition and democracy, and I have not found any modern type so sanely radical or so sanely conservative. But the matter for important comment was here, that when I first went out into the mental atmosphere of the modern world, I found that the modern world was positively opposed on two points to my nurse and to the nursery tales. It has taken me a long time to find out that the modern world is wrong and my nurse was right. The really curious thing was this: that modern thought contradicted this basic creed of my boyhood on its two most essential doctrines. I have explained that the fairy tales founded in me two convictions; first, that this world is a wild and star-tling place, which might have been quite different, but which is quite delightful; second, that before this wildness and delight one may well be modest and submit to the queerest limitations of so queer a kind-ness. But I found the whole modern world running like a high tide against both my tendernesses; and the shock of that collision created two sudden and spontaneous sentiments, which I have had ever since and which, crude as they were, have since hardened into convictions.

First, I found the whole modern world talking scientific fatalism; saying that everything is as it must always have been, being unfolded without fault from the beginning. The leaf on the tree is green because it could never have been anything else. Now, the fairytale philosopher is glad that the leaf is green precisely because it might have been scarlet. He feels as if it had turned green an instant before he looked at it. He is pleased that snow is white on the strictly reason-able ground that it might have been black. Every colour has in it a bold quality as of choice; the red of garden roses is not only decisive but dramatic, like suddenly spilt blood. He feels that something has been *done*. But the great determinists of the nineteenth century were strongly against this native feeling that something had happened an instant before. In fact, according to them, nothing ever really had happened since the beginning of the world. Nothing ever had happened since existence had happened; and even about the date of that they were not very sure.

The modern world as I found it was solid for modern Calvinism, for the necessity of things being as they are. But when I came to ask them I found they had really no proof of this unavoidable repetition in things except the fact that the things were repeated. Now, the mere repetition made the things to me rather more weird than more rational. It was as if, having seen a curiously shaped nose in the street and dismissed it as an accident, I had then seen six other noses of the same astonishing shape. I should have fancied for a moment that it must be some local secret society. So one elephant having a trunk was odd; but all elephants having trunks looked like a plot. I speak here only of an emotion, and of an emotion at once stubborn and subtle. But the repetition in Nature seemed sometimes to be an excited repetition, like that of an angry schoolmaster saying the same thing over and over again. The grass seemed signalling to me with all its fingers at once; the crowded stars seemed bent upon being understood. The sun would make me see him if he rose a thousand times. The recurrences of the universe rose to the maddening rhythm of an incantation, and I began to see an idea.

All the towering materialism which dominates the modern mind rests ultimately upon one assumption; a false assumption. It is supposed that if a thing goes on repeating itself it is probably dead; a piece of clockwork. People feel that if the universe was personal it would vary; if the sun were alive it would dance. This is a fallacy even in relation to known fact. For the variation in human affairs is generally brought into them, not by life, but by death; by the dying down or breaking off of their strength or desire. A man varies his movements because of some slight element of failure or fatigue. He gets into an omnibus because he is tired of walking; or he walks because he is tired of sitting still. But if his life and joy were so gigantic that he never tired of going to Islington, he might go to Islington as regularly as the Thames goes to Sheerness. The very speed and ecstasy of his life would have the stillness of death. The sun rises every morning. I do not rise every morning; but the variation is due not to my activity, but to my inaction. Now, to put the matter in a popular phrase, it might be true that the sun rises regularly because he never gets tired of rising. His routine might be due, not to a lifelessness, but to a rush of life. The thing I mean can be seen, for instance, in children, when they find some game or joke that they specially enjoy. A child kicks his legs rhythmically through excess, not absence, of life. Because children have abounding vitality, because they are in spirit fierce and free, therefore they want things repeated and unchanged. They always say, "Do it again"; and the grownup person does it again until he is nearly dead. For grownup people are not strong enough to exult in monotony. But perhaps God is strong enough to exult in monotony. It is possible that God says every morning, "Do it again" to the sun; and every evening, "Do it again" to the moon. It may not be automatic necessity that makes all daisies alike; it may be that God makes every daisy separately, but has never got tired of making them. It may be that He has the eternal appetite of infancy; for we have sinned and grown old, and our Father is younger than we. The repetition in Nature may not be a mere recurrence; it may be a theatrical encore. Heaven may encore the bird who laid an egg. If the human being conceives and brings forth a human child instead of bringing forth a fish, or a bat, or a griffin, the reason may not be that we are fixed in an animal fate without life or purpose. It may be that our little tragedy has touched the gods, that they admire it from their starry galleries, and that at the end of every human drama man is called again and again before the curtain. Repetition may go on for millions of years, by mere choice, and at any instant it may stop. Man may stand on the earth generation after generation, and yet each birth be his positively last appearance.

This was my first conviction; made by the shock of my childish emotions meeting the modern creed in mid-career. I had always vaguely felt facts to be miracles in the sense that they are wonderful: now I began to think them miracles in the stricter sense that they were *wilful*. I mean that they were, or might be, repeated exercises of some will. In short, I had always believed that the world involved magic: now I thought that perhaps it involved a magician. And this pointed a profound emotion always present and subconscious; that this world of ours has some purpose; and if there is a purpose, there is a person. I had always felt life first as a story: and if there is a story there is a storyteller.

But modern thought also hit my second human tradition. It went against the fairy feeling about strict limits and conditions. The one thing it loved to talk about was expansion and largeness. Herbert Spencer would have been greatly annoyed if anyone had called him an imperialist, and therefore it is highly regrettable that nobody did. But he was an imperialist of the lowest type. He popularized this contemptible notion that the size of the solar system ought to overawe the spiritual dogma of man. Why should a man surrender his dignity to the solar system any more than to a whale? If mere size proves that man is not the image of God, then a whale may be the image of God; a somewhat formless image; what one might call an impressionist portrait. It is quite futile to argue that man is small compared to the cosmos; for man was always small compared to the nearest tree. But Herbert Spencer, in his headlong imperialism, would insist that we had in some way been conquered and annexed by the astronomical universe. He spoke about men and their ideals exactly as the most insolent Unionist talks about the Irish and their ideals. He turned mankind into a small nationality. And his evil influence can be seen even in the most spirited and honourable of later scientific authors; notably in the early romances of Mr. H. G. Wells. Many moralists have in an exaggerated way represented the earth as wicked. But Mr. Wells and his school made the heavens wicked. We should lift up our eyes to the stars from whence would come our ruin.

But the expansion of which I speak was much more evil than all this. I have remarked that the materialist, like the madman, is in prison; in the prison of one thought. These people seemed to think it singularly inspiring to keep on saying that the prison was very large. The size of this scientific universe gave one no novelty, no relief. The cosmos went on forever, but not in its wildest constellation could there be anything really interesting; anything, for instance, such as forgiveness or free will. The grandeur or infinity of the secret of its cosmos added nothing to it. It was like telling a prisoner in Reading gaol that he would be glad to hear that the gaol now covered half the county. The warder would have nothing to show the man except more and more long corridors of stone lit by ghastly lights and empty of all that is human. So these expanders of the universe had nothing to show us except more and more infinite corridors of space lit by ghastly suns and empty of all that is divine.

In fairyland there had been a real law; a law that could be broken, for the definition of a law is something that can be broken. But the machinery of this cosmic prison was something that could not be broken; for we ourselves were only a part of its machinery. We were either unable to do things or we were destined to do them. The idea of the mystical condition quite disappeared; one can neither have the firmness of keeping laws nor the fun of breaking them. The largeness of this universe had nothing of that freshness and airy outbreak which we have praised in the universe of the poet. This modern universe is literally an empire; that is, it is vast, but it is not free. One went into larger and larger windowless rooms, rooms big with Babylonian perspective; but one never found the smallest window or a whisper of outer air.

Their infernal parallels seemed to expand with distance; but for me all good things come to a point, swords for instance. So finding the boast of the big cosmos so unsatisfactory to my emotions I began to argue about it a little; and I soon found that the whole attitude was even shallower than could have been expected. According to these people the cosmos was one thing since it had one unbroken rule. Only (they would say) while it is one thing it is also the only thing there is. Why, then, should one worry particularly to call it large? There is nothing to compare it with. It would be just as sensible to call it small. A man may say, "I like this vast cosmos, with its throng of stars and its crowd of varied creatures." But if it comes to that why should not a man say, "I like this cosy little cosmos, with its decent number of stars and as neat a provision of live stock as I wish to see"? One is as good as the other; they are both mere sentiments. It is mere sentiment to rejoice that the sun is larger than the earth; it is quite as sane a sentiment to rejoice that the sun is no larger than it is. A man chooses to have an emotion about the largeness of the world; why should he not choose to have an emotion about its smallness?

It happened that I had that emotion. When one is fond of anything one addresses it by diminutives, even if it is an elephant or a lifeguardsman. The reason is, that anything, however huge, that can be conceived of as complete, can be conceived of as small. If military moustaches did not suggest a sword or tusks a tail, then the object would be vast because it would be immeasurable. But the moment you can imagine a guardsman you can imagine a small guardsman. The moment you really see an elephant you can call it "Tiny." If you can make a statue of a thing you can make a statuette of it. These people professed that the universe was one coherent thing; but they were not fond of the universe. But I was frightfully fond of the universe and wanted to address it by a diminutive. I often did so; and it never seemed to mind. Actually and in truth I did feel that these dim dogmas of vitality were better expressed by calling the world small than by calling it large. For about infinity there was a sort of carelessness which was the reverse of the fierce and pious care which I felt touching the pricelessness and the peril of life. They showed only a dreary waste; but I felt a sort of sacred thrift. For economy is far more romantic than extravagance. To them stars were an unending income of halfpence; but I felt about the golden sun and the silver moon as a schoolboy feels if he has one sovereign and one shilling.

These subconscious convictions are best hit off by the colour and tone of certain tales. Thus I have said that stories of magic alone can express my sense that life is not only a pleasure but a kind of eccentric privilege. I may express this other feeling of cosmic cosiness by allusion to another book always read in boyhood, *Robinson Crusoe*, which I read about this time, and which owes its eternal vivacity to the fact that it celebrates the poetry of limits, nay, even the wild romance of prudence. Crusoe is a man on a small rock with a few comforts just snatched from the sea: the best thing in the book is simply the list of things saved from the wreck. The greatest of poems is an inventory. Every kitchen tool becomes ideal because Crusoe might have dropped it in the sea. It is a good exercise, in empty or ugly hours of the day, to look at anything, the coal-scuttle or the bookcase, and think how happy one could be to have brought it out of the sinking ship on to the solitary island. But it is a better exercise still to remember how all things have had this hair-breadth escape: everything has been saved from a wreck. Every man has had one horrible adventure: as a hidden untimely birth he had not been, as infants that never see the light. Men spoke much in my boyhood of restricted or ruined men of genius: and it was common to say that many a man was a Great Might-Have-Been. To me it is a more solid and startling fact that any man in the street is a Great Might-Not-Have-Been.

But I really felt (the fancy may seem foolish) as if all the order and number of things were the romantic remnant of Crusoe's ship. That there are two sexes and one sun, was like the fact that there were two guns and one axe. It was poignantly urgent that none should be lost; but somehow, it was rather fun that none could be added. The trees and the planets seemed like things saved from the wreck: and when I saw the Matterhorn I was glad that it had not been overlooked in the confusion. I felt economical about the stars as if they were sapphires (they are called so in Milton's Eden): I hoarded the hills. For the universe is a single jewel, and while it is a natural cant to talk of a jewel as peerless and priceless, of this jewel it is literally true. This cosmos is indeed without peer and without price: for there cannot be another one.

Thus ends, in unavoidable inadequacy, the attempt to utter the unutterable things. These are my ultimate attitudes towards life; the soils for the seeds of doctrine. These in some dark way I thought before I could write, and felt before I could think: that we may proceed more easily afterwards, I will roughly recapitulate them now. I felt in my bones; first, that this world does not explain itself. It may be a miracle with a supernatural explanation; it may be a conjuring trick, with a natural explanation. But the explanation of the conjuring trick, if it is to satisfy me, will have to be better than the natural explanations I have heard. The thing is magic, true or false. Second, I came to feel as if magic must have a meaning, and meaning must have someone to mean it. There was something personal in the world, as in a work of art; whatever it meant it meant violently. Third, I thought this purpose beautiful in its old design, in spite of its defects, such as dragons. Fourth, that the proper form of thanks to it is some form of humility and restraint: we should thank God for beer and Burgundy by not drinking too much of them. We owed, also, an obedience to whatever made us. And last, and strangest, there had come into my mind a vague and vast impression that in some way all good was a remnant to be stored and held sacred out of some primordial ruin. Man had saved his good as Crusoe saved his goods: he had saved them from a wreck. All this I felt and the age gave me no encouragement to feel it. And all this time I had not even thought of Christian theology.

THE PARADOXES OF CHRISTIANITY

The real trouble with this world of ours is not that it is an unreasonable world, nor even that it is a reasonable one. The commonest kind of trouble is that it is nearly reasonable, but not quite. Life is not an illogicality; yet it is a trap for logicians. It looks just a little more mathematical and regular than it is; its exactitude is obvious, but its inexactitude is hidden; its wildness lies in wait. I give one coarse instance of what I mean. Suppose some mathematical creature from the moon were to reckon up the human body; he would at once see that the essential thing about it was that it was duplicate. A man is two men, he on the right exactly resembling him on the left. Having noted that there was an arm on the right and one on the left, a leg on the right and one on the left, he might go further and still find on each side the same number of fingers, the same number of toes, twin eyes, twin ears, twin nostrils, and even twin lobes of the brain. At last he would take it as a law; and then, where he found a heart on one side, would deduce that there was another heart on the other. And just then, where he most felt he was right, he would be wrong.

It is this silent swerving from accuracy by an inch that is the uncanny element in everything. It seems a sort of secret treason in the universe. An apple or an orange is round enough to get itself called round, and yet is not round after all. The earth itself is shaped like an orange in order to lure some simple astronomer into calling it a globe. A blade of grass is called after the blade of a sword, because it comes to a point; but it doesn't. Everywhere in things there is this element of the quiet and incalculable. It escapes the rationalists, but it never escapes till the last moment. From the grand curve of our earth it could easily be inferred that every inch of it was thus curved. It would seem rational that as a man has a brain on both sides, he should have a heart on both sides. Yet scientific men are still organizing expeditions to find the North Pole, because they are so fond of flat country. Scientific men are also still organising expeditions to find a man's heart; and when they try to find it, they generally get on the wrong side of him.

Now, actual insight or inspiration is best tested by whether it guesses these hidden malformations or surprises. If our mathematician from the moon saw the two arms and the two ears, he might deduce the two shoulder-blades and the two halves of the brain. But if he guessed that the man's heart was in the right place, then I should call him something more than a mathematician. Now, this is exactly the claim which I have since come to propound for Christianity. Not merely that it deduces logical truths, but that when it suddenly becomes illogical, it has found, so to speak, an illogical truth. It not only goes right about things, but it goes wrong (if one may say so) exactly where the things go wrong. Its plan suits the secret irregularities, and expects the unexpected. It is simple about the simple truth; but it is stubborn about the subtle truth. It will admit that a man has two hands, it will not admit (though all the Modernists wail to it) the obvious deduction that he has two hearts. It is my only purpose in this chapter to point this out; to show that whenever we feel there is something odd in Christian theology, we shall generally find that there is something odd in the truth.

I have alluded to an unmeaning phrase to the effect that such and such a creed cannot be believed in our age. Of course, anything can be believed in any age. But, oddly enough, there really is a sense in which a creed, if it is believed at all, can be believed more fixedly in a complex society than in a simple one. If a man finds Christianity true in Birmingham, he has actually clearer reasons for faith than if he had found it true in Mercia. For the more complicated seems the coincidence, the less it can be a coincidence. If snowflakes fell in the shape, say, of the heart of Midlothian, it might be an accident. But if snowflakes fell in the exact shape of the maze at Hampton Court, I think one might call it a miracle. It is exactly as of such a miracle that I have since come to feel of the philosophy of Christianity. The complication of our modern world proves the truth of the creed more perfectly than any of the plain problems of the ages of faith. It was in Notting Hill and Battersea that I began to see that Christianity was true. This is why the faith has that elaboration of doctrines and details which so much distresses those who admire Christianity without believing in it. When once one believes in a creed, one is proud of its complexity, as scientists are proud of the complexity of science. It shows how rich it is in discoveries. If it is right at all, it is a compliment to say that it's elaborately right. A stick might fit a hole or a stone a hollow by accident. But a key and a lock are both complex. And if a key fits a lock, you know it is the right key.

But this involved accuracy of the thing makes it very difficult to do what I now have to do, to describe this accumulation of truth. It is very hard for a man to defend anything of which he is entirely convinced. It is comparatively easy when he is only partially convinced. He is partially convinced because he has found this or that proof of the thing, and he can expound it. But a man is not really convinced of a philosophic theory when he finds that something proves it. He is only really convinced when he finds that everything proves it. And the more converging reasons he finds pointing to this conviction, the more bewildered he is if asked suddenly to sum them up. Thus, if one asked an ordinary intelligent man, on the spur of the moment, "Why do you prefer civilisation to savagery?" he would look wildly round at object after object, and would only be able to answer vaguely, "Why, there is that bookcase... and the coals in the coal-scuttle... and pianos... and policemen." The whole case for civilisation is that the case for it is complex. It has done so many things. But that very multiplicity of proof which ought to make reply overwhelming makes reply impossible.

There is, therefore, about all complete conviction a kind of huge helplessness. The belief is so big that it takes a long time to get it into action. And this hesitation chiefly arises, oddly enough, from an indifference about where one should begin. All roads lead to Rome; which is one reason why many people never get there. In the case of this defence of the Christian conviction I confess that I would as soon begin the argument with one thing as another; I would begin it with a turnip or a taximeter cab. But if I am to be at all careful about making my meaning clear, it will, I think, be wiser to continue the current arguments of the last chapter, which was concerned to urge the first of these mystical coincidences, or rather ratifications. All I had hitherto heard of Christian theology had alienated me from it. I was a pagan at the age of twelve, and a complete agnostic by the age of sixteen; and I cannot understand anyone passing the age of seventeen without having asked himself so simple a question. I did, indeed, retain a cloudy reverence for a cosmic deity and a great historical interest in the Founder of Christianity. But I certainly regarded Him as a man; though perhaps I thought that, even in that point, He had an advantage over some of His modern critics. I read the scientific and sceptical literature of my time—all of it, at least, that I could find written in English and lying about; and I read nothing else; I mean I read nothing else on any other note of philosophy. The penny dreadfuls which I also read were indeed in a healthy and heroic tradition of Christianity; but I did not know this at the time. I never read a line of Christian apologetics. I read as little as I can of them now. It was Huxley and Herbert Spencer and Bradlaugh who brought me back to orthodox theology. They sowed in my mind my first wild doubts of doubt. Our grandmothers were quite right when they said that Tom Paine and the freethinkers unsettled the mind. They do. They unsettled mine horribly. The rationalist made me question whether reason was of any use whatever; and when I had finished Herbert Spencer I had got as far as doubting (for the first time) whether evolution had occurred at all. As I laid down the last of Colonel Ingersoll's atheistic lectures the dreadful thought broke across my mind, "Almost thou persuadest me to be a Christian." I was in a desperate way.

This odd effect of the great agnostics in arousing doubts deeper than their own might be illustrated in many ways. I take only one. As I read and reread all the non-Christian or anti-Christian accounts of the faith, from Huxley to Bradlaugh, a slow and awful impression grew gradually but graphically upon my mind—the impression that Christianity must be a most extraordinary thing. For not only (as I understood) had Christianity the most flaming vices, but it had apparently a mystical talent for combining vices which seemed inconsistent with each other. It was attacked on all sides and for all contradictory reasons. No sooner had one rationalist demonstrated that it was too far to the east than another demonstrated with equal clearness that it was much too far to the west. No sooner had my indignation died down at its angular and aggressive squareness than I was called up again to notice and condemn its enervating and sensual roundness. In case any reader has not come across the thing I mean, I will give such instances as I remember at random of this self-contradiction in the sceptical attack. I give four or five of them; there are fifty more.

Thus, for instance, I was much moved by the eloquent attack on Christianity as a thing of inhuman gloom; for I thought (and still think) sincere pessimism the unpardonable sin. Insincere pessimism is a social accomplishment, rather agreeable than otherwise; and fortunately nearly all pessimism is insincere. But if Christianity was, as these people said, a thing purely pessimistic and opposed to life, then I was quite prepared to blow up St. Paul's Cathedral. But the extraordinary thing is this. They did prove to me in Chapter I. (to my complete satisfaction) that Christianity was too pessimistic; and then, in Chapter II., they began to prove to me that it was a great deal too optimistic. One accusation against Christianity was that it prevented men, by morbid tears and terrors, from seeking joy and liberty in the bosom of Nature. But another accusation was that it comforted men with a fictitious providence, and put them in a pink-and-white nursery. One great agnostic asked why Nature was not beautiful enough, and why it was hard to be free. Another great agnostic objected that Christian optimism, "the garment of make-believe woven by pious hands," hid from us the fact that Nature was ugly, and that it was impossible to be free. One rationalist had hardly done calling Christianity a nightmare before another began to call it a fool's paradise. This puzzled me; the charges seemed inconsistent. Christianity could not at once be the black mask on a white world, and also the white mask on a black world. The state of the Christian could not be at once so comfortable that he was a coward to cling to it, and so uncomfortable that he was a fool to stand it. If it falsified human vision it must falsify it one way or another; it could not wear both green and rose-coloured spectacles. I rolled on my tongue with a terrible joy, as did all young men of that time, the taunts which Swinburne hurled at the dreariness of the creed—

"Thou hast conquered, O pale Galilean, the
world has grown gray with Thy breath."

But when I read the same poet's accounts of paganism (as in "Atalanta"), I gathered that the world was, if possible, more gray before the Galilean breathed on it than afterwards. The poet maintained, indeed, in the abstract, that life itself was pitch dark. And yet, somehow, Christianity had darkened it. The very man who denounced Christianity for pessimism was himself a pessimist. I thought there must be something wrong. And it did for one wild moment cross my mind that, perhaps, those might not be the very best judges of the relation of religion to happiness who, by their own account, had neither one nor the other.

It must be understood that I did not conclude hastily that the accusations were false or the accusers fools. I simply deduced that Christianity must be something even weirder and wickeder than they made out. A thing might have these two opposite vices; but it must be a rather queer thing if it did. A man might be too fat in one place and too thin in another; but he would be an odd shape. At this point my thoughts were only of the odd shape of the Christian religion; I did not allege any odd shape in the rationalistic mind.

Here is another case of the same kind. I felt that a strong case against Christianity lay in the charge that there is something timid, monkish, and unmanly about all that is called "Christian," especially in its attitude towards resistance and fighting. The great sceptics of the nineteenth century were largely virile. Bradlaugh in an expansive way, Huxley in a reticent way, were decidedly men. In comparison, it did seem tenable that there was something weak and over patient about Christian counsels. The Gospel paradox about the other cheek, the fact that priests never fought, a hundred things made plausible the accusation that Christianity was an attempt to make a man too like a sheep. I read it and believed it, and if I had read nothing different, I should have gone on believing it. But I read something very different. I turned the next page in my agnostic manual, and my brain turned upside down. Now I found that I was to hate Christianity not for fighting too little, but for fighting too much. Christianity, it seemed, was the mother of wars. Christianity had deluged the world with blood. I had got thoroughly angry with the Christian, because he never was angry. And now I was told to be angry with him because his anger had been the most huge and horrible thing in human history; because his anger had soaked the earth and smoked to the sun. The very people who reproached Christianity with the meekness and nonresistance of the monastries were the very people who reproached it also with the violence and valour of the Crusades. It was the fault of poor old Christianity (somehow or other) both that Edward the Confessor did not fight and that Richard Coeur de Lion did. The Quakers (we were told) were the only characteristic Christians; and yet the massacres of Cromwell and Alva were characteristic Christian crimes. What could it all mean? What was this Christianity which always forbade war and always produced wars? What could be the nature of the thing which one could abuse first because it would not fight, and second because it was always fighting? In what world of riddles was born this monstrous murder and this monstrous meekness? The shape of Christianity grew a queerer shape every instant.

I take a third case; the strangest of all, because it involves the one real objection to the faith. The one real objection to the Christian religion is simply that it is one religion. The world is a big place, full of very different kinds of people. Christianity (it may reasonably be said) is one thing confined to one kind of people; it began in Palestine, it has practically stopped with Europe. I was duly impressed with this argument in my youth, and I was much drawn towards the doctrine often preached in Ethical Societies—I mean the doctrine that there is one great unconscious church of all humanity founded on the omnipresence of the human conscience. Creeds, it was said, divided men; but at least morals united them. The soul might seek the strangest and most remote lands and ages and still find essential ethical common sense. It might find Confucius under Eastern trees, and he would be writing "Thou shalt not steal." It might decipher the darkest hieroglyphic on the most primeval desert, and the meaning when deciphered would be "Little boys should tell the truth." I believed this doctrine of the brotherhood of all men in the possession of a moral sense, and I believe it still—with other things. And I was thoroughly annoyed with Christianity for suggesting (as I supposed) that whole ages and empires of men had utterly escaped this light of justice and reason. But then I found an astonishing thing. I found that the very people who said that mankind was one church from Plato to Emerson were the very people who said that morality had changed altogether, and that what was right in one age was wrong in another. If I asked, say, for an altar, I was told that we needed none, for men our brothers gave us clear oracles and one creed in their universal customs and ideals. But if I mildly pointed out that one of men's universal customs was to have an altar, then my agnostic teachers turned clean round and told me that men had always been in darkness and the superstitions of savages. I found it was their daily taunt against Christianity that it was the light of one people and had left all others to die in the dark. But I also found that it was their special boast for themselves that science and progress were the discovery of one people, and that all other peoples had died in the dark. Their chief insult to Christianity

was actually their chief compliment to themselves, and there seemed
to be a strange unfairness about all their relative insistence on the
two things. When considering some pagan or agnostic, we were to
remember that all men had one religion; when considering some
mystic or spiritualist, we were only to consider what absurd religions
some men had. We could trust the ethics of Epictetus, because ethics
had never changed. We must not trust the ethics of Bossuet, because
ethics had changed. They changed in two hundred years, but not in
two thousand.

This began to be alarming. It looked not so much as if Christianity was bad enough to include any vices, but rather as if any stick
was good enough to beat Christianity with. What again could this
astonishing thing be like which people were so anxious to contradict,
that in doing so they did not mind contradicting themselves? I saw
the same thing on every side. I can give no further space to this
discussion of it in detail; but lest anyone supposes that I have unfairly
selected three accidental cases I will run briefly through a few others.
Thus, certain sceptics wrote that the great crime of Christianity had
been its attack on the family; it had dragged women to the loneliness
and contemplation of the cloister, away from their homes and their
children. But, then, other sceptics (slightly more advanced) said that
the great crime of Christianity was forcing the family and marriage
upon us; that it doomed women to the drudgery of their homes and
children, and forbade them loneliness and contemplation. The
charge was actually reversed. Or, again, certain phrases in the Epis-
tles or the Marriage Service, were said by the anti-Christians to show
contempt for woman's intellect. But I found that the anti-Christians
themselves had a contempt for woman's intellect; for it was their
great sneer at the Church on the Continent that "only women" went
to it. Or again, Christianity was reproached with its naked and
hungry habits; with its sackcloth and dried peas. But the next minute
Christianity was being reproached with its pomp and its ritualism; its
shrines of porphyry and its robes of gold. It was abused for being too
plain and for being too coloured. Again Christianity had always been
accused of restraining sexuality too much, when Bradlaugh the

Malthusian discovered that it restrained it too little. It is often accused in the same breath of prim respectability and of religious extravagance. Between the covers of the same atheistic pamphlet I have found the faith rebuked for its disunion, "One thinks one thing, and one another," and rebuked also for its union, "It is difference of opinion that prevents the world from going to the dogs." In the same conversation a freethinker, a friend of mine, blamed Christianity for despising Jews, and then despised it himself for being Jewish.

I wished to be quite fair then, and I wish to be quite fair now; and I did not conclude that the attack on Christianity was all wrong. I only concluded that if Christianity was wrong, it was very wrong indeed. Such hostile horrors might be combined in one thing, but that thing must be very strange and solitary. There are men who are misers, and also spendthrifts; but they are rare. There are men sensual and also ascetic; but they are rare. But if this mass of mad contradictions really existed, quakerish and bloodthirsty, too gorgeous and too threadbare, austere, yet pandering preposterously to the lust of the eye, the enemy of women and their foolish refuge, a solemn pessimist and a silly optimist, if this evil existed, then there was in this evil something quite supreme and unique. For I found in my rationalist teachers no explanation of such exceptional corruption. Christianity (theoretically speaking) was in their eyes only one of the ordinary myths and errors of mortals. *They* gave me no key to this twisted and unnatural badness. Such a paradox of evil rose to the stature of the supernatural. It was, indeed, almost as supernatural as the infallibility of the Pope. An historic institution, which never went right, is really quite as much of a miracle as an institution that cannot go wrong. The only explanation which immediately occurred to my mind was that Christianity did not come from heaven, but from hell. Really, if Jesus of Nazareth was not Christ, He must have been Antichrist.

And then in a quiet hour a strange thought struck me like a still thunderbolt. There had suddenly come into my mind another explanation. Suppose we heard an unknown man spoken of by many men. Suppose we were puzzled to hear that some men said he was too tall and some too short; some objected to his fatness, some lamented his leanness; some thought him too dark, and some too fair. One explanation (as has been already admitted) would be that he might be an odd shape. But there is another explanation. He might be the right shape. Outrageously tall men might feel him to be short. Very short men might feel him to be tall. Old bucks who are growing stout might consider him insufficiently filled out; old beaux who were growing thin might feel that he expanded beyond the narrow lines of elegance. Perhaps Swedes (who have pale hair like tow) called him a dark man, while negroes considered him distinctly blonde. Perhaps (in short) this extraordinary thing is really the ordinary thing; at least the normal thing, the centre. Perhaps, after all, it is Christianity that is sane and all its critics that are mad—in various ways. I tested this idea by asking myself whether there was about any of the accusers anything morbid that might explain the accusation. I was startled to find that this key fitted a lock. For instance, it was certainly odd that the modern world charged Christianity at once with bodily austerity and with artistic pomp. But then it was also odd, very odd, that the modern world itself combined extreme bodily luxury with an extreme absence of artistic pomp. The modern man thought Becket's robes too rich and his meals too poor. But then the modern man was really exceptional in history; no man before ever ate such elaborate dinners in such ugly clothes. The modern man found the church too simple exactly where modern life is too complex; he found the church too gorgeous exactly where modern life is too dingy. The man who disliked the plain fasts and feasts was mad on entrées. The man who disliked vestments wore a pair of preposterous trousers. And surely if there was any insanity involved in the matter at all it was in the trousers, not in the simply falling robe. If there was any insanity at all, it was in the extravagant entrées, not in the bread and wine.

I went over all the cases, and I found the key fitted so far. The fact that Swinburne was irritated at the unhappiness of Christians and yet more irritated at their happiness was easily explained. It was no longer a complication of diseases in Christianity, but a complication of diseases in Swinburne. The restraints of Christians saddened him simply because he was more hedonist than a healthy man should be. The faith of Christians angered him because he was more pessimist than a healthy man should be. In the same way the Malthusians by instinct attacked Christianity; not because there is anything especially anti-Malthusian about Christianity, but because there is something a little anti-human about Malthusianism.

Nevertheless it could not, I felt, be quite true that Christianity was merely sensible and stood in the middle. There was really an element in it of emphasis and even frenzy which had justified the secularists in their superficial criticism. It might be wise, I began more and more to think that it was wise, but it was not merely worldly wise; it was not merely temperate and respectable. Its fierce crusaders and meek saints might balance each other; still, the crusaders were very fierce and the saints were very meek, meek beyond all decency. Now, it was just at this point of the speculation that I remembered my thoughts about the martyr and the suicide. In that matter there had been this combination between two almost insane positions which yet somehow amounted to sanity. This was just such another contradiction; and this I had already found to be true. This was exactly one of the paradoxes in which sceptics found the creed wrong; and in this I had found it right. Madly as Christians might love the martyr or hate the suicide, they never felt these passions more madly than I had felt them long before I dreamed of Christianity. Then the most difficult and interesting part of the mental process opened, and I began to trace this idea darkly through all the enormous thoughts of our theology. The idea was that which I had outlined touching the optimist and the pessimist; that we want not an amalgam or compromise, but both things at the top of their energy; love and wrath both burning. Here I shall only trace it in relation to ethics. But I need not remind the reader that the idea of this combination is indeed central in orthodox theology. For orthodox theology has specially insisted that Christ was not a being apart from God and man, like an elf, nor yet a being half human and half not, like a centaur, but both things at once and both things thoroughly, very man and very God. Now let me trace this notion as I found it.

All sane men can see that sanity is some kind of equilibrium; that one may be mad and eat too much, or mad and eat too little. Some moderns have indeed appeared with vague versions of progress and evolution which seeks to destroy the μέσον or balance of Aristotle. They seem to suggest that we are meant to starve progressively, or to go on eating larger and larger breakfasts every morning forever. But the great truism of the μέσον remains for all thinking men, and these people have not upset any balance except their own. But granted that we have all to keep a balance, the real interest comes in with the question of how that balance can be kept. That was the problem which Paganism tried to solve: that was the problem which I think Christianity solved and solved in a very strange way.

Paganism declared that virtue was in a balance; Christianity declared it was in a conflict: the collision of two passions apparently opposite. Of course they were not really inconsistent; but they were such that it was hard to hold simultaneously. Let us follow for a moment the clue of the martyr and the suicide; and take the case of courage. No quality has ever so much addled the brains and tangled the definitions of merely rational sages. Courage is almost a contradiction in terms. It means a strong desire to live taking the form of a readiness to die. "He that will lose his life, the same shall save it," is not a piece of mysticism for saints and heroes. It is a piece of everyday advice for sailors or mountaineers. It might be printed in an Alpine guide or a drill book. This paradox is the whole principle of courage; even of quite earthly or quite brutal courage. A man cut off by the sea may save his life if he will risk it on the precipice. He can only get away from death by continually stepping within an inch of it. A soldier surrounded by enemies, if he is to cut his way out, needs to combine a strong desire for living with a strange carelessness about dying. He must not merely cling to life, for then he will be a coward, and will not escape. He must not merely wait for death, for then he will be a suicide, and will not escape. He must seek his life in a spirit of furious indifference to it; he must desire life like water and yet drink death like wine. No philosopher, I fancy, has ever expressed this romantic riddle with adequate lucidity, and I certainly have not done so. But Christianity has done more: it has marked the limits of it in the awful graves of the suicide and the hero, showing the distance between him who dies for the sake of living and him who dies for the sake of dying. And it has held up ever since above the European lances the banner of the mystery of chivalry: the Christian courage, which is a disdain of death; not the Chinese courage, which is a disdain of life.

And now I began to find that this duplex passion was the Christian key to ethics everywhere. Everywhere the creed made a moderation out of the still crash of two impetuous emotions. Take, for instance, the matter of modesty, of the balance between mere pride and mere prostration. The average pagan, like the average agnostic, would merely say that he was content with himself, but not insolently self-satisfied, that there were many better and many worse, that his deserts were limited, but he would see that he got them. In short, he would walk with his head in the air; but not necessarily with his nose in the air. This is a manly and rational position, but it is open to the objection we noted against the compromise between optimism and pessimism—the "resignation" of Matthew Arnold. Being a mixture of two things, it is a dilution of two things; neither is present in its full strength or contributes its full colour. This proper pride does not lift the heart like the tongue of trumpets; you cannot go clad in crimson and gold for this. On the other hand, this mild rationalist modesty does not cleanse the soul with fire and make it clear like crystal; it does not (like a strict and searching humility) make a man as a little child, who can sit at the feet of the grass. It does not make him look up and see marvels; for Alice must grow small if she is to be Alice in Wonderland. Thus it loses both the poetry of being proud and the poetry of being humble. Christianity sought by this same strange expedient to save both of them.

It separated the two ideas and then exaggerated them both. In one way Man was to be haughtier than he had ever been before; in another way he was to be humbler than he had ever been before. In so far as I am Man I am the chief of creatures. In so far as I am *a* man I am the chief of sinners. All humility that had meant pessimism, that had meant man taking a vague or mean view of his whole destiny—all that was to go. We were to hear no more the wail of Ecclesiastes that humanity had no preeminence over the brute, or the awful cry of Homer that man was only the saddest of all the beasts of the field. Man was a statue of God walking about the garden. Man had preeminence over all the brutes; man was only sad because he was not a beast, but a broken god. The Greek had spoken of men creeping on the earth, as if clinging to it. Now Man was to tread on the earth as if to subdue it. Christianity thus held a thought of the dignity of man that could only be expressed in crowns rayed like the sun and fans of peacock plumage. Yet at the same time it could hold a thought about the abject smallness of man that could only be expressed in fasting and fantastic submission, in the grey ashes of St. Dominic and the white snows of St. Bernard. When one came to think of *one's self*, there was vista and void enough for any amount of bleak abnegation and bitter truth. There the realistic gentleman could let himself go—as long as he let himself go at himself. There was an open playground for the happy pessimist. Let him say anything against himself short of blaspheming the original aim of his being; let him call himself a fool and even a damned fool (though that is Calvinistic); but he must not say that fools are not worth saving. He must not say that a man, qua man, can be valueless. Here again, in short, Christianity got over the difficulty of combining furious opposites, by keeping them both, and keeping them both furious. The Church was positive on both points. One can hardly think too little of one's self. One can hardly think too much of one's soul.

Take another case: the complicated question of charity, which some highly uncharitable idealists seem to think quite easy. Charity is a paradox, like modesty and courage. Stated baldly, charity certainly means one of two things—pardoning unpardonable acts, or loving unlovable people. But if we ask ourselves (as we did in the case of pride) what a sensible pagan would feel about such a subject, we shall probably be beginning at the bottom of it. A sensible pagan would say that there were some people one could forgive, and some one couldn't: a slave who stole wine could be laughed at; a slave who betrayed his benefactor could be killed, and cursed even after he was killed. In so far as the act was pardonable, the man was pardonable. That again is rational, and even refreshing; but it is a dilution. It leaves no place for a pure horror of injustice, such as that which is a great beauty in the innocent. And it leaves no place for a mere tenderness for men as men, such as is the whole fascination of the charitable. Christianity came in here as before. It came in startlingly with a sword, and clove one thing from another. It divided the crime from the criminal. The criminal we must forgive unto seventy times seven. The crime we must not forgive at all. It was not enough that slaves who stole wine inspired partly anger and partly kindness. We must be much more angry with theft than before, and yet much kinder to thieves than before. There was room for wrath and love to run wild. And the more I considered Christianity, the more I found that while it had established a rule and order, the chief aim of that order was to give room for good things to run wild.

Mental and emotional liberty are not so simple as they look. Really they require almost as careful a balance of laws and conditions as do social and political liberty. The ordinary aesthetic anarchist who sets out to feel everything freely gets knotted at last in a paradox that prevents him feeling at all. He breaks away from home limits to follow poetry. But in ceasing to feel home limits he has ceased to feel the "Odyssey." He is free from national prejudices and outside patriotism. But being outside patriotism he is outside "Henry V." Such a literary man is simply outside all literature: he is more of a prisoner than any bigot. For if there is a wall between you and the world, it makes little difference whether you describe yourself as locked in or as locked out. What we want is not the universality that is outside all normal sentiments; we want the universality that is inside all normal sentiments. It is all the difference between being free from them, as a man is free from a prison, and being free of them as a man is free of a city. I am free from Windsor Castle (that is, I am not forcibly detained there), but I am by no means free of that building. How can man be approximately free of fine emotions, able to swing them in a clear space without breakage or wrong? *This* was the achievement of this

Christian paradox of the parallel passions. Granted the primary dogma of the war between divine and diabolic, the revolt and ruin of the world, their optimism and pessimism, as pure poetry, could be loosened like cataracts.

St. Francis, in praising all good, could be a more shouting optimist than Walt Whitman. St. Jerome, in denouncing all evil, could paint the world blacker than Schopenhauer. Both passions were free because both were kept in their place. The optimist could pour out all the praise he liked on the gay music of the march, the golden trumpets, and the purple banners going into battle. But he must not call the fight needless. The pessimist might draw as darkly as he chose the sickening marches or the sanguine wounds. But he must not call the fight hopeless. So it was with all the other moral problems, with pride, with protest, and with compassion. By defining its main doctrine, the Church not only kept seemingly inconsistent things side by side, but, what was more, allowed them to break out in a sort of artistic violence otherwise possible only to anarchists. Meekness grew more dramatic than madness. Historic Christianity rose into a high and strange coup de théâtre of morality—things that are to virtue what the crimes of Nero are to vice. The spirits of indignation and of charity took terrible and attractive forms, ranging from that monkish fierceness that scourged like a dog the first and greatest of the Plantagenets, to the sublime pity of St. Catherine, who, in the official shambles, kissed the bloody head of the criminal. Poetry could be acted as well as composed. This heroic and monumental manner in ethics has entirely vanished with supernatural religion. They, being humble, could parade themselves; but we are too proud to be prominent. Our ethical teachers write reasonably for prison reform; but we are not likely to see Mr. Cadbury, or any eminent philanthropist, go into Reading Gaol and embrace the strangled corpse before it is cast into the quicklime. Our ethical teachers write mildly against the power of millionaires; but we are not likely to see Mr. Rockefeller, or any modern tyrant, publicly whipped in Westminster Abbey.

Thus, the double charges of the secularists, though throwing nothing but darkness and confusion on themselves, throw a real light on the faith. It *is* true that the historic Church has at once emphasised celibacy and emphasised the family; has at once (if one may put it so) been fiercely for having children and fiercely for not having children. It has kept them side by side like two strong colours, red and white, like the red and white upon the shield of St. George. It has always had a healthy hatred of pink. It hates that combination of two colours which is the feeble expedient of the philosophers. It hates that evolution of black into white which is tantamount to a dirty grey. In fact, the whole theory of the Church on virginity might be symbolized in the statement that white is a colour: not merely the absence of a colour. All that I am urging here can be expressed by saying that Christianity sought in most of these cases to keep two colours coexistent but pure. It is not a mixture like russet or purple; it is rather like a shot silk, for a shot silk is always at right angles, and is in the pattern of the cross.

So it is also, of course, with the contradictory charges of the anti-Christians about submission and slaughter. It *is* true that the Church told some men to fight and others not to fight; and it *is* true that those who fought were like thunderbolts and those who did not fight were like statues. All this simply means that the Church preferred to use its Supermen and to use its Tolstoyans. There must be *some* good in the life of battle, for so many good men have enjoyed being soldiers. There must be *some* good in the idea of nonresistance, for so many good men seem to enjoy being Quakers. All that the Church did (so far as that goes) was to prevent either of these good things from ousting the other. They existed side by side. The Tolstoyans, having all the scruples of monks, simply became monks. The Quakers became a club instead of becoming a sect. Monks said all that Tolstoy says; they poured out lucid lamentations about the cruelty of battles and the vanity of revenge. But the Tolstoyans are not quite right enough to run the whole world; and in the ages of faith they were not allowed to run it. The world did not lose the last charge of Sir James Douglas or the banner of Joan the Maid. And sometimes this pure gentleness and this pure fierceness met and justified their juncture;

the paradox of all the prophets was fulfilled, and, in the soul of St. Louis, the lion lay down with the lamb. But remember that this text is too lightly interpreted. It is constantly assured, especially in our Tolstoyan tendencies, that when the lion lies down with the lamb the lion becomes lamblike. But that is brutal annexation and imperialism on the part of the lamb. That is simply the lamb absorbing the lion instead of the lion eating the lamb. The real problem is—Can the lion lie down with the lamb and still retain his royal ferocity? *That* is the problem the Church attempted; *that* is the miracle she achieved.

This is what I have called guessing the hidden eccentricities of life. This is knowing that a man's heart is to the left and not in the middle. This is knowing not only that the earth is round, but knowing exactly where it is flat. Christian doctrine detected the oddities of life. It not only discovered the law, but it foresaw the exceptions. Those underrate Christianity who say that it discovered mercy; anyone might discover mercy. In fact everyone did. But to discover a plan for being merciful and also severe—*that* was to anticipate a strange need of human nature. For no one wants to be forgiven for a big sin as if it were a little one. Anyone might say that we should be neither quite miserable nor quite happy. But to find out how far one *may* be quite miserable without making it impossible to be quite happy—that was a discovery in psychology. Anyone might say, "Neither swagger nor grovel"; and it would have been a limit. But to say, "Here you can swagger and there you can grovel"—that was an emancipation.

This was the big fact about Christian ethics; the discovery of the new balance. Paganism had been like a pillar of marble, upright because proportioned with symmetry. Christianity was like a huge and ragged and romantic rock, which, though it sways on its pedestal at a touch, yet, because its exaggerated excrescences exactly balance each other, is enthroned there for a thousand years. In a Gothic cathedral the columns were all different, but they were all necessary. Every support seemed an accidental and fantastic support; every buttress was a flying buttress. So in Christendom apparent accidents balanced. Becket wore a hair shirt under his gold and crimson, and there is much to be said for the combination; for Becket got the benefit of the hair shirt while the people in the street got the benefit of the crimson and gold. It is at least better than the manner of the modern millionaire, who has the black and the drab outwardly for others, and the gold next his heart. But the balance was not always in one man's body as in Becket's; the balance was often distributed over the whole body of Christendom. Because a man prayed and fasted on the Northern snows, flowers could be flung at his festival in the Southern cities; and because fanatics drank water on the sands of Syria, men could still drink cider in the orchards of England. This is what makes Christendom at once so much more perplexing and so much more interesting than the Pagan empire; just as Amiens Cathedral is not better but more interesting than the Parthenon. If anyone wants a modern proof of all this, let him consider the curious fact that, under Christianity, Europe (while remaining a unity) has broken up into individual nations. Patriotism is a perfect example of this deliberate balancing of one emphasis against another emphasis. The instinct of the Pagan empire would have said, "You shall all be Roman citizens, and grow alike; let the German grow less slow and reverent; the Frenchmen less experimental and swift." But the instinct of Christian Europe says, "Let the German remain slow and reverent, that the Frenchman may the more safely be swift and experimental. We will make an equipoise out of these excesses. The absurdity called Germany shall correct the insanity called France."

Last and most important, it is exactly this which explains what is so inexplicable to all the modern critics of the history of Christianity. I mean the monstrous wars about small points of theology, the earthquakes of emotion about a gesture or a word. It was only a matter of an inch; but an inch is everything when you are balancing. The Church could not afford to swerve a hair's breadth on some things if she was to continue her great and daring experiment of the irregular equilibrium. Once let one idea become less powerful and some other idea would become too powerful. It was no flock of sheep the Christian shepherd was leading, but a herd of bulls and tigers, of terrible ideals and devouring doctrines, each one of them strong enough to turn to a false religion and lay waste the world. Remember that the Church went in specifically for dangerous ideas; she was a lion tamer. The idea of birth through a Holy Spirit, of the death of a divine being, of the forgiveness of sins, or the fulfilment of prophecies, are ideas which, anyone can see, need but a touch to turn them into something blasphemous or ferocious. The smallest link was let drop by the artificers of the Mediterranean, and the lion of ancestral pessimism burst his chain in the forgotten forests of the north. Of these theological equalisations I have to speak afterwards. Here it is enough to notice that if some small mistake were made in doctrine, huge blunders might be made in human happiness. A sentence phrased wrong about the nature of symbolism would have broken all the best statues in Europe. A slip in the definitions might stop all the dances; might wither all the Christmas trees or break all the Easter eggs. Doctrines had to be defined within strict limits, even in order that man might enjoy general human liberties. The Church had to be careful, if only that the world might be careless.

This is the thrilling romance of Orthodoxy. People have fallen into a foolish habit of speaking of orthodoxy as something heavy, humdrum, and safe. There never was anything so perilous or so exciting as orthodoxy. It was sanity: and to be sane is more dramatic than to be mad. It was the equilibrium of a man behind madly rushing horses, seeming to stoop this way and to sway that, yet in every attitude having the grace of statuary and the accuracy of arithmetic. The Church in its early days went fierce and fast with any warhorse; yet it is utterly unhistoric to say that she merely went mad along one idea, like a vulgar fanaticism. She swerved to left and right, so as exactly to avoid enormous obstacles. She left on one hand the huge bulk of Arianism, buttressed by all the worldly powers to make Christianity too worldly. The next instant she was swerving to avoid an orientalism, which would have made it too unworldly. The orthodox Church never took the tame course or accepted the conventions; the orthodox Church was never respectable. It would have been easier to have accepted the earthly power of the Arians. It would have been easy, in the Calvinistic seventeenth century, to fall into the bottomless pit of predestination. It is easy to be a madman: it is easy to be a heretic. It is always easy to let the age have its head; the difficult thing is to keep one's own. It is always easy to be a modernist; as it is easy to be a snob. To have fallen into any of those open traps of error and exaggeration which fashion after fashion and sect after sect set along the historic path of Christendom—that would indeed have been simple. It is always simple to fall; there are an infinity of angles at which one falls, only one at which one stands. To have fallen into any one of the fads from Gnosticism to Christian Science would indeed have been obvious and tame. But to have avoided them all has been one whirling adventure; and in my vision the heavenly chariot flies thundering through the ages, the dull heresies sprawling and prostrate, the wild truth reeling but erect.

SCIENCE AND THE SAVAGES

A permanent disadvantage of the study of folklore and kindred subjects is that the man of science can hardly be in the nature of things very frequently a man of the world. He is a student of nature; he is scarcely ever a student of human nature. And even where this difficulty is overcome, and he is in some sense a student of human nature, this is only a very faint beginning of the painful progress towards being human. For the study of primitive race and religion stands apart in one important respect from all, or nearly all, the ordinary scientific studies. A man can understand astronomy only by being an astronomer; he can understand entomology only by being an entomologist (or, perhaps, an insect); but he can understand a great deal of anthropology merely by being a man. He is himself the animal which he studies. Hence arises the fact which strikes the eye everywhere in the records of ethnology and folklore—the fact that the same frigid and detached spirit which leads to success in the study of astronomy or botany leads to disaster in the study of mythology or human origins. It is necessary to cease to be a man in order to do justice to a microbe; it is not necessary to cease to be a man in order to do justice to men. That same suppression of sympathies, that same waving away of intuitions or guesswork which make a man preternaturally clever in dealing with the stomach of a spider, will make him preternaturally stupid in dealing with the heart of man. He is making himself inhuman in order to understand humanity. An ignorance of the other world is boasted by many men of science; but in this matter their defect arises, not from ignorance of the other world, but from ignorance of this world. For the secrets about which anthropologists concern themselves can be best learnt, not from books or voyages, but from the ordinary commerce of man with man. The secret of why some savage tribe worships monkeys or the moon is not to be found even by travelling among those savages and taking down their answers in a notebook, although the cleverest man may pursue this course. The answer to the riddle is in England; it is in London; nay, it is in his own heart. When a man has discovered why men in Bond Street wear black hats he will at the same moment have discovered why men in Timbuktu wear red feathers. The mystery in the heart of some savage war-dance should not be studied in books of scientific travel; it should be studied at a subscription ball. If a man desires to find out the origins of religions, let him not go to the Sandwich Islands; let him go to church. If a man wishes to know the origin of human society, to know what society, philosophically speaking, really is, let him not go into the British Museum; let him go into society.

This total misunderstanding of the real nature of ceremonial gives rise to the most awkward and dehumanized versions of the conduct of men in rude lands or ages. The man of science, not realizing that ceremonial is essentially a thing which is done without a reason, has to find a reason for every sort of ceremonial, and, as might be supposed, the reason is generally a very absurd one— absurd because it originates not in the simple mind of the barbarian, but in the sophisticated mind of the professor. The teamed man will say, for instance, "The natives of Mumbojumbo Land believe that the dead man can eat and will require food upon his journey to the other world. This is attested by the fact that they place food in the grave, and that any family not complying with this rite is the object of the anger of the priests and the tribe." To anyone acquainted with humanity this way of talking is topsy-turvy. It is like saying, "The English in the twentieth century believed that a dead man could smell. This is attested by the fact that they always covered his grave with lilies, violets, or other flowers. Some priestly and tribal terrors were evidently attached to the neglect of this action, as we have records of several old ladies who were very much disturbed in mind because their wreaths had not arrived in time for the funeral." It may be of course that savages put food with a dead man because they think that a dead man can eat, or weapons with a dead man because they think that a dead man can fight. But personally I do not believe that they think anything of the kind. I believe they put food or weapons on the dead for the same reason that we put flowers, because it is an exceedingly natural and obvious thing to do. We do not understand, it is true, the emotion which makes us think it obvious and natural; but that is because, like all the important emotions of human existence it is essentially irrational. We do not understand the savage for the same reason that the savage does not understand himself. And the savage does not understand himself for the same reason that we do not understand ourselves either.

The obvious truth is that the moment any matter has passed through the human mind it is finally and forever spoilt for all purposes of science. It has become a thing incurably mysterious and infinite; this mortal has put on immortality. Even what we call our material desires are spiritual, because they are human. Science can analyse a pork-chop, and say how much of it is phosphorus and how much is protein; but science cannot analyse any man's wish for a pork-chop, and say how much of it is hunger, how much custom, how much nervous fancy, how much a haunting love of the beautiful. The man's desire for the pork-chop remains literally as mystical and ethereal as his desire for heaven. All attempts, therefore, at a science of any human things, at a science of history, a science of folklore, a science of sociology, are by their nature not merely hopeless, but crazy. You can no more be certain in economic history that a man's desire for money was merely a desire for money than you can be certain in hagiology that a saint's desire for God was merely a desire for God. And this kind of vagueness in the primary phenomena of the study is an absolutely final blow to anything in the nature of a science. Men can construct a science with very few instruments, or with very plain instruments; but no one on earth could construct a science with unreliable instruments. A man might work out the whole of mathematics with a handful of pebbles, but not with a handful of clay which was always falling apart into new fragments, and falling together into new combinations. A man might measure heaven and earth with a reed, but not with a growing reed.

As one of the enormous follies of folklore, let us take the case of the transmigration of stories, and the alleged unity of their source. Story after story the scientific mythologists have cut out of its place in history, and pinned side by side with similar stories in their museum of fables. The process is industrious, it is fascinating, and the whole of it rests on one of the plainest fallacies in the world. That a story has been told all over the place at some time or other, not only does not prove that it never really happened; it does not even faintly indicate or make slightly more probable that it never happened. That a large number of fishermen have falsely asserted that they have caught a pike two feet long, does not in the least affect the question of whether anyone ever really did so. That numberless journalists announce a Franco-German war merely for money is no evidence one way or the other upon the dark question of whether such a war ever occurred. Doubtless in a few hundred years the innumerable Franco-German wars that did not happen will have cleared the scientific mind of any belief in the legendary war of '70 which did. But that will be because if folklore students remain at all, their nature will be unchanged; and their services to folklore will be still as they are at present, greater than they know. For in truth these men do something far more godlike than studying legends; they create them.

There are two kinds of stories which the scientists say cannot be true, because everybody tells them. The first class consists of the stories which are told everywhere, because they are somewhat odd or clever; there is nothing in the world to prevent their having happened to somebody as an adventure any more than there is anything to prevent their having occurred, as they certainly did occur, to some-body as an idea. But they are not likely to have happened to many people. The second class of their "myths" consist of the stories that are told everywhere for the simple reason that they happen every-where. Of the first class, for instance, we might take such an example as the story of William Tell, now generally ranked among legends upon the sole ground that it is found in the tales of other peoples. Now, it is obvious that this was told everywhere because whether true or fictitious it is what is called "a good story;" it is odd, exciting, and it has a climax. But to suggest that some such eccentric incident can never have happened in the whole history of archery, or that it did not happen to any particular person of whom it is told, is stark impu-dence. The idea of shooting at a mark attached to some valuable or beloved person is an idea doubtless that might easily have occurred to any inventive poet. But it is also an idea that might easily occur to any boastful archer. It might be one of the fantastic caprices of some storyteller. It might equally well be one of the fantastic caprices of some tyrant. It might occur first in real life and afterwards occur in legends. Or it might just as well occur first in legends and afterwards occur in real life. If no apple has ever been shot off a boy's head from the beginning of the world, it may be done tomorrow morning, and by somebody who has never heard of William Tell.

This type of tale, indeed, may be pretty fairly paralleled with the ordinary anecdote terminating in a repartee or an Irish bull. Such a retort as the famous "*Je ne vois pas la necessité*" we have all seen attributed to Talleyrand, to Voltaire, to Henri Quatre, to an anony-mous judge, and so on. But this variety does not in any way make it more likely that the thing was never said at all. It is highly likely that it was really said by somebody unknown. It is highly likely that it was really said by Talleyrand. In any case, it is not any more difficult to believe that the mot might have occurred to a man in conversation than to a man writing memoirs. It might have occurred to any of the men I have mentioned. But there is this point of distinction about it, that it is not likely to have occurred to all of them. And this is where the first class of so-called myth differs from the second to which I have previously referred. For there is a second class of incident found to be common to the stories of five or six heroes, say to Sigurd, to Hercules, to Rustem, to the Cid, and so on. And the peculiarity of this myth is that not only is it highly reasonable to imagine that it really happened to one hero, but it is highly reasonable to imagine that it really happened to all of them. Such a story, for instance, is that of a great man having his strength swayed or thwarted by the mysterious weakness of a woman. The anecdotal story, the story of William Tell, is as I have said, popular, because it is peculiar. But this kind of story, the story of Samson and Delilah, of Arthur and Guinevere, is obviously popular because it is not peculiar. It is popular as good, quiet fiction is popular, because it tells the truth about people. If the ruin of Samson by a woman, and the ruin of Hercules by a woman, have a common legendary origin, it is gratifying to know that we can also explain, as a fable, the ruin of Nelson by a woman and the ruin of Parnell by a woman. And, indeed, I have no doubt whatever that, some centuries hence, the students of folklore will refuse altogether to believe that Elizabeth Barrett eloped with Robert Browning, and will prove their point up to the hilt by the unquestionable fact that the whole fiction of the period was full of such elopements from end to end.

Possibly the most pathetic of all the delusions of the modern students of primitive belief is the notion they have about the thing they call anthropomorphism. They believe that primitive men attributed phenomena to a god in human form in order to explain them, because his mind in its sullen limitation could not reach any further than his own clownish existence. The thunder was called the voice of a man, the lightning the eyes of a man, because by this explanation they were made more reasonable and comfortable. The final cure for all this kind of philosophy is to walk down a lane at night. Anyone who does so will discover very quickly that men pictured something semi-human at the back of all things, not because such a thought was natural, but because it was supernatural; not because it made things more comprehensible, but because it made them a hundred times more incomprehensible and mysterious. For a man walking down a lane at night can see the conspicuous fact that as long as nature keeps to her own course, she has no power with us at all. As long as a tree is a tree, it is a top-heavy monster with a hundred arms, a thousand tongues, and only one leg. But so long as a tree is a tree, it does not frighten us at all. It begins to be something alien, to be something strange, only when it looks like ourselves. When a tree really looks like a man our knees knock under us. And when the whole universe looks like a man we fall on our faces.

ON THE NEGATIVE SPIRIT

Much has been said, and said truly, of the monkish morbidity, of the hysteria which as often gone with the visions of hermits or nuns. But let us never forget that this visionary religion is, in one sense, necessarily more wholesome than our modern and reasonable morality. It is more wholesome for this reason, that it can contemplate the idea of success or triumph in the hopeless fight towards the ethical ideal, in what Stevenson called, with his usual startling felicity, "the lost fight of virtue." A modern morality, on the other hand, can only point with absolute conviction to the horrors that follow breaches of law; its only certainty is a certainty of ill. It can only point to imperfection. It has no perfection to point to. But the monk meditating upon Christ or Buddha has in his mind an image of perfect health, a thing of clear colours and clean air. He may contemplate this ideal wholeness and happiness far more than he ought; he may contemplate it to the neglect of exclusion of essential things; he may contemplate it until he has become a dreamer or a driveller; but still it is wholeness and happiness that he is contemplating. He may even go mad; but he is going mad for the love of sanity. But the modern student of ethics, even if he remains sane, remains sane from an insane dread of insanity.

The anchorite rolling on the stones in a frenzy of submission is a healthier person fundamentally than many a sober man in a silk hat who is walking down Cheapside. For many such are good only through a withering knowledge of evil. I am not at this moment claiming for the devotee anything more than this primary advantage, that though he may be making himself personally weak and miserable, he is still fixing his thoughts largely on gigantic strength and happiness, on a strength that has no limits, and a happiness that has no end. Doubtless there are other objections which can be urged without unreason against the influence of gods and visions in morality, whether in the cell or street. But this advantage the mystic morality must always have—it is always jollier. A young man may keep himself from vice by continually thinking of disease. He may keep himself from it also by continually thinking of the Virgin Mary. There may be question about which method is the more reasonable, or even about which is the more efficient. But surely there can be no question about which is the more wholesome.

I remember a pamphlet by that able and sincere secularist, Mr. G. W. Foote, which contained a phrase sharply symbolizing and dividing these two methods. The pamphlet was called *Beer and Bible*, those two very noble things, all the nobler for a conjunction which Mr. Foote, in his stern old Puritan way, seemed to think sardonic, but which I confess to thinking appropriate and charming. I have not the work by me, but I remember that Mr. Foote dismissed very contemptuously any attempts to deal with the problem of strong drink by religious offices or intercessions, and said that a picture of a drunkard's liver would be more efficacious in the matter of temperance than any prayer or praise. In that picturesque expression, it seems to me, is perfectly embodied the incurable morbidity of modern ethics. In that temple the lights are low, the crowds kneel, the solemn anthems are uplifted. But that upon the altar to which all men kneel is no longer the perfect flesh, the body and substance of the perfect man; it is still flesh, but it is diseased. It is the drunkard's liver of the New Testament that is marred for us, which we take in remembrance of him.

Now, it is this great gap in modern ethics, the absence of vivid pictures of purity and spiritual triumph, which lies at the back of the real objection felt by so many sane men to the realistic literature of the nineteenth century. If any ordinary man ever said that he was horrified by the subjects discussed in Ibsen or Maupassant, or by the plain language in which they are spoken of, that ordinary man was lying. The average conversation of average men throughout the whole of modern civilization in every class or trade is such as Zola would never dream of printing. Nor is the habit of writing thus of these things a new habit. On the contrary, it is the Victorian prudery and silence which is new still, though it is already dying. The tradition of calling a spade a spade starts very early in our literature and comes down very late. But the truth is that the ordinary honest man, whatever vague account he may have given of his feelings, was not either disgusted or even annoyed at the candour of the moderns. What disgusted him, and very justly, was not the presence of a clear realism, but the absence of a clear idealism. Strong and genuine religious sentiment has never had any objection to realism; on the contrary, religion was the realistic thing, the brutal thing, the thing that called names. This is the great difference between some recent developments of Nonconformity and the great Puritanism of the seventeenth century. It was the whole point of the Puritans that they cared nothing for decency. Modern Nonconformist newspapers distinguish themselves by suppressing precisely those nouns and adjectives which the founders of Nonconformity distinguished themselves by flinging at kings and queens. But if it was a chief claim of religion that it spoke plainly about evil, it was the chief claim of all that it spoke plainly about good. The thing which is resented, and, as I think, rightly resented, in that great modern literature of which Ibsen is typical, is that while the eye that can perceive what are the wrong things increases in an uncanny and devouring clarity, the eye which sees what things are right is growing mistier and mistier every moment, till it goes almost blind with doubt. If we compare, let us say, the morality of the *Divine Comedy* with the morality of Ibsen's *Ghosts*, we shall see all that modern ethics have really done. No one, I imagine, will accuse the author of the *Inferno* of an Early Victorian prudishness or a Podsnapian optimism. But Dante describes three moral instruments—Heaven, Purgatory, and Hell, the vision of perfection, the vision of improvement, and the vision of failure. Ibsen has only one—Hell. It is often said, and with perfect truth, that no one could read a play like *Ghosts* and remain indifferent to the necessity of an ethical self-command. That is quite true, and the same is to be said of the most monstrous and material descriptions of the eternal fire. It is quite certain the realists like Zola do in one sense promote morality—they promote it in the sense in which the hangman promotes it, in the sense in which the devil promotes it. But they only affect that small minority which will accept any virtue of courage. Most healthy people dismiss these moral dangers as they dismiss the possibility of bombs or microbes. Modern realists are indeed Terrorists, like the dynamiters; and they fail just as much in their effort to create a thrill. Both realists and dynamiters are well-meaning people engaged in the task, so obviously ultimately hopeless, of using science to promote morality.

I do not wish the reader to confuse me for a moment with those vague persons who imagine that Ibsen is what they call a pessimist. There are plenty of wholesome people in Ibsen, plenty of good people, plenty of happy people, plenty of examples of men acting wisely and things ending well. That is not my meaning. My meaning is that Ibsen has throughout, and does not disguise, a certain vagueness and a changing attitude as well as a doubting attitude towards what is really wisdom and virtue in this life—a vagueness which contrasts very remarkably with the decisiveness with which he pounces on something which he perceives to be a root of evil, some convention, some deception, some ignorance. We know that the hero of *Ghosts* is mad, and we know why he is mad. We do also know that Dr. Stockman is sane; but we do not know why he is sane. Ibsen does not profess to know how virtue and happiness are brought about, in the sense that he professes to know how our modern sexual tragedies are brought about. Falsehood works ruin in *The Pillars of Society*, but truth works equal ruin in *The Wild Duck*. There are no cardinal virtues of Ibsenism. There is no ideal man of Ibsen. All this is not only admitted, but vaunted in the most valuable and thoughtful of all the eulogies upon Ibsen, Mr. Bernard Shaw's "Quintessence of Ibsenism." Mr. Shaw sums up Ibsen's teaching in the phrase, "The golden rule is that there is no golden rule." In his eyes this absence of an enduring and positive ideal, this absence of a permanent key to virtue, is the one great Ibsen merit. I am not discussing now with any fullness whether this is so or not. All I venture to point out, with an increased firmness, is that this omission, good or bad, does leave us face to face with the problem of a human consciousness filled with very definite images of evil, and with no definite image of good. To us light must be henceforward the dark thing—the thing of which we cannot speak. To us, as to Milton's devils in Pandemonium, it is darkness that is visible. The human race, according to religion, fell once, and in falling gained knowledge of good and of evil. Now we have fallen a second time, and only the knowledge of evil remains to us.

A great silent collapse, an enormous unspoken disappointment, has in our time fallen on our Northern civilization. All previous ages have sweated and been crucified in an attempt to realize what is really the right life, what was really the good man. A definite part of the modern world has come beyond question to the conclusion that there is no answer to these questions, that the most that we can do is to set up a few notice-boards at places of obvious danger, to warn men, for instance, against drinking themselves to death, or ignoring the mere existence of their neighbours. Ibsen is the first to return from the baffled hunt to bring us the tidings of great failure.

Every one of the popular modern phrases and ideals is a dodge in order to shirk the problem of what is good. We are fond of talking about "liberty"; that, as we talk of it, is a dodge to avoid discussing what is good. We are fond of talking about "progress"; that is a dodge to avoid discussing what is good. We are fond of talking about "education"; that is a dodge to avoid discussing what is good. The modern man says, "Let us leave all these arbitrary standards and embrace liberty." This is, logically rendered, "Let us not decide what is good, but let it be considered good not to decide it." He says, "Away with your old moral formulae; I am for progress." This, logically stated, means, "Let us not settle what is good; but let us settle whether we are getting more of it." He says, "Neither in religion nor morality, my friend, lie the hopes of the race, but in education." This, clearly expressed, means, "We cannot decide what is good, but let us give it to our children."

Mr. H. G. Wells, that exceedingly clear-sighted man, has pointed out in a recent work that this has happened in connection with economic questions. The old economists, he says, made generalizations, and they were (in Mr. Wells's view) mostly wrong. But the new economists, he says, seem to have lost the power of making any generalizations at all. And they cover this incapacity with a general claim to be, in specific cases, regarded as "experts," a claim "proper enough in a hairdresser or a fashionable physician, but indecent in a philosopher or a man of science." But in spite of the refreshing rationality with which Mr. Wells has indicated this, it must also be said that he himself has fallen into the same enormous modern error. In the opening pages of that excellent book *Mankind in the Making*, he dismisses the ideals of art, religion, abstract morality, and the rest, and says that he is going to consider men in their chief function, the function of parenthood. He is going to discuss life as a "tissue of births." He is not going to ask what will produce satisfactory saints or satisfactory heroes, but what will produce satisfactory fathers and mothers. The whole is set forward so sensibly that it is a few moments at least before the reader realises that it is another example of unconscious shirking. What is the good of begetting a man until we have settled what is the good of being a man? You are merely handing on to him a problem you dare not settle yourself. It is as if a man were asked, "What is the use of a hammer?" and answered, "To make hammers"; and when asked, "And of those hammers, what is the use?" answered, "To make hammers again." Just as such a man would be perpetually putting off the question of the ultimate use of carpentry, so Mr. Wells and all the rest of us are by these phrases successfully putting off the question of the ultimate value of the human life.

The case of the general talk of "progress" is, indeed, an extreme one. As enunciated today, "progress" is simply a comparative of which we have not settled the superlative. We meet every ideal of religion, patriotism, beauty, or brute pleasure with the alternative ideal of progress—that is to say, we meet every proposal of getting something that we know about, with an alternative proposal of getting a great deal more of nobody knows what. Progress, properly understood, has, indeed, a most dignified and legitimate meaning. But as used in opposition to precise moral ideals, it is ludicrous. So far from it being the truth that the ideal of progress is to be set against that of ethical or religious finality, the reverse is the truth. Nobody has any business to use the word "progress" unless he has a definite creed and a cast-iron code of morals. Nobody can be progressive without being doctrinal; I might almost say that nobody can be progressive without being infallible—at any rate, without believing in some infallibility. For progress by its very name indicates a direction; and the moment we are in the least doubtful about the direction, we become in the same degree doubtful about the progress. Never perhaps since the beginning of the world has there been an age that had less right to use the word "progress" than we. In the Catholic twelfth century, in the philosophic eighteenth century, the direction may have been a good or a bad one, men may have differed more or less about how far they went, and in what direction, but about the direction they did in the main agree, and consequently they had the genuine sensation of progress. But it is precisely about the direction that we disagree. Whether the future excellence lies in more law or less law, in more liberty or less liberty; whether property will be finally concentrated or finally cut up; whether sexual passion will reach its sanest in an almost virgin intellectualism or in a full animal freedom; whether we should love everybody with Tolstoy, or spare nobody with Nietzsche;—these are the things about which we are actually fighting most. It is not merely true that the age which has settled least what is progress is this "progressive" age. It is, moreover, true that the people who have settled least what is progress are the most "progressive" people in it. The ordinary mass, the men who have never troubled about progress, might be trusted perhaps to progress. The particular individuals who talk about progress would certainly fly to the four winds of heaven when the pistol-shot started the race. I do not, therefore, say that the word "progress" is unmeaning; I say it is unmeaning without the previous definition of a moral doctrine, and that it can only be applied to groups of persons who hold that doctrine in common. Progress is not an illegitimate word, but it is logically evident that it is illegitimate for us. It is a sacred word, a word which could only rightly be used by rigid believers and in the ages of faith.

THE ESCAPE FROM PAGANISM

The modern missionary, with his palm-leaf hat and his umbrella, has become rather a figure of fun. He is chaffed among men of the world for the ease with which he can be eaten by cannibals and the narrow bigotry which makes him regard the cannibal culture as lower than his own. Perhaps the best part of the joke is that the men of the world do not see that the joke is against themselves. It is rather ridiculous to ask a man just about to be boiled in a pot and eaten, at a purely religious feast, why he does not regard all religions as equally friendly and fraternal. But there is a more subtle criticism uttered against the more old-fashioned missionary; to the effect that he generalises too broadly about the heathen and pays too little attention to the difference between Mahomet and Mumbo-Jumbo. There was probably truth in this complaint, especially in the past; but it is my main contention here that the exaggeration is all the other way at present. It is the temptation of the professors to treat mythologies too much as theologies; as things thoroughly thought out are seriously held. It is the temptation of the intellectuals to take much too seriously the fine shades of various schools in the rather irresponsible metaphysics of Asia.

Above all it is their temptation to miss the real truth implied in the idea of *Aquinas contra Gentiles* or *Athanasius contra mundum*.

If the missionary says, in fact, that he is exceptional in being a Christian, and that the rest of the races and religions can be collectively classified as heathen, he is perfectly right. He may say it in quite the wrong spirit, in which case he is spiritually wrong. But in the cold light of philosophy and history, he is intellectually right. He may not be right minded, but he is right. He may not even have a right to be right, but he is right. The outer world to which he brings his creed really is some thing subject to certain generalisations covering all its varieties, and is not merely a variety of similar creeds. Perhaps it is in any case too much of a temptation to pride or hypocrisy to call it heathenry. Perhaps it could be better simply to call it humanity. But there are certain broad characteristics of what we call humanity while it remains in what we call heathenry. They are not necessarily bad characteristics; some of them are worthy of the respect of Christendom; some of them have been absorbed and transfigured in the substance of Christendom. But they existed before Christendom and they still exist outside Christendom, as certainly as the sea existed before a boat and all round a boat; and they have as strong and as universal and as unmistakable a savour as the sea.

For instance, all real scholars who have studied the Greek and Roman culture say one thing about it. They agree that in the ancient world religion was one thing and philosophy quite another. There was very little effort to rationalise and at the same time to realise a real belief in the gods. There was very little pretense of any such real belief among the philosophers. But neither had the passion or perhaps the power to persecute the others save in particular and peculiar cases; and neither the philosopher in his school nor the priest in his temple seems ever to have seriously contemplated his own concept as covering the world. A priest sacrificing to Artemis in Calydon did not seem to think that people would some day sacrifice to her instead of to Isis beyond the sea; a sage following the vegetarian rule of the Neo-Pythagoreans did not seem to think it would universally prevail and exclude the methods of Epictetus or Epicurus.

We may call this liberality if we like; I am not dealing with an argument but describing an atmosphere. All this, I say, is admitted by all scholars; but what neither the learned nor the unlearned have fully realised, perhaps, is that this description is really an exact description of all non-Christian civilisation today; and especially of the great civilisations of the East. Eastern paganism really is much more all of a piece, just as ancient paganism was much more all of a piece, than the modern critics admit. It is a many-coloured Persian Carpet as the other was a varied and tessellated Roman pavement; but the one real crack right across that pavement came from the earthquake of the Crucifixion.

The modern European seeking his religion in Asia is reading his religion into Asia. Religion there is something different; it is both more and less. He is like a man mapping out the sea as land; marking waves as mountains; not understanding the nature of its peculiar permanence. It is perfectly true that Asia has its own dignity and poetry and high civilisation. But it is not in the least true that Asia has its own definite dominions of moral government, where all loyalty is conceived in terms of morality; as when we say that Ireland is Catholic or that New England was Puritan. The map is not marked out in religions, in our sense of churches. The state of mind is far more subtle, more relative, more secretive, more varied and changing, like the colours of the snake. The Moslem is the nearest approach to a militant Christian; and that is precisely because he is a much nearer approach to an envoy from western civilisation. The Moslem in the heart of Asia almost stands for the soul of Europe. And as he stands between them and Europe in the matter of space so he stands between them and Christianity in the matter of time. In that sense the Moslems in Asia are merely like the Nestorians in Asia. Islam, historically speaking, is the greatest of the Eastern heresies. It owed something to the quite isolated and unique individuality of Israel; but it owed more to Byzantium and the theological enthusiasm of Christendom. It owed something even to the Crusades. It owed nothing whatever to Asia. It owed nothing to the atmosphere of the ancient and traditional world of Asia, with its immemorial etiquette and its bottomless or bewildering philosophies. All that ancient and actual Asia felt the entrance of Islam as something foreign and western and warlike, piercing it like a spear.

Even where we might trace in dotted lines the domains of Asiatic religions, we should probably be reading into them something dogmatic and ethical belonging to our own religion. It is as if a European ignorant of the American atmosphere were to suppose that each 'state' was a separate sovereign state as patriotic as France or Poland; or that when a Yankee referred fondly to his 'home town' he meant he had no other nation, like a citizen of ancient Athens or Rome. As he would be reading a particular sort of loyalty into America, so we are reading a particular sort of loyalty into Asia. There are loyalties of other kinds; but not what men in the West mean by being a believer, by trying to be a Christian, by being a good Protestant or a practising Catholic. In the intellectual world it means something far more vague and varied by doubts and speculations. In the moral world it means something far more loose and drifting. A professor of Persian at one of our great universities, so passionate a partisan of the East as practically to profess a contempt for the West, said to a friend of mine: 'You will never understand oriental religions, because you always conceive religion as connected with ethics. This kind has really nothing to do with ethics.' We have most of us known some Masters of the Higher Wisdom, some Pilgrims upon the Path to Power, some eastern esoteric saints and seers, who had really nothing to do with ethics. Something different, something detached and irresponsible, tinges the moral atmosphere of Asia and touches even that of Islam. It was very realistically caught in the atmosphere of Hassan; and a very horrible atmosphere too. It is even more vivid in such glimpses as we get of the genuine and ancient cults of Asia. Deeper than the depths of metaphysics, far down in the abysses of mystical meditations under all that solemn universe of spiritual things, is a secret, an intangible and a terrible levity. It does not really very much matter what one does. Either because they do not believe in a devil, or because they do believe in a destiny, or because experience here is everything and eternal life something totally different, but for some reason they are totally different. I have read somewhere that there were three great friends famous in medieval Persia for their unity of mind. One became the responsible and respected Vizier of the Great King; the second was the poet Omar, pessimist and epicurean, drinking wine in mockery of Mahomet; the third was the Old Man of the Mountain who maddened his people with hashish that they might murder other people with daggers. It does not really much matter what one does.

The Sultan in Hassan would have understood all those three men; indeed he was all those three men. But this sort of universalist cannot have what we call a character; it is what we call a chaos. He cannot choose; he cannot fight; he cannot repent; he cannot hope. He is not in the same sense creating something; for creation means rejection. He is not, in our religious phrase, making his soul. For our doctrine of salvation does really mean a labour like that of a man trying to make a statue beautiful; a victory with wings. For that there must be a final choice, for a man cannot make statues without rejecting stone. And there really is this ultimate unmorality behind the metaphysics of Asia. And the reason is that there has been nothing through all those unthinkable ages to bring the human mind sharply to the point; to tell it that the time has come to choose. The mind has lived too much in eternity. The soul has been too immortal, in the special sense that it ignores the idea of mortal sin. It has had too much of eternity, in the sense that it has not had enough of the hour of death and the day of judgement. It is not crucial enough; in the literal sense that it has not had enough of the cross. That is what we mean when we say that Asia is very old. But strictly speaking Europe is quite as old as Asia; indeed in a sense any place is as old as any other place. What we mean is that Europe has not merely gone on growing older. It has been born again.

Asia is all humanity; as it has worked out its human doom. Asia, in its vast territory, in its varied populations, in its heights of past achievement and its depths of dark speculation, is itself a world; and represents something of what we mean when we speak of the world. It is a cosmos rather than a continent. It is the world as man has made it; and contains many of the most wonderful things that man has made. Therefore Asia stands as the one representative of paganism and the one rival to Christendom. But everywhere else where we get glimpses of that mortal destiny, they suggest stages in the same story. Where Asia trails away into the southern archipelagoes of the savages, or where a darkness full of nameless shapes dwells in the heart of Africa, or where the last survivors of lost races linger in the cold volcano of prehistoric America, it is all the same story; sometimes perhaps later chapters of the same story. It is men entangled in the forest of their own mythology; it is men drowned in the sea of their own metaphysics. Polytheists have grown weary of the wildest of fictions. Monotheists have grown weary of the most wonderful of truths. Diabolists here and there have such a hatred of heaven and earth that they have tried to take refuge in hell. It is the Fall of Man; and it is exactly that fall that was being felt by our own fathers at the first moment of the Roman decline. We also were going down that side road; down that easy slope; following the magnificent procession of the high civilisations of the world.

If the Church had not entered the world then, it seems probable that Europe would be now very much what Asia is now. Something may be allowed for a real difference of race and environment, visible in the ancient as in the modern world. But after all we talk about the changeless East very largely because it has not suffered the great change. Paganism in its last phase showed considerable signs of becoming equally changeless. This would not mean that new schools or sects of philosophy would not arise; as new schools did arise in Antiquity and do arise in Asia. It does not mean that there would be no real mystics or visionaries; as there were mystics in Antiquity and are mystics in Asia. It does not mean that there would be no social codes, as there were codes in Antiquity and are codes in Asia. It does not mean that there could not be good men or happy lives, for God has given all men a conscience and conscience can give all men a kind of peace. But it does mean that the tone and proportion of all these things, and especially the proportion of good and evil things, would be in the unchanged West what they are in the changeless

East. And nobody who looks at that changeless East honestly, and with a real sympathy, can believe that there is anything there remotely resembling the challenge and revolution of the Faith.

In short, if classic paganism had lingered until now, a number of things might well have lingered with it; and they would look very like what we call the religions of the East. There would still be Pythagoreans teaching reincarnation, as there are still Hindus teaching reincarnation. There would still be Stoics making a religion out of reason and virtue, as there are still Confucians making a religion out of reason and virtue. There would still be Neo-Platonists studying transcendental truths, the meaning of which was mysterious to other people and disputed even amongst themselves; as the Buddhists still study a transcendentalism mysterious to others and disputed among themselves. There would still be intelligent Apollonians apparently worshipping the sun-god but explaining that they were worshipping the divine principle; just as there are still intelligent Parsees apparently worshipping the sun but explaining that they are worshipping the deity. There would still be wild Dionysians dancing on the mountain as there are still wild Dervishes dancing in the desert. There would still be crowds of people attending the popular feasts of the gods, in pagan Europe as in pagan Asia. There would still be crowds of gods, local and other, for them to worship. And there would still be a great many more people who worshipped them than people who believed in them. Finally there would still be a very large number of people who did worship gods and did believe in gods; and who believed in gods and worshipped gods simply because they were demons. There would still be Levantines secretly sacrificing to Moloch as there are still Thugs secretly sacrificing to Kalee. There would still be a great deal of magic; and a great deal of it would be black magic. There would still be a considerable admiration of Seneca and a considerable imitation of Nero; just as the exalted epigrams of Confucius could coexist with the tortures of China. And over all that tangled forest of traditions growing wild or withering would brood the broad silence of a singular and even nameless mood; but the nearest name of it is nothing. All these things, good and bad, would have an indescribable air of being too old to die.

None of these things occupying Europe in the absence of Christendom would bear the least likeness to Christendom. Since the Pythagorean Metempsychosis would still be there, we might call it the Pythagorean religion as we talk about the Buddhist religion. As the noble maxims of Socrates would still be there, we might call it the Socratic religion as we talk about the Confucian religion. As the popular holiday was still marked by a mythological hymn to Adonis, we might call it the religion of Adonis as we talk about the religion of Juggernaut. As literature would still be based on the Greek mythology, we might call that mythology a religion, as we call the Hindu mythology a religion. We might say that there were so many thousands or millions of people belonging to that religion, in the sense of frequenting such temples or merely living in a land full of such temples. But if we called the last tradition of Pythagoras or the lingering legend of Adonis by the name of a religion, then we must find some other name for the Church of Christ.

If anybody says that philosophic maxims presented through many ages, or mythological temples frequented by many people, are things of the same class and category as the Church, it is enough to answer quite simply that they are not. Nobody thinks they are the same when he sees them in the old civilisation of Greece and Rome; nobody would think they were the same if that civilisation had lasted two thousand years longer and existed at the present day; nobody can in reason think they are the same in the parallel pagan civilisation in the East, as it is at the present day. None of these philosophies or mythologies are anything like a Church; certainly nothing like a Church Militant. And, as I have shown elsewhere, even if this rule were not already proved, the exception would prove the rule. The rule is that pre-Christian or pagan history does not produce a Church Militant; and the exception, or what some would call the exception, is that Islam is at least militant if it is not Church. And that is precisely because Islam is the one religious rival that is not pre-Christian and therefore not in that sense pagan. Islam was a product of Christianity;

even if it was a by-product; even if it was a bad product. It was a heresy or parody emulating and therefore imitating the Church. It is no more surprising that Mahomedanism had something of her fighting spirit than that Quakerism had something of her peaceful spirit. After Christianity there are any number of such emulations or extensions. Before it there are none.

The Church Militant is thus unique because it is an army marching to effect a universal deliverance. The bondage from which the world is thus to be delivered is something that is very well symbolised by the state of Asia as by the state of pagan Europe. I do not mean merely their moral or immoral state. The missionary, as a matter of fact, has much more to say for himself than the enlightened imagine even when he says that the heathen are idolatrous and immoral. A touch or two of realistic experience about Eastern religion, even about Moslem religion, will reveal some startling insensibilities in ethics; such as the practical indifference to the line between passion and perversion. It is not prejudice but practical experience which says that Asia is full of demons as well as gods. But the evil I mean is in the mind. And it is in the mind wherever the mind has worked for a long time alone. It is what happens when all dreaming and thinking have come to an end in an emptiness that is at once negation and necessity. It sounds like an anarchy, but it is also a slavery. It is what has been called already the wheel of Asia; all those recurrent arguments about cause and effect or things beginning and ending in the mind, which make it impossible for the soul really to strike out and go anywhere or do anything. And the point is that it is not necessarily peculiar to Asiatics; it would have been true in the end of Europeans--if something had not happened. If the Church Militant had not been a thing marching, all men would have been marking time. If the Church Militant had not endured a discipline, all men would have endured a slavery.

What that universal yet fighting faith brought into the world was hope. Perhaps the one thing common to mythology and philosophy was that both were really sad; in the sense that they had not this hope even if they had touches of faith or charity. We may call

Buddhism a faith; though to us it seems more like a doubt. We may call the Lord of Compassion a Lord of Charity, though it seems to us a very pessimist sort of pity. But those who insist most on the antiquity and size of such cults must agree that in all their ages they have not covered all their areas with that sort of practical and pugnacious hope. In Christendom hope has never been absent; rather it has been errant, extravagant, excessively fixed upon fugitive chances. Its perpetual revolution and reconstruction has at least been an evidence of people being in better spirits. Europe did very truly renew its youth like the eagles; just as the eagles of Rome rose again over the legions of Napoleon, or we have seen soaring but yesterday the silver eagle of Poland. But in the Polish case ever revolution always went with religion. Napoleon himself sought a reconciliation with religion. Religion could never be finally separated even from the most hostile of the hopes; simply because it was the very source of the hopefulness. And the cause of this is to be found simply in the religion itself. Those who quarrel about it seldom even consider it in itself. There is neither space nor place for such a full consideration here; but a word may be said to explain a reconciliation that always recurs and still seems to require explanation.

There will be no end to the weary debates about liberalising theology, until people face the fact that the only liberal part of it is really the dogmatic part. If dogma is incredible, it is because it is incredibly liberal. If it is irrational, it can only be in giving us more assurance of freedom than is justified by reason. The obvious example is that essential form of freedom which we call free-will. It is absurd to say that a man shows his liberality in denying his liberty. But it is tenable that he has to affirm a transcendental doctrine in order to affirm his liberty. There is a sense in which we might reasonably say that if man has a primary power of choice, he has in that fact a super-natural power of creation, as if he could raise the dead or give birth to the unbegotten. Possibly in that case a man must be a miracle; and certainly in that case he must be a miracle in order to be a man; and most certainly in order to be a free man. But it is absurd to forbid him to be a free man and do it in the name of a more free religion.

But it is true in twenty other matters. Anybody who believes at all in God must believe in the absolute supremacy of God. But in so far as that supremacy does allow of any degrees that can be called liberal or illiberal, it is self-evident that the illiberal power is the deity of the rationalists and the liberal power is the deity of the dogmatists. Exactly in proportion as you turn monotheism into monism you turn it into despotism. It is precisely the unknown God of the scientist, with his impenetrable purpose and his inevitable and unalterable law, that reminds us of a Prussian autocrat making rigid plans in a remote tent and moving mankind like machinery. It is precisely the God of miracles and of answered prayers who reminds us of a liberal and popular prince, receiving petitions, listening to parliaments and considering the cases of a whole people. I am not now arguing the rationality of this conception in other respects; as a matter of fact it is not, as some suppose, irrational; for there is nothing irrational in the wisest and most well-informed king acting differently according to the action of those he wishes to save. But I am here only noting the general nature of liberality, or of free or enlarged atmosphere of action. And in this respect it is certain that the king can only be what we call magnanimous if he is what some call capricious. It is the Catholic, who has the feeling that his prayers do make a difference, when offered for the living and the dead, who also has the feeling of living like a free citizen in something almost like a constitutional commonwealth. It is the monist who lives under a single iron law who must have the feeling of living like a slave under a sultan. Indeed I believe that the original use of the word suffragium, which we now use in politics for a vote, was that employed in theology about a prayer. The dead in Purgatory were said to have the suffrages of the living. And in this sense, of a sort of right of petition to the supreme ruler, we may truly say that the whole of the Communion of Saints, as well as the whole of the Church Militant, is founded on universal suffrage.

But above all, it is true of the most tremendous issue; of that tragedy which has created the divine comedy of our creed. Nothing short of the extreme and strong and startling doctrine of the divinity of Christ will give that particular effect that can truly stir the popular sense like a trumpet; the idea of the king himself serving in the ranks like a common soldier. By making that figure merely human we make that story much less human. We take away the point of the story which actually pierces humanity; the point of the story which was quite literally the point of a spear. It does not especially humanise the universe to say that good and wise men can die for their opinions; any more than it would be any sort of uproariously popular news in an army that good soldiers may easily get killed. It is no news that King Leonidas is dead any more than that Queen Anne is dead; and men did not wait for Christianity to be men, in the full sense of being heroes. But if we are describing, for the moment, the atmosphere of what is generous and popular and even picturesque, any knowledge of human nature will tell us that no sufferings of the sons of men, or even of the servants of God, strike the same note as the notion of the master suffering instead of his servants. And this is given by the theological and emphatically not by the scientific deity. No mysterious monarch, hidden in his starry pavilion at the base of the cosmic campaign, is in the least like that celestial chivalry of the Captain who carries his five wounds in the front of battle.

What the denouncer of dogma really means is not that dogma is bad; but rather that dogma is too good to be true. That is, he means that dogma is too liberal to be likely. Dogma gives man too much freedom when it permits him to fall. Dogma gives even God too much freedom when it permits him to die. That is what the intelligent sceptics ought to say; and it is not in the least my intention to deny that there is something to be said for it. They mean that the universe is itself a universal prison; that existence itself is a limitation and a control; and it is not for nothing that they call causation a chain. In a word, they mean quite simply that they cannot believe these things; not in the least that they are unworthy of belief. We say not lightly but very literally, that the truth has made us free. They say that it makes us so free that it cannot be the truth. To them it is like believing in fairyland to believe in such freedom as we enjoy. It is like believing in men with wings to entertain the fancy of men with wills. It is like accepting a fable about a squirrel in conversation with a mountain to believe in a man who is free to ask or a God who is free to answer. This is a manly and a rational negation for which I for one shall always show respect. But I decline to show any respect for those who first of all clip the wings and cage the squirrel, rivet the chains and refuse the freedom, close all the doors of the cosmic prison on us with a clang of eternal iron, tell us that our emancipation is a dream and our dungeon a necessity; and then calmly turn round and tell us they have a freer thought and a more liberal theology.

The moral of all this is an old one; that religion is revelation. In other words it is a vision, and a vision received by faith; but it is a vision of reality. The faith consists in a conviction of its reality. That, for example, is the difference between a vision and a day-dream. And that is the difference between religion and mythology. That is the difference between faith and all that fancy-work, quite human and more or less healthy, which we considered under the head of mythology. There is something in the reasonable use of the very word vision that implies two things about it; first that it comes very rarely, possibly that it comes only once; and secondly that it probably comes once and for all. A day-dream may come every day. A day-dream may be different every day. It is something more than the difference between telling ghost-stories and meeting a ghost.

But if it is not a mythology neither is it a philosophy. It is not a philosophy because, being a vision, it is not a pattern but a picture. It is not one of those simplifications which resolve everything into an abstract explanation; as that everything is recurrent; or everything is relative; or everything is inevitable; or everything is illusive. It is not a process but a story. It has proportions, of the sort seen in a picture or a story; it has not the regular repetitions of a pattern or a process; but it replaces them by being convincing as a picture or a story is convincing. In other words, it is exactly, as the phrase goes, like life. For indeed it is life. An example of what is meant here might well be found in the treatment of the problem of evil. It is easy enough to make a plan of life of which the background is black, as the pessimists do; and then admit a speck or two of star-dust more or less accidental, or at least in the literal sense insignificant. And it is easy enough to make another plan on white paper, as the Christian Scientists do, and explain or explain away somehow such dots or smudges as may be difficult to deny. Lastly it is easiest of all perhaps, to say as the dualists do, that life is like a chess-board in which the two are equal, and can as truly be said to consist of white squares on a black board or of black squares on a white board. But every man feels in his heart that none of these three paper plans is like life; that none of these worlds is one in which he can live. Something tells him that the ultimate idea of a world is not bad or even neutral; staring at the sky or the grass or the truths of mathematics or even a new-laid egg, he has a vague feeling like the shadow of that saying of the great Christian philosopher, St. Thomas Aquinas, 'Every existence, as such, is good.' On the other hand, something else tells him that it is unmanly and debased and even diseased to minimise evil to a dot or even a blot. He realises that optimism is morbid. It is if possible even more morbid than pessimism. These vague but healthy feelings, if he followed them out, would result in the idea that evil is in some way an exception but an enormous exception; and ultimately that evil is an invasion or yet more truly a rebellion. He does not think that everything is right or that every thing is wrong, or that everything is equally right and wrong. But he does think that right has a right to be right and therefore a right to be there, and wrong has no right to be wrong and therefore no right to be there. It is the prince of the world; but it is also a usurper. So he will apprehend vaguely what the vision will give to him vividly; no less than all that strange story of treason in heaven and the great desertion by which evil damaged and tried to destroy a cosmos that it could not create. It is a very strange story and its proportions and its lines and colours are as arbitrary and absolute as the artistic composition of a picture. It is a vision which we do in fact symbolise in pictures by titanic limbs and passionate tints of plumage; all that abysmal vision of falling stars and the peacock panoplies of the night. But that strange story has one small advantage over the diagrams. It is like life.

Another example might be found, not in the problem of evil, but in what is called the problem of progress. One of the ablest agnostics of the age once asked me whether I thought mankind grew better or grew worse or remained the same. He was confident that the alternative covered all possibilities. He did not see that it only covered patterns and not pictures; processes and not stories. I asked him whether he thought that Mr. Smith of Golder's Green got better or worse or remained exactly the same between the age of thirty and forty. It then seemed to dawn on him that it would rather depend on Mr. Smith; and how he chose to go on. It had never occurred to him that it might depend on how mankind chose to go on; and that its course was not a straight line or an upward or downward curve, but a track like that of a man across a valley, going where he liked and stopping where he chose, going into a church or falling down in a ditch. The life of man is a story; an adventure story; and in our vision the same is true even of the story of God.

The Catholic faith is the reconciliation because it is the realisation both of mythology and philosophy. It is a story and in that sense one of a hundred stories; only it is a true story. It is a philosophy and in that sense one of a hundred philosophies; only it is a philosophy that is like life. But above all, it is a reconciliation because it is something that can only be called the philosophy of stories. That normal narrative instinct which produced all the fairy tales is something that is neglected by all the philosophies--except one. The Faith is the justification of that popular instinct; the finding of a philosophy for it or the analysis of the philosophy in it. Exactly as a man in an adventure story has to pass various tests to save his life, so the man in this philosophy has to pass several tests and save his soul. In both there is an idea of free will operating under conditions of design; in other words, there is an aim and it is the business of a man to aim at it; we therefore watch to see whether he will hit it. Now this deep and democratic and dramatic instinct is derided and dismissed in all the other philosophies. For all the other philosophies avowedly end where they begin; and it is the definition of a story that it ends differently; that it begins in one place and ends in another. From Buddha and his wheel to Akhen Aten and his disc, from Pythagoras with his abstraction of number to Confucius with his religion of routine, there is not one of them that does not in some way sin against the soul of a story. There is none of them that really grasps this human notion of the tale, the test, the adventure; the ordeal of the free man. Each of them starves the story-telling instinct, so to speak, and does something to spoil human life considered as a romance; either by fatalism (pessimist or optimist) and that destiny that is the death of adventure; or by indifference and that detachment that is the death of drama; or by a fundamental scepticism that dissolves the actors into atoms; or by a materialistic limitation blocking the vista of moral consequences; or a mechanical recurrence making even moral tests monotonous; or a bottomless relativity making even practical tests insecure. There is such a thing as a human story; and there is such a thing as the divine story which is also a human story; but there is no such thing as a Hegelian story or a Monist story or a relativist story or a determinist story; for every story, yes, even a penny dreadful or a cheap novelette, has something in it that belongs to our universe and not theirs. Every short story does truly begin with creation and end with a last judgement.

And that is the reason why the myths and the philosophers were at war until Christ came. That is why the Athenian democracy killed Socrates out of respect for the gods; and why every strolling sophist gave himself the airs of a Socrates whenever he could talk in a superior fashion of the gods; and why the heretic Pharaoh wrecked his huge idols and temples for an abstraction and why the priests could return in triumph and trample his dynasty under foot; and why Buddhism had to divide itself from Brahminism, and why in every age and country outside Christendom there has been a feud for ever between the philosopher and the priest. It is easy enough to say that the philosopher is generally the more rational; it is easier still to forget that the priest is always the more popular. For the priest told the people stories; and the philosopher did not understand the philosophy of stories. It came into the world with the story of Christ.

And this is why it had to be a revelation or vision given from above. Any one who will think of the theory of stories or pictures will easily see the point. The true story of the world must be told by somebody to somebody else. By the very nature of a story it cannot be left to occur to anybody. A story has proportions, variations, surprises, particular dispositions, which cannot be worked out by rule in the abstract, like a sum. We could not deduce whether or no Achilles would give back the body of Hector from a Pythagorean theory of number or recurrence; and we could not infer for ourselves in what way the world would get back the body of Christ, merely from being told that all things go round and round upon the wheel of Buddha. A man might perhaps work out a proposition of Euclid without having heard of Euclid; but he would not work out the precise legend of Eurydice without having heard of Eurydice. At any rate he would not be certain how the story would end and whether Orpheus was ultimately defeated. Still less could he guess the end of our story; or the legend of our Orpheus rising, not defeated from, the dead.

To sum up; the sanity of the world was restored and the soul of man offered salvation by something which did indeed satisfy the two warring tendencies of the past; which had never been satisfied in full and most certainly never satisfied together. It met the mythological search for romance by being a story and the philosophical search for truth by being a true story. That is why the ideal figure had to be a historical character, as nobody had ever felt Adonis or Pan to be a historical character. But that is also why the historical character had to be the ideal figure; and even fulfil many of the functions given to these other ideal figures; why he was at once the sacrifice and the feast, why he could be shown under the emblems of the growing vine or the rising sun. The more deeply we think of the matter the more we shall conclude that, if there be indeed a God, his creation could hardly have reached any other culmination than this granting of a real romance to the world. Otherwise the two sides of the human mind could never have touched at all; and the brain of man would have remained cloven and double; one lobe of it dreaming impossible dreams and the other repeating invariable calculations. The picture-makers would have remained forever painting the portrait of nobody. The sages would have remained for ever adding up numerals that came to nothing. It was that abyss that nothing but an incarnation could cover; a divine embodiment of our dreams; and he stands above that chasm whose name is more than priest and older even than Christendom; Pontifex Maximus, the mightiest maker of a bridge.

But even with that we return to the more specially Christian symbol in the same tradition; the perfect pattern of the keys. This is a historical and not a theological outline, and it is not my duty here to defend in detail that theology, but merely to point out that it could not even be justified in design without being justified in detail--like a key. Beyond the broad suggestion of this chapter I attempt no apologetic about why the creed should be accepted. But in answer to the historical query of why it was accepted and is accepted, I answer for millions of others in my reply; because it fits the lock, because it is like life. It is one among many stories; only it happens to be a true story. It is one among many philosophies; only it happens to be the truth. We accept it; and the ground is solid under our feet and the road is open before us. It does not imprison us in a dream of destiny or a consciousness of the universal delusion. It opens to us not only incredible heavens but what seems to some an equally incredible earth, and makes it credible. This is the sort of truth that is hard to explain because it is a fact; but it is a fact to which we can call witnesses. We are Christians and Catholics not because we worship a key, but because we have passed a door; and felt the wind that is the trumpet of liberty blow over the land of the living.